The
Passing
of
Modernity

COMMUNICATIONS

George Gerbner and Marsha Siefert, Editors
The Annenberg School of Communications
University of Pennsylvania, Philadelphia

The
Passing
of
Modernity

*Communication
and the Transformation
of Society*

Hamid Mowlana
*The American University
Washington, D.C.*
and
Laurie J. Wilson
Brigham Young   University

Longman
New York & London

HD
76
M68
1990

The Passing of Modernity

Longman 95 Church Street, White Plains, N.Y. 10601
A division of Addison-Wesley Publishing Co., Inc.

Associated companies:
Longman Group Ltd., London
Longman Cheshire Pty., Melbourne
Longman Paul Pty., Auckland
Copp Clark Pitman, Toronto

Executive editor: Gordon T. R. Anderson
Production editor: Marie-Josée Anna Schorp
Cover design: Michael Jung
Text art: Vantage Art, Inc.

Library of Congress Cataloging-in-Publication Data

Mowlana, Hamid, 1937–
    The passing of modernity.
    (Communications)
    Bibliography: p.
    1. Communication in economic development.
I. Wilson, Laurie J. II. Title. III. Series:
Communications (Annenberg School of Communications
(University of Pennsylvania))
HD76.M68 1990   303.48'33   89–31791
ISBN 0–8013–0409–1

ABCDEFGHIJ-MA-99 98 97 96 95 94 93 92 91 90 89

To Kubra, Tahereh, and Tayyebeh
who graciously accepted
the transformation of their society

Contents

Preface

Events have taken development theorists by surprise. Until 1978, almost no one in the West credited the traditional people and leaders of Iran with the ability to inspire a large-scale revolution. Thus, no one foretold the resurgence of Islam and its consequences in the region. The Solidarity movement in Poland, other reforms in the socialist countries of Eastern Europe, and the processes of change in the Soviet Union under *perestroika* and *glasnost* were not on the syllabus of courses on political and social development, anymore than were the AIDS and drug-related social problems threatening the social fabric of American society. Similarly, the Palestinian uprising *intifada* in the occupied territories, which received worldwide attention everywhere, was as unpredicted as the rise of the students' movement for democracy in the People's Republic of China. Development studies focused on the modernization of societies, on growth, and on the decline of traditionalism. If the rise of neoconservatism in the West surprised social scientists, the realignment and the reported decline of the superpowers was indeed astonishing.

Today there is hardly a major political, social, or economic problem in the developing world that cannot be observed in some degree in both the capitalist and the socialist industrialized regions. We are now witnessing an unprecedented phenomenon of societal transformation everywhere which cannot be explained merely by orthodox political and economic theories of social change. It is in the simulacrum and the digital world that the experience of life in a secular environment must be understood. Modernity, as we have come to know it, is not an inevitable culminating stage in the evolution of societies. Some have chosen to leave it behind or to go beyond it. The monistic/emancipatory models of societal transformation are challenging the dualism of modernity as much as dominant Western political-moral ideologies are eroding in their liberal and Marxist forms. Indeed, as it is argued in this volume, these systems of implicit legitimation have been eroding for some time, and the search for *Lebensraum* in societies dominated by impersonal bureaucratic organization is already underway, with the state unable to control the flow. This chaotic evolutionary process can be understood only if we shift our attention from politico-economic models to communication and force-field theories of transformation.

As we shift our focus from development to transformation, we must redefine the conceptual signification of international communication as well as the way in which development communication studies are constituted within this field. This reconstruction of development and communication studies is necessary given the erosion of a rational framework of reference, the global socio-political context of the field, and its inability to provide itself with a unified and stable logo. One of the parameters with which we can chart our new conceptualization of communication and change is the development of a global level of communicative effect.

Modernity used to mean a process of societal rationalization involving the intermingling of a particular world view and a set of external factors, leading to the industrialization of Europe and of the United States and to market-regulated economic systems in which the state played a complimentary role. The process of secularization, in which the Christian church lost its role in international relations, was one of the major outcomes of modernity and delegated global responsibility to the institutions and to the legal order of modernized societies. Immediately after the turn of the century, the institutionalization of purposive-rational action based on Western models thus became the mainstream framework for developmental schemes everywhere. The modern structure of consciousness which was established with capitalism was only partial then. With the emergence of socialism in Europe, the Soviet Union, and elsewhere around the world, modernity—although diverse in its many politico-economic levels—acquired an almost universal legitimacy, becoming the super-paradigm of societal development in industrialized countries both in the West and in the East. In short, modernity in its broad sense, meant some form of Occidental rationalism which required the creation of new social organizations to replace the traditional ones, an industrialization of the economy, secularization, and the development of the nation-state in small and large-scale communities. The objectification of interpersonal relations through bureaucratic and state intervention also meant that with modernity, the collective and the impersonal alone are real. Material conditions—not spirituality—determined the outlook, behavior, and modes of thought of individuals in a society where there are no objective standards or eternal truth. Since World War II, development theorists and historians have usually sought their models for social, political, and economic structures in Western history, and primarily in the history of the modernity syndrome. In contrast, we argue that social behavior and societal transformations in any system must, indeed, be understood and planned on their own terms. To understand these transformations, we should give primary attention to the world views of these societies and to their own account of their inner and outer worlds, to the terms in which individuals, groups, and nations explain their choices.

This book is not rejecting modernity in order to celebrate what is known as post-modernism. It sees modernity—and old social models associated with it—as only part of the large picture in the transformation of society. The book synthesizes a wide range of scholarly and experimental materials on a broad range of development and communication phenomena. It offers the additional advantage, also uncommon in current literature, of addressing history in depth, when dealing with development theories and communication policies. Attempts have been made not only to provide the reader with a comprehensive critique of the main perspectives in development theories but also to present a systematic synthesis of many of the themes of modernization and social change that have preoccupied major writers since World War II. In short, this volume covers three interrelated objectives: (1) to provide a systematic and critical analysis of development and communication theories in a historical context; (2) to construct a new conceptual framework for a critical theory of societal transformation which goes beyond modernity; (3) to evaluate the usefulness of current information and communication technologies in economic, political, and cultural changes. The book approaches these tasks through a combination of conceptual analyses, systematic reviews, and critical reconstructions of theories by such thinkers as Marx, Weber, Habermas, Foucault, Lyotard, Baudrillard, in the West or Ibn Khaldun, Khomeini, and Mutahhari in other cultures.

More than three decades have gone by since the publication of Daniel Lerner's *Passing of Traditional Society: Modernizing the Middle East* in 1958. The story of that book began in 1949 with the initiation of the Truman Doctrine and its Point IV Program and was followed by a period of unchallenged supremacy of the United States, as well as by the *development* decades at the United Nations. Since then, the world has changed considerably but not in the direction of Lerner's projection. The Middle East, Latin America, Asia, Africa, and indeed Europe and the United States have become different places from what they were in the post-World War II years.

This book, represents two decades of efforts and reflections on the questions of development and communication. I joined the faculty of the School of International Service at The American University in 1968, and established the International Communication Program with a number of graduate courses and seminars on communication and socio-economic and political development. As we began to celebrate the twentieth anniversary of the

Program at the end of 1988, the boundaries and frontiers of the field of development were still in a state of flux and evolution. Cultural and ecological issues had extended the political and economic frontiers to information and communication as the foci of analysis. In the intervening twenty years of turbulence and profound transformation which characterized many societies, I have traveled to many parts of the world as a visiting professor and scholar in such countries as England, Argentina, the Soviet Union, Nigeria, Japan, Egypt, Iran, Turkey, Poland, and many regions in the controversial East-West and North-South belts. The initial drafts of a number of chapters were written from these lectures and research tours as I interviewed many of the leaders and planners of these countries. In the last five years alone, I returned a number of times to Iran, Turkey, and other East and West European countries in search of new data and interviews.

These observations offer the data and the background for some of the new perspectives presented in the pages that follow. For example, the discussion on culture, society, and communication in Chapter 4 can trace its origin to the opening paper I delivered at the World Congress of the International Association of Mass Communication Research in Warsaw, Poland, at the eve of the Islamic revolution in Iran and of the initial formation of the Solidarity groups in Poland. Over the last decade, a number of revisions of this particular chapter were prepared to reflect the changing environments of the world at large, as well as those of cultural studies on communication. Chapters 3 and 5, analyzing contending approaches to development and communication, have been tested in university fora in such cities as Cairo, Tehran, and Ljubljana. A considerable amount of data as well as debates were analyzed in the context of the Asian and Pacific regions, especially when I had the good fortune of serving as a Fellow at the East-West Center in Hawaii and on the panels of various symposia that took place in New Delhi and Tokyo.

All these have convinced me that a new appraisal and review of the global shift in development and communication were indeed needed. The so-called "developing world" was in transition with problems of personal identity, of revolutionary ideology, and struggling for everyday life. The "Western world" has had different—but not milder—problems. The demand for a New International Economic Order and the quest for a New World Information and Communication Order of the 1970s, have been transformed to a new global economic competitiveness and crisis and to a call for a new cultural and information ecology. The North-South issues have been crystallized but not resolved, and the East-West and West-West relationships have entered a new political, economic, and technological era. The result is a paradox and a good deal of uncertainty and insecurity.

This book owes its origin to both individuals and institutions. In 1984, I was commissioned by UNESCO to prepare a study which attempted to describe and analyze the contribution of communication technology to development from different geographical, socio-economic, and cultural perspectives to provide a status report on various strategies and experiences throughout the world. I then invited Laurie J. Wilson to collaborate with me in that project. The result was published under the title of *Communication Technology and Development* by UNESCO in its series, "Reports and Papers on Mass Communications," No. 101 © UNESCO, 1988. The present volume is, in part, an outgrowth of that project, and although the opinions expressed therein do not necessarily represent the views of UNESCO, I want to thank that organization for the permission to use that material as part of this book. Thanks is also due to Sage Publications for their kind permission to incorporate part of my article, "Mass Media and Culture: Toward an Integrated Theory," in William B. Gudykunst, ed. *Intercultural Communication Theory: Current Perspectives,* Copyright © 1983 by Sage Publications Inc., Beverly Hills, California, in Chapter 4 of this volume.

In short, this volume attempts to integrate the many threads of the complex problems of development and communication into a coherent frame of reference so that we may better understand the dynamics of change now taking place in our world. The first chapter surveys various attempts of social philosophers and social scientists to understand the process of societal development in its economic, political, and psychocultural contexts and gives an historical analysis of the trend toward development theory. Chapter 2 outlines a new framework for integrating the concepts of development and communication into a coherent whole, and it sketches out a world view concept of societal transformation. Chapter 3 reviews and classifies contending theories and approaches to communication and development; it also describes and identifies a set of monistic/emancipatory models as alternatives to the more orthodox approaches of the past. Chapter 4 focuses on the relationships between culture, society, and communication, reviewing theories from several different disciplines of the social sciences. These theories may be used to build a set of concepts relevant not only at the national level but also when the complex nature of international relations and international communication are concerned. Chapter 5 discusses some implications of communication and transformation theory in the emerging field of communication policies and planning. Chapters 6 through 8 evaluate the applications of development theories in practice. These chapters discuss various experiments that have been attempted as a result of past theories and policies. Some five hundred experimental projects at both macro and micro levels dealing with the impact of information and communication technologies on social and economic development have been analyzed. Finally, Chapter 9 summarizes some of the findings, arguing that we must go beyond the development and underdevelopment syndrome and adds a tentative postscript on communication and the transformation of society.

Clearly, such an undertaking must acknowledge the contribution of a number of individuals and institutions, such as those we have cited in the text, the notes, and the bibliography. Special gratitude is due to Ann Jaussi who assisted in the preparation and editing of this work from start to finish; to Bruce Kotz, whose research and synthesis of information were invaluable; and to Ginger Smith, who provided encouragement, support, and the willingness to help in any aspect. We truly appreciate the dedication and assistance of these three individuals, as well as the contributions of all others cited elsewhere in this book.

Hamid Mowlana
Washington, D.C.

CHAPTER 1

Development: A Field in Search of Itself

Any critique and discussion of communication and development should naturally begin with the more basic analysis not only of the relationship between them, but more important, of their separate conceptual meanings. In short, one cannot discuss the interaction of communication and development without understanding the natures of the concepts themselves. Unfortunately, since the end of World War II, as the terms have come into prominent usage in the scholarly literature as well as in policy circles, they have not been systematically and critically analyzed.

This is not to suggest that the area of communication and development has not been critically examined. On the contrary, one can cite a number of highly critical and analytical essays and monographs that have examined the current literature.[1] What is lacking is a historical and evolutionary analysis of the concepts employed as well as a systematic treatment of the relationship between communication and development in its sociological, epistemological, and methodological context. In the next few chapters, we will examine the historical growth of the term *development*, critique the notion of communication and communications, and examine the utility of the term *development* in studying a series of social processes, which although previously defined differently, are now commonly included in the definition of development.

We will begin with a number of theses and contentions, which are the result of a rather thorough examination of the literature and will be explained and elaborated on as we progress. First, it is argued that the concept of development as it has been increasingly used since the 1940s has become a residual conceptual category for a number of otherwise ambiguous notions of individual, institutional, societal, and international change. It consequently lacks the rigorous epistemological, conceptual, and at times, methodological power to be of any real value in enhancing our understanding of some of the most complex historical, social, political, economic, and spiritual occurrences of our times. It has neither the narrow connotation of *development*, in terms of the economic and technological processes evidenced in the early history of the term, nor the rigor and explanatory power of the more general notion of historical change for which it claims ownership. In short, the term has been misused, abused, and at times, corrupted and may eventually prove beyond salvation.

Second, although perhaps less abused than *development*, the term *communication*, or *communications*, has also been used in rather ambiguous ways. Whereas *communication* refers to the process of exchange and sharing, the term *communications* implies the means by which this process operates. Any attempt to relate the term communication to the entire process of what is called "development" requires an explanation of the meaning of the former.

Third, contrary to the general belief that the paradigm of communication and development has gone through a change, not only has there been no radical change in the dominant paradigm but also a natural prerequisite for such a change is the rejection of the current conceptualization of *development*.[2] In fact, the real challenge to the dominant paradigm may come not from the "developmentalists" but from those who have abandoned this term and have more clearly defined their objectives, what they hope to achieve, and what specific human processes they wish to examine.

Further, the understanding of the relationship between communication and what is now termed development is rooted in the contemporary history of all nations and societies, if not in the entire history of the civilization of mankind. A systematic and thorough examination of the relationship between communication and such specific concepts as revolution, reform, industrialization, economic growth, and cultural and spiritual renaissance could provide us with a wealth of information, particularly if compared cross-nationally or cross-culturally, in order to design new concepts and categories that may eventually replace the general term *development*.

Finally, the term *development* in its current usage, both nationally and internationally, has become the cornerstone of such numerous rationalizations and legitimizations that instead of being a force of "liberation" and "emancipation," "progress" and "democracy," "human growth" and "global community," it has gradually deteriorated into a repository for otherwise unrelated and fragmentary policies, programs, and objectives.

THE HISTORICAL GROWTH
OF THE TERM DEVELOPMENT

The role of communication in general—and the technology of mass media in particular—in the process of social change, economic growth, and political upheaval in the so-called less industrialized and developing countries has been studied as early as the 19th century. In fact, examination of events in the Middle East, Latin America, and Asia during the current century shows the direct intermingling of both old and new communication institutions with the nation-building process. Indeed, one can draw a direct parallel between reformists and revolutionaries on the one hand, and journalists, writers, orators, or political pamphleteers on the other.[3] The relationship between the two in the Third World over the last 100 years cannot be separated. It can be said that in all these countries, there have been direct relationships between the press and reform, telecommunications and modernization, and traditional institutions and revolution.

The rise of European liberalism and the spread of post-French revolutionary nationalism in Asia, Latin America, and Africa in the closing decades of the 19th century (especially in such countries as Iran, Egypt, Turkey, and Japan), and the spread of socialism from its center in Europe to Russia in the early decades of the 20th century, all contributed immensely to the study of the relationship between communication institutions and the entire process of political rebellion, revolution, and social reform. In fact, some of the most important works during the first two decades of the 20th century in the Middle East and Asia, and to a degree in Latin America, deal directly with the relationships among the press, public opinion, and political reforms and revolutions.

Indeed, the study and the role of communication in the process of political and economic "modernization" became a central point in the changes taking place in such countries as Iran and Turkey in the 1920s and 1930s. The propaganda role of modern telecommunications and technology, especially the radio, was brought to the forefront not only by the rise of totalitarianism and fascism in Europe but also by the rise of a process of Europeanization and Westernization in the secular modern nation states in Asia and Latin America. The rise of socialism in Russia and the entire process of economic and political change, which eventually led to consolidation of power by the revolutionaries in what became the Soviet Union, were directly tied to both communication as a process and communications as a mobilizing force using media technologies. In short, the current literature and research in communication and development has its roots primarily in the processes of social change spanning the decades between 1890 and 1940.

It must be noted that during the early period of this century, the terms used in communication and mass media were directly linked to specific and rather well-defined areas of societal and national change. If there was a movement of intellectuals embracing European ideas and ideals, there was no ambiguity in their rhetoric. They wrote of industrialization, secularization, liberalism, parliamentary democracy, and a score of other specifically defined experiences prevalent at the time. Moreover, there were few ambiguities in the messages of revolutionary socialists or their moderate counterparts. When there was opposition on national objectives that ran contrary to modern European thinking and modernization, these too lacked ambiguity. For example, some of the Islamic intellectuals of the late 19th century who sought reform and revolution but opposed secularization and Europeanization, were indeed clear about their objectives and the types of societies and democracies they envisioned. In short, until World War II, and in the absence of a general concept like "development," the objectives, policies, and programs of the specific actors could be traced to well-defined areas of activities, even though they ranged from very evolutionary to very revolutionary types of programs.

In sum, the term *development* as an all-encompassing concept referring to such widely different processes as "modernization," "Westernization," "Europeanization," "industrialization," "economic growth," "political change," "nation building," and a score of other economic, political, social, and cultural activities and changes was not used extensively in the literature until the end of World War II. Yet for over half a century, prior to the outbreak of the war, the relationship between communication as a social process and communications as a means and technology of the modern age was studied in the context of such specific phenomena as revolution, reform, economic growth, democracy, and political mobilization as well as education, literacy, and cultural activities. Experiments and studies were implemented not only in the highly industrialized countries of the West but also in a number of less industrialized and agricultural economies such as the Soviet Union, Japan, Egypt, Iran, Turkey, and Mexico. One important characteristic of this period was the clear-cut relation between a given communication technology (and medium) and a specific "developmental" goal. Thus the role of the press as an organizer, an agitator, and a propagandist was recognized, as was its place in the democratization, surveillance, and cultural transformation of societies and nations. The central role of telecommunication, specifically the telephone, telegraph, and submarine cables, in economic growth and trade was recognized, and more attention was given to the role of the press in urban development and the role of radio in agricultural and rural extension services.

The widespread use of "development" as a conceptual framework for a number of individual, institutional, national, and international changes, and for "progress," is a post-World War II phenomenon. In the 1940s and especially in the 1950s and the 1960s, (the term *development* became synonomous with growth, modernization, change, democracy, productivity, industrialization, and a score of related Western historical and evolutionary changes.) Popularized first by (and among) the American scholars and policy makers, and soon introduced to Europe and especially the less industrialized countries of the world, the term *development* became a major issue in international organizations despite its ill-defined and less than universally recognized meaning. The term was popular, especially among American scholars and policy makers, for several reasons.

1. The United States was the dominant world power at the end of World War II, and the attempt was made to transform defeated countries (Germany, Japan, and Italy) as well as emerging non-Western and less industrialized countries of Asia, Latin America, and Africa into "Western-style" democracies through peaceful means and gradual reforms and reconstructions. Thus, "development" in both Western and non-Western societies was perceived as a gradual but multi-stage evolution, rather than as a revolutionary process.

2. Through the Marshall Plan to assist western European reconstruction; the Truman Doctrine's Four Point program of economic and technical assistance to countries such as Greece, Iran, and Turkey; the increase in the amount of U.S. foreign aid to a number of countries on the path of "modernization" such as Pakistan, Thailand, and South Korea; and the subsequent establishment of the U.S. Agency for International Development (USAID), with its various programs and activities, the term *development* acquired a special meaning from the viewpoint of the United States as donor and a number of countries as recipients.

3. The establishment of the United Nations system and its affiliated agencies involved with aspects of national, regional, and international activities of an economic, monetary, financial, technical, educational, scientific, cultural, and political nature further helped to enhance the concept of "development," especially in the context of the political and economic modernization and growth of less industrialized countries and emerging nations. Indeed, the 1950s and the 1960s became known as the decades of "development," when many countries in Africa, Asia, and Latin America, after years of struggle for independence and decolonialization, were within reach of developmental models that they envisioned would improve their standards of living, establish economic and political infrastructures, and help them join the community of nations as a participant and "equal partner." Without a doubt, these events had an important role in popularizing the term *development* in international usage. Furthermore, in its general

context, the term was a convenient name and a residual category under which a number of ad hoc programs, projects, and ideas could be grouped together without offending the ideological and philosophical orientations of the parties concerned. It provided a nice vocabulary, with all its charm and controversy, and a forum for discussions and commentaries, experiments and experiences, celebrations and joy, and of course, frustration. Yet it meant different things to different people.

4. And finally, the keen interest of the United States' scholarly community, and later of the scholars of Europe and other areas, in the study of non-Western societies under the rubric of "developing" countries was largely responsible not only for the further popularity of the term *development* but also its conceptual and methodological growth. In short, after years of scattered references to non-Western societies as "backward," "non-industrialized," and "underdeveloped," this quasi-academic term replaced the old clichés without offending new nations and their peoples. No doubt the sharpening of research and investigatory tools and improved means of collecting, storing, retrieving, and sharing the data gathered from, now, the "developing" world were important consequences to the scholarly community's interest in an interdisciplinary approach to the process of change in large areas of the globe.

Development had become both a legitimate and a convenient term on which a number of otherwise diversified research interests could converge. As was evidenced in the case of the United States, development studies were expanded and somewhat solidified as a result of a number of scholarly projects in the areas of politics, economics, cultural anthropology, rural sociology, international relations, and international communication. For example, one study found that communication and development was the area of the greatest growth in scholarly investigation because of communication-oriented studies dealing with international problems.[4] Further, the study found that the amount of research on development and communication in specific cultural and geographical areas corresponded roughly to the level of U.S. political involvement in those areas. In fact, the factor of involvement seemed to have heavily influenced what domestic studies were undertaken and what foreign works were translated. In short, by the early 1960s, development as a field of academic and social inquiry had undergone extraordinary growth under the influence of the dominant modernization paradigm, with a great deal of emphasis being placed on economic, technological, and institutional factors.

The Turning Point: Abandon or Embrace?

Beginning with the 1960s and continuing well into the 1970s, two trends were seen in both the theoretical and the policy spheres of development studies. The first, the emergence of contending models of social, economic, and political development in the socialist countries, was almost entirely ignored by the developmentalists. This trend was crystallized with the "developmental" changes occurring in the People's Republic of China and in Cuba, both of which seemed to be successful in specific economic and social spheres such as agriculture, health, and education, thus providing alternative models to change in less industrialized countries. The second, equally significant trend was that "the passing of traditional societies," anticipated by many Western social scientists, was running into trouble in such countries as Pakistan, Turkey, and Iran. Indeed, the Third World was generally concerned that the model of development propagated in the 1940s and 1950s was not suited to the needs of the culturally diverse nations of Asia, Latin America, and Africa. This was a crucial conclusion and could have become a turning point in the field of development had scholars chosen to make it so. The term *development* by now had moved from a narrow definition of purely economic growth to encompass a broad sphere of political and social activities, including political, social, and cultural development. At the same time, the meaning of *development* in noneconomic spheres was not specified.

In the face of these ambiguities, the scholarly community was in a position either to further legitimize or to destroy the conceptual and practical position of development in the overall paradigm of academic and social thought. Here there were two clear choices: Realizing the ambiguities of the term and the conceptual weaknesses of the model, scholars could have dismissed the notion of development as least satisfactory and rigorous for describing the phenomena under investigation, and they might have searched for fresh concepts that would better describe the dynamics of diverse social, economic, and political activities; or in light of contending models and approaches, they could have attempted to retain the term but to modify, redefine, and tailor it to a variety of real individual, institutional, and societal needs. Enamored by the popularity of the term and perhaps victimized by the lack of a rigorous epistemological debate on the phenomenon itself, scholarly communities almost collectively chose to enter the battle of development and the debate already underway rather than rejecting the utility of the concept in the first place.

The next decade or so, therefore, became a period in which the "paradists" of development joined with the "apologists" of underdevelopment and, hand in hand with the "consciousness seekers," injected further epistemological biases into an already complex and controversial concept. The result was the emergence of what were called new paradigms and new approaches ranging from dependency theory in all its varieties to human emancipatory and liberation models to neoclassic approaches to development now modified as a result of past experiences. If the contending approaches to "so-called" development theories are examined rather carefully, it is arguable whether or not the development paradigm had truly undergone a fundamental change in the first place. It raises questions as to whether or not a scientific revolution in the Kuhnian sense had really occurred: It had not.

This is not to suggest, of course, that there have been no attempts to redirect the theories, strategies, and policies of development from their initial course of the 1940s and 1950s. Indeed, the term itself has undergone a reconceptualization, as have related strategies and tactics. What is suggested, however, is that the change in the paradigm was neither sufficient to change theories nor to change methodologies and models. The paradigmatic shift could have been accomplished if the fundamental notions of social developmental phenomena and the method for their study were abandoned, giving their place not only to new terminologies but also to a fundamentally restructured epistemology as well.

The crucial contention here is that the very notion and concept of development as a framework of analysis in describing the complex nature of human and societal development has not been challenged. Nor has it been abandoned and replaced by a more rigorous concept. The fact remains that the yet to be defined term *development* tends to be an umbrella under which all other phenomena, ranging from human and spiritual development to nationalism and community development, from organizational change to managerial techniques, have become related and somewhat subordinate. One can claim that every sphere of human and societal activity in its community, national, and international context is part of the field of development, and every part of development studies is part of each social science, biological, and physiological discipline. In short, "development" is everything, and everything is "development."

The popularity and diversity of the use of *communication* in relation to developmental activities, especially during the last decade or so, has added to the complexity of the phenomenon under investigation. In the early stages of convergence, the term *communication* was used to refer to communication technologies, particularly the mass media and a variety of journalistic activities. But with the communications revolution, and especially with the increased use of communication satellites and computers, even the technological meaning of *communication* has been expanded to encompass everything from the printing press to complex electronic and space technologies. At the same time, it has been perspicaciously recognized that there can be no communication analysis without taking into account the complex networks of human, interpersonal, and group communication. Unlike what took place in the early years of the post-World War II era, the tendency now is to view communication as an integrated complex whole in which both human and technological dimensions ought to be considered in interrelationship.[5]

The Meaning of Development

"Development" as a concept was perhaps initially introduced by Ibn Khaldun (A.D. 1332–1406), an Islamic social thinker, in his *Muqaddimah* (*An Introduction to History*).[6] Ibn Khaldun, a Tunisian who some view as the founder of sociology and demography, used the Arabic term *ilm-al-umran* to describe a new *science of development* or of society—that is, sociology. His work with this new science was thus, basically, a paradigm and methodology of sociology. The notion of development was used to consider the basic causes of historical evolution, causes that Ibn Khaldun thought to be in the economic and social structures of societies. According to Toynbee, Sorokin, and Gumplowicz, who consider Ibn Khaldun's work beyond that of some of the classical sociologists, he stood far above his age in sociological theorizing and historical research. He used the term *development* in its broadest sense to mean the development of human societies in space and time. Therefore, to Ibn Khaldun, the science of development or sociology (*ilm-al-umran*) was allied with history in its scientific context, for it was a way of reading and understanding history (*tarikh*).

In showing the dynamic relationships of nomadic, tribal, rural, and urban societies, Ibn Khaldun showed how societies move from simple to complex social organizations, *asabiya*—group solidarity and social cohesion —being stronger among members of tribal societies. He thus saw two main types of society: primitive and elementary society (*jawam al-bedoun*) and civilized and complex society (*jawam al-hazari*). The latter, which resulted from urbanization, depended on three factors: population, natural resources, and the quality of government. The quality and the duration, however, of a given "development," which Ibn Khaldun equated with the science of a given society, were not confined to quantitative progression in terms of economic, labor, and institutional expansion. A number of social, psychological, cultural, and political factors were essential as well for the continuity and qualitative development of a "civilized" society. Thus, Ibn Khaldun saw the increasing monopoly of power by the ruler and governmental institutions; the expansion of unnecessary consumption and indulgence in luxury by the population; and the decline of the *asabiya*, or social solidarity and cohesion, and the corresponding rise in individual alienation in society as some of the primary disintegrating features of "civilized," "urban," and "developed" societies.

Implicit and explicit in Ibn Khaldun's notion of societal development was the direct relationship between religion and politics. He saw no separation between the two; the leader, in the role of the Prophet, should be both a spiritual and a political guide for the community. It is interesting to note that Ibn Khaldun emphasized the peaceful relationships of nations and was one of the first social thinkers to recognize the importance of communication, common goals, and economic and cultural exchange as prerequisite to the attainment of peace.

For about two centuries, Ibn Khaldun's work remained the single most comprehensive analysis of societal development and social organization. Beginning with the 17th century and continuing into the 19th and 20th centuries, European philosophers, social thinkers, economists, and sociologists alike paid particular attention to the broad notion of development in terms of transformation from a rural, communal, and agrarian society to the urban, rational, contractual, and industrial nation-state system. Whereas Ferdinand Tönnies[7] (Germany) spoke of *Gemeinschaft* (community relationships based on traditional association) and *Gesellschaft* (contracted associations based on rationally established relationships) and George Simmel[8] (Germany) of rural and urban communities, Auguste Comte[9] (France) emphasized static versus dynamic societies, and both Max Weber[10] (Germany) and Émile Durkheim[11] (France) advanced a more detailed as well as an optimistic view of societal development, arguing that the division of labor and societal relationships are the bases of organic solidarity in modern society.

The process of societal development as economic activity was initially studied by Adam Smith,[12] David Ricardo,[13] and Karl Marx,[14] followed by a host of other economic thinkers such as Robert Owen[15] in England and Pierre Joseph Proudhon[16] in France. Whereas the mercantilists of the 15th and 16th centuries analyzed development in terms of pragmatic notions of capital formation and wealth, the classical liberals of the later centuries translated this into classical political economy, advocating the accumulation of capital as the basis for economic expansion and consequently societal development. It was Karl Marx who transcended both the thinking of the utopian socialists as well as classical liberal economists, devising a theory of surplus value and a synthesis of economics and politics that provided an overall theory of societal development based on dialectical materialism and class struggle.

In 1776 when Adam Smith published his *Wealth of Nations*, which is often regarded as the first attempt to analyze economic development, classic economic liberalism was on the rise. Newtonian science had already made a significant impact on the theory of development in general by breaking away from the static concept of a designed earth. This conceptual innovation, combined with Jean-Jacques Rousseau's more idealistic insistence on the rights of all individuals to freedom of action, had made the doctrine of *laissez-faire* espoused by Adam Smith an influencial liberating concept, introducing a belief in unlimited technical progress. David Ricardo and his theories of comparative advantage further justified this notion of development, as trade and commerce flourished between Europe and the rest of the world.

The modernization process occurring in Europe and North America from 1750 to about 1917 comprises the "classical model" of economic and socio-political development. By the 19th century, economic development, which was analyzed in terms of the growth of national production, occupied the central position in national development in Europe. Earlier, the mercantilists looked at economic development not so much as an end in itself but as a means for building a nation-state system. As the focus was directed to achievement and performance norms for acquiring manufactured goods, the principle of "rationality" in economic decision making was developed. The questions of unemployment, business recession, and poverty, as well as the tendency toward imperialist expansion, were partially rationalized with the Malthusian theory of population, in which the poor are blamed for their misery because they simply have too many children. In the political sphere, the concepts of "freedom" and "equality" achieved great prominence, and democracy combined with a representative form of government was advocated. Equality was defined in terms of certain basic civil rights and equality before the law. Freedom largely meant "individualism," or individual liberty and freedom from government control. This classical model of development, among other things, encompassed

1. Nationalism and imperialism
2. The industrial and technical revolution
3. Economic growth and materialism
4. Democracy and individual rights and
5. Bureaucratic and rationalistic forms of organization

After World War I, the foundation of the classical model of development was shaken by a number of events, including the Bolshevik revolution in Russia, the rise of fascism in Europe, and the Great Depression and advocacy of the welfare state in Europe and the United States by such political and economic leaders as Franklin D. Roosevelt and Maynard Keynes, who put the classical model on a new foundation through government interference and reform measures.

The critics of the classical model of development, most notably Karl Marx and his followers, viewed its inherent contradictions as so significant as to cause its downfall, rendering "development" impossible. They asserted that five basic types of production relations are exemplified in human history: primitive society; slavery; feudalism; capitalism; and socialism, the first face of communism. The underlying commonality is a definite form of ownership of the instruments and means of production. In explaining what determines the development of society, Marxists argued that economic laws form the basis and determine the great variety of socio-economic relations among people, that is, relations in the sphere of production, distribution, exchange, and consumption. Besides these specific economic laws, there are others that apply to all socio-economic formations. Among these is the law that production relations correspond to the character of the productive forces. This law examines the necessary connections and interdependencies between the two aspects of socio-production: production forces and production relations.

One of the most important features of the Marxist model of development is the argument that the nature of economic activities in colonial areas depended on what was taking place in the developed capitalist countries. It was Lenin who, in his analysis of the highest and last stage of capitalism, saw the phenomenon of imperialism and argued that the uneven economic and political development of capitalism during the imperialist epoch would become the basis for proletarian revolution. As Marx put it, labor alone is the substance of value; the more labor required for the production of a commodity, the greater its value and cost. Lenin argued that "value is a relation between two persons . . . a relation disguised as a relation between things."[17] In this Marxist-Leninist tradition of political economy, the later critics of capitalism, especially the dependency theorists of the 1960s and 1970s, attributed the condition of underdevelopment to the economic dependency of less dominant nations on dominant nations.

Thus, the notion of development as a generic and overall concept for societal change had come full circle since Ibn Khaldun's time in the 14th century. Whereas Ibn Khaldun succeeded in incorporating the socio-psychological dynamism of *asabiya*, or social solidarity and social cohesion, as one of the main concepts of his development scheme and had identified excessive use of material goods and luxury as indices of societal decline, the classical and neo-classical thinkers of the 17th to the 20th centuries, in the traditions of both liberalism and Marxism, were now emphasizing material growth as a basis of modern industrial society. At the turn of the century, as a result of industrialization, the secularization of thought, and the rise of modern nationalism in terms of the nation-state system, the process of societal development had come to be focused on accumulation of wealth within capitalism and the general theories of the motion of capital formulated by Marx.

Despite the prominence of the concept of societal development in the work of these scholars, from the turn of this century until the end of World War II, "development" as an all-encompassing concept of societal transformation and growth was not systematically used in the literature except in the discussion of economic and industrial growth and measurement. Yet Western theories of human development, both liberal-democratic and Marxist, proceeded from a shared assumption that the development of societies requires modern economic and social organization to replace traditional structure. Firmly adopted in Europe and North America and diffused among the elites of the less industrialized countries, this assumption included, among other things, industrialization in the economy; secularization in thought and personality; and modernization modeled on some variation of capitalism, socialism, liberalism, or communism—"reform" or "revolution." In most instances, this "development" implied Westernization or Europeanization. With the increased popularity of the term *development* during the early decades of the post-war era, the ethnocentric description of the majority of the world's population and societies as "backward" and "non-Western" was gradually being replaced by the more respectable adjectives *underdeveloped* and *developing*.

Since the 1950s, but more particularly since the 1960s, a tremendous amount of literature has been generated by theorists, from both orthodox and radical schools, who have used the term *development* to explain an enormous range of political, economic, social, psychological, cultural, and ecological phenomena in almost all levels of human activity. This unrestricted usage has led to a certain development fetish and developmentalism, in which the term has lost both its previously identifiable meaning and its specific intellectual reference. This plethora of application makes the task of analysis awesome and difficult for anyone who attempts to draw the boundaries of the field.

From "Modernization" to "Dependency" and Beyond

Development, both as a process and generic notion and as a concept referring to several specific evolutionary or revolutionary phenomena, has been used since World War II to describe phenomena in four broad literary themes:

1. Modernization, nationalism, and political development
2. Economic development and technological diffusion
3. Imperialism and underdevelopment
4. Revolution, liberation, and human development

Whereas the first two themes tend to be evolutionary and functional in their orientations, the last two take a more radical view of the processes under investigation and are directed toward basic and fundamental structural changes. It is difficult, however, to label each group by its precise politico-economic and socio-cultural orientation because there are both overlapping theories and imprecision in the terminologies employed among the adherents to these intellectual themes.

Modernization, Nationalism, and Political Development. During the 1950s and 1960s, modernization, nationalism, and political development were the dominant approaches to development and nation building, especially among the political scientists, sociologists, and social psychologists in the United States.[18] The series initiated under the leadership of Gabriel Almond and sponsored by the Committee on Comparative Politics of the Social Science Research Council at Princeton University began to compile cross-cultural data necessary for a discussion of modernization and political development. Among the political scientists who stressed modernization and political development and who were in search of universal indicators for these processes were Gabriel A. Almond and G. Bingham Powell, Jr., Samuel P. Huntington, David Apter, Leonard Binder, Sidney Verba, James C. Coleman, and Myron Weiner.

There were those such as Lucian W. Pye, Ithiel de Sola Pool, Frederick W. Frey, and Richard Fagen, who thought of communication as a key function common to all political systems. Here the literature on political development and modernization tended to distinguish political from economic development. The writers emphasized the importance of Western democracy, as well as institution building and citizen participation. The emphasis was on formal institutional channels of politics, mostly along the lines of parliamentary democracy. Multi-party system, secularization in thought, and the sovereignty of the nation-state system were strongly advocated and supported. Political development was viewed primarily as a process of national integration, as movement from less to more national unity. Associated with this theory were two problems: the necessity to link previously autonomous units to each other, and the requirement to bridge the gap between national elites and others of the same system. Political development also meant extending central communication networks into and across previously isolated sectors of the society. Modernization, the political development process, involved (1) increased structural differentiation in the political system, (2) movement away from ascription criteria and toward achievement criteria in political recruitment and evaluation, (3) a widening of the effective scope of political activity, and (4) increased secularization and "rationalization."

The last product of the Committee on Comparative Politics was the final deliberations of its members, and it promised a theoretical framework for less biased and least culture-bound political variables. Under a "political development syndrome," Leonard Binder and his colleagues offered the following explanation to the study of crisis and sequences of development.

> The political development process is a continuous interaction among processes of structural *differentiation*, the imperative of *equality*, and the integrative, responsive, and adaptive *capacity* of a political system. Political development implies successful institutionalism of: (1) New patterns of integration and *penetration* regulating and containing the tensions and conflicts produced by increased *differentiation;* (2) New patterns of *participation* and resource *distribution* adequately responsive to the demands generated by the imperative of *equality.* The acquisition of such a performance *capacity* is, in turn, a decisive factor in resolving problems of both *identity* and *legitimacy.*[19]

Development syndrome was thus the interaction of differentiation, equality, and capacity—the elements of political development. Differentiation referred to the process of progressive separation and specialization of roles, institutional spheres, and associations in societies undergoing modernization.

Equality had three components that were indicative of and significant for political development: national citizenship, a universalistic legal order, and achievement norms. Capacity was an integrative, responsive, adaptive, and innovative element in response to tensions.

Three decades of study on political development by the mainstream of American political scientists did not produce any new theory about political development. Although Binder and his colleagues were able to overcome some of the early orthodoxy of the field, their conceptualization was either too general or too overlapping to be of significant use in understanding the many problems of traditional and non-Western societies. Their approach drew considerably on Weberian ideal types, and development meant a movement from old to new and from traditional to modern. As late as 1976, this theoretical orthodoxy, with an implicit belief in the superiority of Western ideas, particularly American political values and institutions, had remained alive, as was shown in the definition of modernization and development offered by Samuel P. Huntington and Joan M. Nelson in their study of political participation in developing countries:

> We will use the words "modernization" or "development" to refer to the overall process of social, economic, intellectual, political, and cultural change that are associated with the movement of societies from relatively poor, rural, agrarian conditions to relatively affluent, urban, industrial conditions. Our usage is comparable to that of Cyril E. Black, *The Dynamics of Modernization* (New York: Harper and Row, 1966). We will use the phrase "socio-economic development" to refer to those portions of this overall process that involve urbanization, industrialization, commercialization of agriculture, media and communication development, diversification of the occupational structure, and related processes, which are often subsumed under the two concepts "economic development" and "social mobilization." See Samuel P. Huntington, *Political Order in Changing Societies* (New Haven: Yale University Press, 1968) pp. 33-34. We will use the phrase "economic growth" to refer to the increase in overall economic wealth of a society as measured, typically, by per capita gross domestic product.[20]

Still, there are those who have dealt with the question of modernization, nationalism, and development from the standpoint of a wide variety of disciplines and perspectives. Representative of those generating data through field research are the sociologists Daniel Lerner, S. N. Eisenstadt, and Everett Rogers; the psychologist David McClelland; and the political scientist Karl Deutsch, who has studied the process of nationalism and nation building from a perspective of communication and cybernetics theories.

Among the early studies, Lerner's work on modernization theory is probably the most important and influential because it represents the first attempt in cross-national studies to formulate a universal model of moderni-zation.[21] Lerner developed a general theory of modernization based on a "behavioral system" of an interactive life-style, and he then tested it with survey and fieldwork in a number of countries in the Middle East. Lerner primarily searches for the manner in which societies pass from traditional to transitional stages, eventually achieving modernity, and how that modernity can be communicated. Modernity is defined as a participant life-style; mod-ern society is a participant society. The characteristics of participant society are those found in the West, where people attend school, read newspapers, receive monetary compensation for their work, purchase commodities, vote, and have opinions on a variety of subjects. To explain the society's transition from the traditional to the transitional and modern way of life, Lerner ad-vances three major propositions. First, modernization in developing countries has to follow the historical model of Western development because "Western society still provides the most developed model of societal attributes (power, wealth, skill, rationality) which Middle Eastern spokesmen continue to advo-cate as their own goal."[22] Lerner does not elaborate on who these spokesmen are, but one assumes that he is referring to the ruling political and economic elite, who are more or less Westernized and at the time are the dominant powers in their societies. Second, the key to modernization is a dynamic psychological component called "empathy." Empathy, according to Lerner, "is the capacity to see oneself in the other fellow's situation."[23] Lerner then clarifies "the process whereby the high empathizer tends to become also the cash customer, the radio listener, the voter."[24] Third, the process of moderni-zation is facilitated by mass media, which act as an agent and index of change.

The Western pattern of modernization is presented as a universal model because it is based on historical reality. Secularism (indifference to or rejec-tion of religious consideration) in thought must be followed, as was the case in Europe and later in the United States:

> Secular enlightenment does not easily replace sacred revelation in the guid-ance of human affairs. Sacred codes, once revealed and transmitted through the shepherd, provide simple rules of conduct for all the flock—who can remain ignorant or more profoundly, innocent. But secular enlight-enment each man must get for himself. Many individuals must struggle through the loss of ignorance-is-bliss in the making of a new secular "climate of opinion."[25]

The Western model of progression to modern society comprises, accord-ing to Lerner, four sequential phases. First is urbanization, then literacy; next is media exposure, which leads finally to integration into modern participant society, resulting in economic and political development:

The Western model of modernization exhibits certain components and sequences whose relevance is global. Everywhere, for example, increasing urbanization has tended to raise literacy; rising literacy has tended to increase media exposure; increasing media exposure has "gone with" wider economic participation (per capita income) and political participation (voting). The model evolved in the West is a historical fact.[26]

Lerner's work on development and his modernization theory were highly influential in the research of American sociologists who were interested in the process of social change in developing countries. Everett M. Rogers's definition of modernization and development is an illustration. According to Rogers and F. F. Shoemaker, development is "a type of social change in which new ideas are introduced into a social system in order to produce higher per capita income levels of living through more modern production methods and improved social organization." Thus, development was defined as "modernization at the social systems level."[27]

The notion of development is also associated with the literature on nationalism. Here, one can cite the works of Carlton J. H. Hayes, Louis L. Snyder, Hans Kohn, and Boyd C. Shafer, who trace theories of nationalism to the French Revolution and associate it with the concept of the nation-state and the emergence of modern countries since World Wars I and II. In describing new nationalism and the nation-building process, Karl W. Deutsch attempts to determine what makes an individual nationalistic and what makes one feel a part of a nation-state. He writes of a nationality as "a people among whom there exists a significant movement toward political, economic, and cultural autonomy."[28] The "significant movement" can be determined by investigating the overlapping clusters of interaction patterns, that is, the volume and frequency of actual communication and traffic. Deutsch's attempt to measure the process of nationalism and social communication quantitatively. His model, based for the most part on elements of modernization and assimilation, can and has been adequately used to explain the growth of nations in many years.

Nevertheless, little has been said about areas where nation building is not the case, but the maintenance of ethnic identity vis-à-vis national identity is apparent. Several scholars have claimed that Deutsch's theory fails to explain the historical incidence of ethnic states and solidarities outside the context of social and economic modernization (such as the Germanic states and the medieval political community of western Europe) and instances in which societies emerge from the experience of modernization without an ethnically defined political identity or ability to assume a dual identity.[29]

That nationalism provides ideological, psychological, and moral support for development has been noted by many scholars who have related the growth of modern nationalism in the developing countries to the question of nation-state, liberalism, socialism, and communism but have failed to examine the phenomenon of nationalism beyond the nation-state system. For example, in the study of nationalism in the Middle East or certain Islamic societies, such discussions have failed to demonstrate the contradiction between nationalism and modernization based on Western experiences of development and the centuries-old Islamic concept of *ummah*, or community, which includes all the Islamic people regardless of race, nationality, and geographical proximity.

The confusion also arises when the writers fail to distinguish between a nation-state and an Islamic state. The two are completely opposed to each other and are thus incompatible. Whereas the nation-state is a political state, the Islamic state is *muttagi* (God-fearing), a major instrument of divine purpose on earth. This was definitely the case with those who became completely confused in the analysis of both the constitutional revolution in Iran during 1906–1911 and the Islamic revolution of 1978–1979. By relating nationalism to religion and Islam, and impressed by the wane of modern liberal ideas of the West, their conceptualization of the events underway did not transcend the formal institutions of authorities in the modern sense; they also ignored or failed to understand the theoretical and Islamic underpinning of the government, according to the *Qur'an* (*Koran*) and *Hadith* (the sayings of the Prophet). In Islamic doctrine, politics cannot be separated from ethics and thus religion. According to the Islamic perception, a political leader cannot be qualified to lead a community or an Islamic state without possessing *taqwa* (piety).

The question of nationalism versus the world socialist movement has also been debated in the literature on development. There have been attempts to relate Marxism to both nationalism and internationalism, the first being the prerequisite of the second. That Lenin, Stalin, and Mao had divergent views on nationalism cannot be questioned. Whereas Marx and Engels viewed nationalism primarily from the viewpoint of western European economic and political development, the revolutions in Russia, China, and Cuba have given new perspectives to the question of nationalism and socialist movements around the world, occupying the attention of many scholars now and for years to come.

Economic Development and Technological Diffusion. From an economic and technological perspective, the post-World War II period, and especially the decades of the 1950s and 1960s, was a period when development was viewed as synonymous with economic growth measured in aggregate terms—a perspective that still has many adherents today. Here, the major deficit of national development or societal development is seen to be a deficit of economic resources. As was pointed out earlier, the "classical" school of development (which counted among its members Adam Smith, Thomas Malthus, John Stuart Mills, and David Ricardo) focused its attention on economic growth. The total economic output was seen as dependent on the size of the labor force, the supply of land, the stock of capital, the proportions in which these factors of production were combined, and the level of technology. In his discussion of economic growth, Karl Marx used the same basic production function as did the classicists, but he viewed the decline of the capitalist system as stemming from social revolution rather than from the stagnation caused by the fundamental contradictions between the roles of the capitalists and the working classes.

The strategy of direct economic investment in developing countries to increase the rate of their economic growth became very popular in the years immediately after the war. This thesis, which became the backbone of the Marshall Plan and related programs of the United States, formed the basis for much of the economic aid flowing from developed to developing countries since the 1950s. It was said that economic aid supports a two-factor theory of productivity: (1) Society and the individual have a productive potential, and (2) external resources provide the necessary ingredients for realizing that potential. Economic aid supplies the second factor but not the first. Thus, society and the individual will benefit from economic aid only when the first factor is present and the second is absent.

One result was the attempt to reduce the development process to oversimplified mathematical models based on diverse production functions. In developing countries, the narrow goal became the speed of economic growth defined as a function of the investment rate divided by the capital-output ratio. Later, such factors as technological innovation were added (at a given rate) to the equation. One of the most influential, and now largely orthodox, views of development is W. W. Rostow's theory of economic growth, which identified five stages:[30] (1) traditional society; (2) precondition for take-off, in which certain requisites were fulfilled; (3) take-off; (4) drive and climb to maturity; and finally, (5) high levels of mass consumption. This "non-communist manifesto" was based on the belief that a steady increase in per capita income, especially during the "take-off" stage, through the mechanism of savings and investment and the emergence of a political and social framework capable of exploiting the impulses to expansion would underline the "drive to maturity," resulting in development.

One of the critics of the Rostow model was Alexander Gerschenkron, who proposed an alternative model based on the degree of "economic backwardness" of the country under study. The more backward a country, the greater the growth spurt experienced, thus allowing for a different progression through the various stages.[31] Two other perspectives that defined development in terms of its growth dimension were the dualistic and strategic approaches. In the dualistic model, it was common for a money economy in the advanced urban sector to exist alongside a traditional subsistence economy in the rural areas. Here, development was conceived as the mere expansion of the money economy and elimination of the subsistence factor.[32] The strategic approach viewed the controversy in development in terms of balanced and unbalanced growth. The balanced growth theorists advocated a synchronized and complementary large-scale investment plan as necessary for development.[33] The unbalanced growth theorists countered this observation by arguing that the best approach would instead be in maximizing induced investment decisions by maintaining strategically unbalanced growth, thus accelerating pressure and encouraging people to invest in related areas of development.[34]

Whereas the stage models of "take-off" and "great spurt" were faulty in that they attempted to fit all the developing countries into a universal formula that ignored their diverse characteristics, the dualistic and strategic approaches were also equally limited in that they overlooked many vital aspects of development and assumed the existence of resources that are actually most scarce in developing countries. Furthermore, these various growth models—classical, mathematical, historical, dualistic, strategic— either ignored all non-economic and human factors relevant to development or subordinated them to the practical requirements of their originators and planners. Development was thus seen as a much wider phenomenon than economic growth, political development, and the promotion of social change.

By the mid-1960s, many economists, political scientists, sociologists, and anthropologists, although not minimizing the significance of the more obvious and generally recognized economic and political obstacles and the inadequacy of many governmental, legal, social, and cultural institutions, suggested that the way people in developing countries think and their cultural and social philosophies may give different meaning to development and bear on the prospects of not only economic growth but also the entire realm of societal development.[35] Development thus came to mean more than mere economic growth and the implementation of technological innovations; it was recognized that structural change was also necessary. One of the first proponents of the growth plus structural change concept of development was Simon Kuznets, who in underlining the complexities of the development process, concluded that development did not consist solely of technological innovation and increased output but must also incorporate the "institutional and ideological adjustments" needed to promote and sustain growth.[36] Irma Adelman and Cynthia Morris, in an empirical study of 44 countries to determine what independent variables affected the dependent variable of income distribution, found that economic growth benefited the poorer groups in society only when accompanied by broad-based efforts to improve the human resource base of the economy; otherwise the development process takes a trickle-up shape in favor of the middle class and the rich.[37] As some economists decried the "trickle-down" theory, in which high growth rates would eventually filter down to the masses, Rostow added "the search for quality" as a sixth stage in this theory of development.[38] This new perspective of the social orientation of economic development was clearly stated in 1972 by World Bank President Robert S. McNamara:

> It is becoming increasingly clear that the critical issue within developing countries is not simply the pace of growth, but the nature of growth. The developing nations achieved an overall average annual growth rate of more than the targeted 5% by the end of the sixties. But the social impact of that growth was so severely skewed, and the numbers of individuals all but passed by so absolutely immense, that the simple statistical achievement of that target was misleading.[39]

Indeed, after two successive United Nations Development Decades, a rise in Gross National Product (GNP) per capita was accompanied by a rise in unemployment, a rise in inequality, and a rise in poverty as reflected in malnutrition, starvation, and illiteracy rates: As economists came to realize that development constitutes more than just growth, a number of sociologists, psychologists, and anthropologists sought to determine the factors affecting change in social and cultural parameters to allow for economic progress. Thus, there emerged a sociology of development in which some argued that values and attitudes must change prior to economic growth and development, whereas others argued that necessary values, attitudes, and behavior would follow when opportunities and incentives were offered. Nevertheless, there was consensus on the need for change, especially among American scholars.[40]

One of the economists who discarded the economic theories of development and sought for plausible explanations of development outside his discipline was Everett Hagen. His conception of the ideal "traditional society" postulated that behavior is governed by custom, not law, and that in such a society the individual's position is normally inherited rather than achieved. Consequently, economic productivity is low.[41] Hagen argued that the problem is inherent within a culture in terms of the types of personalities—widespread authoritarianism and aggressiveness—that limit creativity. A high degree of human creativity is what brings about the forces producing economic growth, and thus "the interactions between personality and social structure are such as to make it clear that social change will not occur without change in personalities."[42] Hagen proposed that for successful economic growth, the traditional authoritarian personality must yield to the innovative (or creative) personalities, which he defined as

> openness to experience and a tendency to perceive phenomena . . . as forming systems of interacting forces whose action is explainable, creative imagination, of which the central component is the ability to let one's unconscious process work on one's behalf; confidence and content in one's

own evaluations, satisfaction in facing and attacking problems and in solving confusion or inconsistency; a sense that one has a duty or responsibility to achieve; intelligence; energy; and . . . a perception that the world is somewhat threatening and that one must strive perpetually if one is to be able to cope with it.[43]

Here, the model tends to be modern industrial people in the West who are capable of ordering their behavior by secular-rational norm; their philosophy of being practical and instrumental, their secular attitudes toward life, all promote the use of reason as the dominant tool for comprehending and controlling both human and natural environment. Although the world is perceived as threatening, work and technology are harnessed to the satisfaction of needs. The self is glorified, and individual ambition and competitiveness are encouraged.

It is interesting to note that Hagen explained the origins of the authoritarian personality in terms of Erik Erikson's life-stage model, which focuses on childhood socialization patterns.[44] The elements embodied in the authoritarian syndrome come to be altered by what Hagen terms "the withdrawal of status respect"—certain groups in society come to acquire new values, which they perceive are in conflict with the larger society. This conflict results in the creation of an environment that is conducive to the development of the innovational personality.

A similar theory was developed by David McClelland, whose concept of the achieving society is based on the premise that a society with a generally high level of "need achievement" will produce more entrepreneurs, who in turn, produce more rapid economic development.[45] As with Hagen, McClelland studied the sources of need achievement (n achievement) in child-rearing techniques. He advocated not only the modification of child socialization patterns but also the development of achievement motivation through educational techniques.

McClelland defined n achievement as "a desire to do well, not so much for the sake of social recognition or prestige, but to attain an inner feeling of personal accomplishment," which he found to be high among middle-class Americans and entrepreneurial individuals.[46] Max Weber's description of the personality created by the Protestant Reformation—probing values such as self-reliance and hard work and generating the spirit and implementation of modern capitalism—is very similar to the personality description formulated by McClelland. According to McClelland, the high level of achievement motivation is responsible in part for the economic development in the West. He also saw a direct relationship between a high level of n achievement and a higher rate of technological growth. Here, a high level of production and a high level of consumption are projected. People who have high levels of n achievement will act like entrepreneurs: producing more goods than they can consume.

Although the human factor was introduced into the literature of economic development, the meaning of development remained the same. The dominant paradigm, regardless of the disciplinary training of the researchers and writers, always emphasized Western-style modernization, political development, and economic growth. The shift in focus from things to people did not include the "relative" nature of development: for whom and for what?

Imperialism and Underdevelopment. During the post-World War II period, especially since the 1970s, the question of development has been debated within the broader framework of theories of imperialism and underdevelopment, including both Marxist and non-Marxist perspectives. Both the intellectual and policy traditions in this area were further stimulated by the fact that traditional approaches to development as applied to developing countries were not successful, and the notion of the dependency of lesser developed countries on the center of the developed industrialized world was gaining acceptance and visibility through debate.

The older theories of imperialism come in two varieties, the political, which displays great emphasis on power politics and geopolitics, and the economic, which like classic Marxist-Leninist theories relies mainly on economic factors and class analysis, as opposed to a power political model of the world. More recent interpretation of imperialism includes not only political and economic dimensions but equally, if not more, the social and cultural aspects as well. This new approach to imperialism sees the phenomena in a multi-dimensional process and relates it to "neo-colonialism," "cultural imperialism," and "underdevelopment."

The early classical political interpretation of imperialism was based on the notion of a preeminent imperial ruler having sovereignty over numerous, far-flung territories. As the forceful extension of hegemony by a state to encompass areas not previously included in the state system, imperialism reoriented the expansion of great power competition to new fields of battle in the less industrialized world. This idea of imperialism was closely linked to nationalism, which exalted the nation-state above all other competing values and loyalties. Other political theories of imperialism based on such concepts as Social Darwinism and racism were explored in the pre-World War I era as well as in Nazi Germany in the 1920s and 1930s.[47]

Although imperialism had often been linked by analysts and ideologues to economic motives, such as mercantilism, it was James Hobson who provided the first significant theoretical work in the field. Hobson linked imperialism not simply to national aggrandizement but also to the search for profitable overseas investment as an outlet for surplus capital. Imperialism thus served the needs of investors and banks whose domestic investments garnered diminishing returns and who hoped to maximize profit by investing abroad. It was these sectors of society who, according to Hobson, benefited from imperialism. Hobson also believed that radical reform to redistribute wealth could create renewed opportunities for profitable investment at home by increasing purchasing power and consumer demand; thus, Hobson, although not rejecting capitalism, did call for a new social and economic order.[48] Older economic theories were rooted in the notion that the possibilities of internal capitalistic growth were not unlimited, and therefore the development of overseas markets was necessary. Imperialism was seen as a means of achieving this end. Hobson was the leading critic of this kind of reasoning. For Hobson, who published his work at the turn of the century, imperialism served to perpetuate and expand the power and interests of the wealthy few at the expense of the subsistence masses and the nation as a whole. This argument was buttressed by the assertion that the ruling elite, to gain support for its imperialistic policies, used the communication media to manipulate the masses into a nationalistic passion. They were able to do so in spite of what Hobson saw as the true implications of imperialism for the masses.

Joseph Schumpeter, another of the "older" economic theorists, saw imperialism as a lingering vestige of feudalism in the modern industrial, capitalist world.[49] War and imperialism existed because of the persistence of archaic political forms in which were sown the interests of an absolutist aristocracy; nationalism, too, was such an archaic phenomenon. Schumpeter's socioeconomic theory of imperialism, written in response to Marxist theory, was based on Max Weber's older notions of domestic and international prestige. Weber saw the prestige potential of imperialism as particularly appealing to elites, especially those associated with economic interests. Thus, it is not nations that compete for power but rather their privileged aristocratic classes.

Although Marx himself devoted little time to imperialism, seeing it as the extension of colonialism and, historically, as an advanced force replacing older social forms, with capitalism as a precursor to socialism, Marxists and Marxist-Leninists began to analyze imperialism more elaborately as it flourished in the late 1800s and early 1900s. Rudolf Hilferding presented the earliest fully developed Marxist theory of imperialism, postulating that it was a necessary part of advanced capitalism.[50] Emphasizing the role of "finance capital," Hilferding argued that imperialist expansion became necessary to maintain the rate of finance capital profit, thus bringing new areas into the capitalist system.

Rosa Luxemburg was another scholar who linked imperialism to the capitalist search for surplus value. Because opportunities for exploitation were faltering at home, capitalists were forced to look abroad to maintain profit without internal reform. It was a means of expanding the accumulation possibilities of the capitalist classes and, as such, was the political expression of their competitive struggle for what was still left of the non-capitalist regions of the world.[51]

Marxist theories of imperialism reached an apogee with Lenin's contribution, which for the most part synthesizes the works of Hobson and Hilferding with the adoption of Luxemburg's notion of imperialism as being a form of capitalism at its highest stage.[52] Lenin saw imperialism as a mechanism by which capitalism could postpone the resolution of the internal contradictions that would eventually result in its destruction. Again, this represented the "highest stage" of capitalism, in which monopolies and monopolistic finance capital dominated capitalist societies while exporting surplus capital to underdeveloped areas abroad, dividing up the world among the capitalist powers. Although most of the writings on imperialism to this point were centered on the evolution of industrial and capitalist countries, it was mainly with the work of Lenin that attention was also directed to the less industrialized world's development and that an alliance with national liberation movements and revolutionary forces was sought.

An orthodox Marxist, although countering many of Lenin's and the Bolsheviks' ideas of international development and imperialism, Karl Kautsky in Germany advanced the notion of "peaceful resolution of imperialism" and argued that there will be a collective exploitation of the world by international finance and industry.[53] A critic of the Bolshevik revolution, he believed that the revolution in Russia was followed by the dictatorship of the party in power and not the entire proletariat, as Marx had envisioned it.

More recent interpretations of imperialism include Herbert Luthy's claim that it was mainly a work of education and civilization,[54] and Ronald Robinson and John Gallagher's "informal empire," which breaks away from the traditional definition of imperialism exclusively in terms of colonial territories and relates it to a continuous involvement of non-governmental character.[55] Other interpretations of the term proposed the notion of "periphery imperialism," which meant that the unsatisfactory conditions of the colonies, such as those in Africa and Central America, was a major factor in the development of imperialism, thus placing the center of gravity in the less industrialized countries themselves.[56] Among the Marxist scholars there were attempts to reinterpret imperialism in light of Marx's and Lenin's work. For example, Paul Baran and Paul Sweezy wrote of "state monopoly capitalism" as a new phase of state intervention in the economic affairs of the industrial capitalist countries,[57] and Harry Magdoff discussed imperialism in the context of conglomerate monopolies.[58]

Thus, by the 1950s and 1960s, two major propositions were advanced in regard to development and imperialism. One was the general notion of neocolonialism presented by the leaders of the Third World in the mid-1950s, which charged the indirect exploitation of developing countries and former colonial territories by means of unequal trade and political relationships.[59] The second, which was rooted in the dependency school of thought advanced mostly by Latin American writers and supported by their North American counterparts in the 1960s, argued that development and underdevelopment were interrelated and continuous processes—two sides of a single coin.[60] A perspective of the dependency approach to development was evolved from the structuralist viewpoint of the Economic Commission for Latin America (ECLA), which linked Latin American underdevelopment to the international economic system. Others who took a more Marxist perspective wove the dependency approach into their Marxist-Leninist theory of imperialism.

The gap between the increasing economic decline of the ·developing countries and the capital accumulation by international industrial monopolies was emphasized by André Gunder Frank[61] who wrote chiefly on Latin America, and Samir Amin[62] and others, whose presentations were drawn mainly from the experience of former French and English colonies. They argued that the capitalist world system is basically opposed to the development of the Third World and therefore tends to increase its dependency on the industrial world. The dependency theory emphasizes the international division of labor and advances a more or less economic and socio-political approach to the problems of imperialism and underdevelopment.

Johan Galtung, in a tradition of neo-Marxist interpretation of imperialism and critical theory of sociology, has identified five types of imperialism: economic, political, military, cultural, and communication, based on the ideas of the "peripheral school," and he defines imperialism as a form of structural dependence between central and peripheral nations.[63] This feudal relationship between the centers and the peripheries is based partially on the cooperation of indigenous ruling elites whose values are very similar to those of the center metropolis.

Related to the broader question of economic structuralism and international development is the work of Immanuel Wallerstein, who views the world economic system as a single system with three basic elements: a single market dominated by a capitalist world system, a series of state structures or countries that determine the working conditions of the market, and an exploitative process involving the center and the periphery.[64] The transnational corporations have proven to be effective in organizing this system. It must be pointed out that Wallerstein's work is on the world system level and not on the national or international economic scale. Thus his work is an elaboration of the world capitalist system and is not a theory of national development.

In this brief review of the literature on imperialism and underdevelopment, a number of common characteristics have become evident. First, the literature takes an economic perspective of the phenomenon under discussion, with occasional political and social frameworks. Second, it shows more concern with the causes of "development" and "underdevelopment" than with the meaning and analysis of "development" itself. Third, it investigates the causes and aspects of underdevelopment in terms of external factors and from the viewpoint of industrial and capitalist competition rather than from the point of view of the Third World, or "underdeveloped" areas. Fourth, it is somewhat vague and general in its use of such notions as dependency and center-periphery relations. These terms are often used to point to the ideological commitment of the writers rather than being any serious attempt to delineate and define them. Thus, the notion of dependency, used by the early writers to refer to a particular and specific case of economic or political relationship, is now being used as a residual notion to signal general relationships.

For example, if capitalism is an international system, as it is being claimed, how can we justify the use of the term *dependence*, to show a particular part of that system when, by definition, all parts of a system are dependent on each other. Furthermore, instead of using *dependence* to refer to all kinds of relationships, we can employ such concepts as domination, integration, incorporation, interconnectedness, and interdependence to describe a variety of activities that are diverse, unique, and multi-dimensional. Seen from this perspective, the impediments to *development* are neither solely structural nor behavioral in nature, but rather are integrated in a way that requires more than an economic or political analysis.

Revolution, Liberation, and Human Development. Despite the enthusiasm expressed by the advocates, the theorists, and the planners of the orthodox theories of development, it was clear by the 1960s and the early 1970s that the philosophies as well as the strategies either had failed to meet their desired goals, or in the case of successful implementations, were becoming dysfunctional, creating sharp criticism from within and without the system. This was the beginning of what we might call a new wave—a process and a continuous stream of criticism, rebellion, protest, revolution, self-evaluation, and search for alternatives—which reached its most crucial period in the late 1970s, culminating and manifesting itself in many events of the period. This new wave eschews all the orthodox models of development, both liberal and Marxist. Unlike the previous approaches it cannot be identified on either geopolitical or national divisions; neither is it exclusively a phenomenon to be seen in the Third World countries alone. It finds its support and manifestations in the industrial and "developing" countries of both East and West. It has its roots in more humane, monistic, ethical, traditionalist, anti-bloc, self-reliance theories of human and social development.[65]

By the middle of the 1980s, it had become clear that this new emerging perspective, which we call monistic/emancipatory, was gaining popularity and influence and had pushed the two dominant orthodox models of development—the liberal/capitalist and the Marxist/socialist—to a position of conservative, defensive, and *status quo* seeking perspectives. The underlying, philosophical and theoretical, as well as practical, reasons for the emergence of this new wave were many, but chief among them were the following:

1. The developmental plans under the liberal/capitalist model, which expressed the prevailing views about the relationship between socio-economic "backwardness" and inequality and political development and which found the answers to these "ills" in rapid economic modernization and industrialization, had failed in almost all the Third World and developing countries. In the three decades between 1946 and 1976, not only had the gap between the rich and the poor widened internationally, but also on the national level in such regions as Asia, Latin America, and Africa economic modernization had resulted in autocratic regimes, military dictatorships, political instability, and even revolution. Even in the wealthier nations that were members of the Organization of Petroleum Exporting Countries (OPEC), the increase in GNP and national wealth had not led to participatory political democracy. The "passing of traditional society" and the "modernizing of the Middle East," which Daniel Lerner had predicted two decades earlier, turned out to be the Islamic revolution, which set the seal on Iran's historic referendum designed finally to lay to rest the Western paradigm, and with it, its main agent, the Pahlavi dynasty, which had ruled Iran for over a century. In short, the Iranian case provided empirical evidence of the demise of the model of "modernization" through industrialization; however, its most profound impact is the impetus it has given to a number of indigenous developmental strategies and policies not only in Iran but in the Islamic world as a whole.[66]

2. The Marxist/socialist model, too, though successful in many areas of development, especially in the People's Republic of China, had run into some difficulties of its own both in the lands of its origins and in its application to the problems of development in the Third World. Some of these obstacles were political in nature, but others had social and even economic roots. That the straight-jacket model of Marxism/socialism was in conflict with many of the values and traditions of developing countries and thus incompatible with some indigenous developmental goals in these societies could not be denied.

3. Despite the contrasting points of view, both the liberal/capitalist and Marxist/socialist models of development represented a single super-paradigm of development. Both approaches took mainly economic and material views to development; the variables were chiefly socio-economic in nature, and the difference in measurement secured was minimal. Both the liberal and especially the neo-Marxist began from the premise that the causal flow of development would be from economics to politics rather than the reverse. Although the orthodox Marxist point of view emphasized political factors and revolution, it too, like the liberal model, gave primacy to politico-economic varia-

bles over cultural, communication, human, and spiritual factors. Both models grew out of historical experiences in the West—primarily in Europe. Both were secular, nation-state oriented, and linear, one emphasizing indigenous factors and the other exogenous factors of development. Both failed to take an integrative view of development on individual and societal levels.

4. The dependency theory in all its variations, like the earlier social democratic analyses of development (such as the ones expressed by Gunnar Myrdal and Robert McNamara), was not a new model of development but only a collection of critiques of the orthodox approaches. The critiques dealt primarily with various perceived causes of underdevelopment rather than establishing new meanings of development. Both reformed neo-classical economists/developmentalists and dependency-oriented structuralists again accepted the nation-state as the primary unit of analysis. Ultimately, all were committed to the notion of "development," and none was willing to question the fundamental validity and acceptability of the term or the process. Whereas the liberal pluralists and neo-classic reformists continued to talk about such items as "an irrefutable relationship between violence and economic backwardness,"[67] offering data to demonstrate the positive relationship between economic development and democracy,[68] the Marxists, neo-Marxists, and their various structural strategists were debating such issues as the mode of production controversy and the role of merchant capital and unequal exchange in underdevelopment.[69]

5. As disappointment mounted, more and more writers, analysts, thinkers, and policy makers, found the source of frustration in the unwarranted assumptions of the dominant models of development, which formed the super-paradigm of social change. The main flaws in these models included ethnocentrism, biologism, and ahistoricity.

For example, it was realized that development was a much more complicated process than that envisioned by the practitioners of the orthodox theories. Instead of neatly woven but sometimes overlapping schemes—such as the stage theories, which explained development as an automatic step-by-step process; the index theories, which claimed that socio-cultural indices of developmental change related directly to economic indices; the differentiation theories, which sought answers to development in increasing differentiation of structures and functions; and the diffusion theories, which suggested that development begins with the spread of certain ideas, motivations, attitudes, and behaviors—development may actually be described as a dialectical process involving trade-offs in which sequences lag and consequences vary from society to society. Furthermore, the theories of exogenously induced change and economic growth, deemed to be the *sine qua non* of progress, supported by capital-intensive technology imported from the West with Western ideas, centralized planning and encouraged a philosophy that underdevelopment had internal causes.

Inherent in the orthodox theories was a logical positivist bias, combined with what may be termed biologism, which assigned precedence to the laws of nature, regarded humankind simply as another link in the chain of scientific discovery along the line of biological and physical sciences, and separated human spirituality from the notion of human development. When focused on ahistoricity, the problem of underdevelopment can be set in the context of a world capitalist economy in which the West takes advantage of the poor South, a theme that prompted a new understanding on the part of structuralists, dependency theorists, and the new diffusionists.

Indeed, it can be said that whereas the Third World accepted the orthodox models of development such as industrialization, the West conceptualized it as civilization, which embraced a number of economic, political, and social dimensions. As Lerner had conceptualized, "The Western Model of modernization [that] exhibits certain components and sequences whose relevance is global . . ."[70] and "what America is . . . the modernizing Middle East seeks to become."[71] The "traditional" person was going through "transition" to become "modern." "The traditional," according to Lerner, "cares nothing, wants nothing, can do nothing about this world."[72] As was expressed by Wilbur Schramm, "A developing country . . . cannot choose to import the mechanical side of modern civilization while retaining old social institutions that are inconsistent with industry."[73] Lerner and his colleagues had overstated themselves. As the outcome of the social processes revealed itself in the Middle East during the 1970s and 1980s, the traditional person may know, care, and want more than his or her apparent "apathy" reveals to the outsider.

It can be said that the period beginning with the late 1960s and continuing well through the mid-1970s turned out to be one of apology and rethinking.[74] In one interview, Lerner was asked if he had any new thoughts on the subject of his modernization theory and if there were any changes he would make in his model. "The most important change that I want to make," Lerner responded, "is not to call the whole process 'modernization' anymore but rather 'change' . . . I would think of the factors not as indicators of modernity but as 'propensity to change' or readiness to try new things." But Lerner did not elaborate on what direction this "change" should go or what he meant by "new things."

Samuel P. Huntington, Everett Rogers, and Wilbur Schramm are among those who modified their earlier ideas on "modernization." In 1976, Huntington and his colleague concluded that "the liberal model of development has been shown to be methodologically weak, empirically questionable, and historically irrelevant, except under specialized circumstances."[75] Nevertheless, these critiques remained faithful to the principles of the orthodox theories and super-paradigm without proposing a new one. For example, alternatives to liberal models, according to Huntington and Nelson, included overlapping and conceptually contradictory vague and redundant models labeled "bourgeois, autocratic, populist, and technocratic."[76]

6. Finally, a number of world events precipitated criticisms of the orthodox models of development and helped lead to their rejection as a realistic and viable standard for development theory. First, modern nationalism had run into difficulty, and ardent and zealous leaders such as Mohammed Mossadegh of Iran, Gamal Abdul Nasser of Egypt, and Sukarno of Indonesia had not been so successful in dealing with a number of important developmental questions both internally and externally. Their brand of "liberal democracy," "popular socialism," and "guided democracies" had been disappointing both to their followers and to the public in general. Second, the nonaligned movement headed by Nehru of India and Tito of Yugoslavia and the 1973 oil embargo and crisis demonstrated that, if they work together, less developed countries can indeed represent a bargaining power to establish international "rules of the game." Third, the mounting economic, political, and social problems in industrialized countries coupled with improved public health, family planning and other developmental progress in the People's Republic of China presented new alternatives and possibilities for developmental planners. And fourth, the environmental and ecological realization that industrial technology was hazardous to human health and to the ecological balance prompted suggestions to slow down the industrial technology race as much as possible. Additionally, population pressures further moved the debate away from concentrating solely on economic growth and opened the door to a more general goal referred to as quality of life. One of the most important recent developments, of course, is the growing influence of religion, as is demonstrated by the Islamic revolution in Iran and the resurgence of Islam as a revolutionary social, cultural, and political force.

As the concept of development became broader and more general, its elasticity kept changing: Why and how should we measure human satisfaction and "happiness'" instead of measuring only income. This was the question that, if answered, would provide a new meaning of development. During the 1970s and 1980s, contributions to the new meaning of development have come from diverse and varied schools of thought, geographical areas, and personalities. They include the Islamic response of Ayatollah Ruhollah Khomeini,[77] his disciple Murtaza Mutahhari,[78] and Iranian sociologist Ali Shari'ati;[79] the Latin American discourse of such writers as Paulo Freire[80] and Gustavo Gutierrez Merino;[81] and the African challenge by Frantz Fanon,[82] Julius K. Nyerere,[83] and several others. A number of these thinkers definitely are major contributors to the newly emerging school of thought in development, which we have labeled monistic/emancipatory.

For example, this notion of development is well illustrated by Gutierrez, a Peruvian theologian and social activist: "The term development conveys a pejorative connotation . . . [and] is gradually being replaced by the term liberation."[84] Gutierrez, a major spokesman for the "theology of liberation" movement in Latin America was referring to liberation from the domination of capitalist Western countries and from virtual enslavement by the national oligarchies of many Latin American nations.

One of the central questions is this: If "development" has to take place and if the process of social change is an ongoing and continuous one, which cultural peculiarities are to be allowed and which are to be eliminated when they interfere with "societal progress"? Who should determine just how fast, by whom, for what, under what conditions, and in what way values in a developing society are to be altered? It is deemed appropriate that societies should decide for themselves which elements they will emphasize and which they will alter, in recognition of the value of self-determination. Denis Goulet, one of the critics of orthodox approaches to development, emphasized the importance of the collective cultural perspective to an individual's survival and self-esteem. He identified "existence rationality," with core values as its base, as the crucial aspect in effecting social change.[85] Recognizing the ethical components of development, Goulet argued that it is necessary for the alien rationality of modernization to be critically linked, by the people themselves, to traditional and cultural values.[86] And as Ivan Illich has pointed out, these solutions were not forthcoming from the advanced industrialized countries, where social imagination was overshadowed by material life.[87]

The new notion of development emphasizes not only traditional and cultural values but also self-reliance, grass-roots initiatives, and an ideology of its own, independent from traditional liberalism and Marxism. One of its spokespersons, Julius Nyerere, president of Tanzania, tried to create an African ideology that is independent from Western philosophies. Criticizing capitalism, colonialism, and European socialism, and dismissing them as either harmful to or inconsistent with Tanzanian social and economic realities, he attempted to create "African socialism" based on the concept of *ujamaa*, a Swahili word meaning "familyhood." The concept of *ujamaa* is supported by the similarities between communal philosophy and tribal culture. It incorporates a positive valuation of shared ownership of land and property, equal distribution of wealth, and non-exploitation of people. To Nyerere, the individual is the most important element in the success of developmental efforts. Nyerere's ideas, though somewhat general and less successful in practice, did raise enthusiasm on the part of many for an alternative strategy for and philosophy of development. By the 1970s, Mahatma Gandhi's earlier comment that there is no road to self-reliance because self-reliance *is* the road had gained a new respect and popularity among the development planners, especially in the Third World. In simple, yet compelling language, Nyerere divorced himself from those who regarded development as merely an economic advancement and technological and bureaucratic growth:

> Development brings freedom, provided it is development of people. But people cannot be developed; they can only develop themselves. For while it is possible for an outsider to build a man's house, an outsider cannot give the man pride and self-confidence in himself. [88]

Development or liberation and emancipation? This question spurred related thoughts among a number of scholars who felt that development pedagogy must take its course by encouraging in each individual the emergence of an inquiring mind. One of the most provocative formulations of a strategy of this type was that of Paulo Freire and his liberating theory; the new term *conscientizacao* (Portuguese for *conscientiazation*) referred to the process of learning to perceive social, political, and economic realities and contradictions in peoples' lives and of taking action against the oppressive elements in a given situation as a whole. *Conscientizacao* enables humankind to enter the historical process as subjects, not as objects, as had been the case for so many centuries, specifically in the Third World and the Latin American societies to which Freire implicitly directs his theory. People can then take it upon themselves to change the structure of an oppressive society. Freire was considered a reformist who wanted to bring certain political and social reforms to northeastern Brazil, where he lived. But when the Brazilian government invited him to leave the country, and when he spent six years in Chile and in the United States, his writings tended to become even more revolutionary. Indeed, some of his best writings concern education as a means for promoting revolutionary action: "It is only when the oppressed find the oppressor out and become involved in the organized struggle for their liberation that they begin to believe in themselves."[89]

On the theme of freedom, oppression, human dignity, and organized revolutionary action, Freire's work was validated by a number of contemporary social and religio-political thinkers who had addressed themselves to these questions. For example, the phenomenon of the psychological alienation of black people in a white-dominated world, their inferiority complex, the quest for whiteness, and the depersonalization that characterized the colonial era were all part of the theme of Frantz Fanon's writings. Mutahhari and

Shari'ati, like Freire and Fanon, believe that the oppressed cannot clearly perceive the "order" that serves the interests of the oppressors, whose image they have internalized.[90]

Certainly the most novel, critical, and fundamental aspects of the emerging paradigm of development is its monistic, emancipatory, and spiritual nature. In that it goes beyond secular humanism and existentialism, it takes an integrated view of human development as it relates to God, humanity, and nature. It has a strong religious and spiritual quality. Many of the leaders of this tradition come from religious educations in Christianity, Islam, and Buddhism. Yet there are many among them and among their followers who have had no formal religious education. For example, Freire is deeply religious, and this commitment no doubt has shaped his thoughts about human society and individual development. To Freire, humankind is essentially defined by the relationship first to God and second to other humans, and dehumanization in the form of disintegration of this relationship is destructive to true human nature and dignity. Thus, Freire, Fanon, and Shari'ati all speak of human nature in the most optimistic terms. Yet it is the inseparably integrated function of religion, politics, and emancipatory revolution that has characterized the mainstream of the emerging paradigms of development. This point was well captured by Ayatollah Khomeini, its most outspoken leader and advocate in this century: "A religion which does not stipulate war against oppression is an incomplete religion."[91]

Thus, although one of the primary realizations resulting from dissatisfaction with the liberal/capitalist and Marxist/socialist super-paradigm was that there are many pathways to development, some common elements in this new conception (which for the lack of a better description we have termed monistic/emancipatory) have clearly emerged. Here we can define *development* as a much wider phenomenon than economic, political, and social constructs to produce change. Development, if it is accepted in the first place, can be defined as the entire gamut of processes and means by which a social system moves away from a condition of life widely perceived as unsatisfactory in some way toward conditions regarded as humanly better.

Some of its main characteristics can be summarized as follows:

- Unity of God, humanity, and nature, its monistic and monotheistic world view
- Importance of ethics, aesthetics, and spirituality
- Dimensions of emancipation, human revolution, and elimination of oppression
- Primacy of value and cultural systems over economic and political variables
- Emphasis on communication as a process of sharing and on dialogue over communications as the means for technological innovations and manipulation

- Commitment and loyalty to individual, community, and global concepts rather than a nation-state level of analysis
- Anti-bloc, self-reliance, and independence in development with an emphasis on the potential of local resources
- Integration of the traditional and modern system and a non-linear view of development
- Popular participation in self-development planning and execution, a bottom-up rather than a top-down development strategy
- Negation of capitalism and state monopoly socialism in favor of alternative, indigenous politico-economic systems.

The paradox of development is its contradictions and ironic nature. That development should take place is unquestionably accepted almost by all, and most certainly by those in the social sciences. Yet the major focus of the argument, as directed to the problems of the so-called developing societies, is that development has no universally applicable model. One might argue that a society that has refused to accept development as a useful concept for its survival and growth is better adapted to the requirements of a satisfactory, harmonious, and peaceful life than a modern developed state. In this context, there is a major gap in the literature on development, a kind of imbalance and ethnocentrism that has kept the field of inquiry narrow and parochial. Lacking are the analyses of both small- and large-scale social liberation and religious movements that have important historical and cultural roots, and which provide the core of the emerging dialectic between the state and society, the individual and community, ideology and technology, the truth and knowledge, and a score of other points and counterpoints.

The contemporary resurgence and rebirth of Islam manifested in the Islamic revolution of Iran and portrayed in the protest and Islamization movements in the Middle East, Asia, Africa, and other regions can be studied as the most challenging and visible response to the dominant paradigm(s) of development.[92] Comparison and contrast of those movements with recent religious resurgence and trends in the highly developed Western nations may further support the notion presented herein that development is not merely growth and change of societies; it is a fundamental social, economic, political, and spiritual emancipation of individuals.

NOTES

1. Examples include Hamid Mowlana, "Toward a Theory of Communication Systems: A Developmental Approach," *Gazette: International Journal for Mass Communication Studies*, XVII, 1/2, 1971, pp. 17–28; and his "Mass Communication and National Development Objectives," in Albert L. Hester and Richard R. Cole, eds., *Mass Communication in Mexico* (Proceedings of the March 11–15, 1974, Seminar in Mexico, DF), International Communication Division of

the Association for Education in Journalism and the University of Iberoamericana, Brookings, Department of Journalism and Mass Communication, South Dakota State University, pp. 115–120; Peter Golding, "Media Role in National Development: Critique of a Theoretical Orthodoxy," *Journal of Communication*, 24: 3, Summer 1974, pp. 39–53; Everett M. Rogers, ed., *Communication and Development: Critical Perspectives*, Beverly Hills, CA, Sage, 1976; Wilbur Schramm and Daniel Lerner, eds., *Communication and Change: The Last Ten Years—and the Next*, Honolulu, The University of Hawaii Press, 1976; Kaarle Nordenstreng and Herbert I. Schiller, "Communication and National Development: Changing Perspectives," in Kaarle Nordenstreng and Herbert I. Schiller, eds., *National Sovereignty and International Communication*, Norwood, NJ, Ablex Publishing, 1979, pp. 3–8; Majid Tehranian, "Development Theory and Communication Policy: The Changing Paradigms," in Melvin J. Voigt and Gerhard J. Hanneman, eds., *Progress in Communication Sciences, Volume I*, Norwood, NJ, Ablex Publishing, 1979, pp. 119–166; Georg-Michael Luyken, "25 Jahre 'Communication and Development'—Forschung in den USA: Wissenschaft oder Ideologie?" *Rundfunk und Fernsehen* (Hans-Bredow Institut für Rundfunk und Fernsehen an der Universität Hamburgs), 28 Jahrgang 1980/1, pp. 110–122. Some of the more recent reviews include Wimal Dissanayake, "Development and Communication: Four Approaches," *Media Asia*, 8: 4, 1981, pp. 217–227; Maria Cornelio, "The Sociology of Development and the New World Information Order," paper presented at the Conference on Communications, Mass Media and Development, Northwestern University, Chicago, October 1983; and Jan Servaes, "Communication and Development for Whom and for What?" paper presented at the International Association for Mass Communication Research (IAMCR), Prague, August 27–31, 1984.

2. See Thomas S. Kuhn, *The Structure of Scientific Revolutions*, 2nd ed., Chicago, University of Chicago Press, 1970.

3. For example, see Edward G. Brown, *The Persian Revolution*, Cambridge, England, Cambridge University Press, 1910; and his *The Press and Poetry in Modern Persia*, Cambridge, England, Cambridge University Press, 1914; V. I. Lenin, *What Is to Be Done?* Moscow, Progress Publishers, 1947; Hamid Mowlana, "Mass Media Systems and Communication Behaviour," in Michael Adams, ed., *The Middle East: A Handbook*, London, Anthony Blond, 1971, pp. 584–598; and his "Mass Communication, Elites and National Systems in the Middle East," in *Der Anteil der Massenmedien bei der Herausbildung des Bewußtseins in der sich wandelnden Welt* (Proceedings of the IXth General Assembly and Scientific Conference of the International Association for Mass Communication Research, September 17–21, 1974), Leipzig, Vol. 1, pp. 55–71; and George Gerbner, ed., *Mass Media Policies in Changing Cultures*, New York, Wiley, 1977.

4. Hamid Mowlana, "Trends in Research on International Communication in the United States," *Gazette: International Journal for Mass Communication Studies*, XIX: 2, 1973, pp. 79–90.

5. Hamid Mowlana, *Global Information and World Communication*, White Plains, NY, Longman, 1985, pp. 1–18.

6. Ibn Khaldun, *The Muqaddimah: An Introduction to History* (translated from the Arabic by Franz Rosenthal), London, Routledge & Kegan Paul, 1967.

7. Ferdinand Tönnies, *Gemeinschaft and Gesellschaft* (translated by C. P. Loomis as *Fundamental Concepts of Sociology)*, New York, American Books, 1940.

8. See *The Sociology of George Simmel* (translated and edited by Kurt Wolff), New York, Free Press, 1950.

9. The *Positive Philosophy of Auguste Comte* (translated and condensed by Harriet Martineau), Vol. III, London, Bell, 1896.

10. Max Weber, *The Protestant Ethic and Spirit of Capitalism* (translated by Talcott Parsons), New York, Scribner, 1930; and his *The Theory of Social and Economic Organization*, New York, Oxford University Press, 1947.

11. Émile Durkheim, *The Division of Labor in Society* (translated by G. Simpson), Glencoe, IL, Free Press, 1933.

12. Adam Smith, *The Wealth of Nations,* New York, Modern Library, Random House, 1937.

13. David Ricardo, in Piero Sraffa, ed., *Works and Correspondence of David Ricardo,* Vol. 1, Cambridge, England, Cambridge University Press, 1951.

14. Karl Marx, *Capital,* 3 vols., Moscow, Foreign Languages Publishing House, 1959.

15. For a discussion of Robert Owen and Pierre Joseph Proudhon, see Louis Dupré, *The Philosophical Foundation of Marxism,* New York, Harcourt Brace Jovanovich, 1966.

16. Proudhon was the leading figure of French socialism in the 1850s and the author of *Philosophy of Poverty.* Marx attacked the political economy of Proudhon in his *The Poverty of Philosophy,* which he wrote while in exile in Paris.

17. V. I. Lenin, "On Dialectics," *Marx, Engels, Marxism,* Moscow, Progress Publishers, 1963, p. 272.

18. For example, see Gabriel A. Almond and G. Bingham Powell, Jr., *Comparative Politics: A Developmental Approach,* Boston, Little, Brown, 1966; Gabriel A. Almond and Sidney Verba, *Civic Culture,* Boston, Little, Brown, 1963; David Apter, *The Politics of Modernization,* Chicago, University of Chicago Press, 1965; Lucian W. Pye and Sidney Verba, eds., *Political Culture and Political Development,* Princeton, NJ, Princeton University Press, 1965; Samuel P. Huntington, *Political Order in Changing Societies,* New Haven, CT, Yale University Press, 1968; Karl W. Deutsch, *Nationalism and Social Communication,* Cambridge, MA, MIT Press, 1953; Lucian W. Pye, ed., *Communication and Political Development,* Princeton, NJ, Princeton University Press, 1963; Daniel Lerner, *The Passing of Traditional Society: Modernizing the Middle East,* Glencoe, IL, Free Press, 1958; David McClelland, *The Achieving Society,* Princeton, NJ, Van Nostrand, 1961; Everett M. Rogers, *Modernization Among Peasants: The Impact of Communication,* New York, Holt, Rinehart and Winston, 1969; and Leonard Binder, James C. Coleman, Joseph La Palombara, Lucian W. Pye, Sidney Verba, and Myron Weiner, *Crises and Sequences in Political Development,* Princeton, NJ, Princeton University Press, 1971.

19. Binder, et al., *Crises and Sequences in Political Development,* pp. 86–87.

20. Samuel P. Huntington and Joan M. Nelson, *No Easy Choice: Political Participation in Developing Countries,* Cambridge, MA, Harvard University Press, 1976, p. 17.

21. Lerner, *The Passing of Traditional Society,* pp. 1–99.

22. Ibid., p. 47.
23. Ibid., p. 50.
24. Ibid.
25. Ibid., p. 43.
26. Ibid., p. 46.
27. E. M. Rogers and F. F. Shoemaker, *Communication of Innovations: A Cross-Cultural Approach*, New York, Free Press, 1971, p. 11.
28. Deutsch, *Nationalism and Social Communication*, pp. 86–90.
29. Hamid Mowlana and Ann Elizabeth Robinson, "Ethnic Mobilization and Communication Theory," in Abdul A. Said and Luis R. Simmons, eds., *Ethnicity in an International Context*, New Brunswick, NJ, Transaction Books, 1976, pp. 48–63.
30. W. W. Rostow, *The Stages of Economic Growth: A Non-Communist Manifesto*, Cambridge, England, Cambridge University Press, 1960."
31. Alexander Gerschenkron, *Economic Backwardness in Historical Perspective*, Cambridge, MA, Harvard University Press, 1962.
32. Benjamin Higgins, "The Dualist Theory of Underdeveloped Areas," *Economic Development and Cultural Change*, January 1956.
33. Ragner Nurkse, *The Problem of Capital Formation in Underdeveloped Countries*, Oxford, England, Basil Blackwell and Mott, 1953.
34. Albert Hirschman, "Obstacles to Development: A Classification and a Quasi-Vanishing Act," *Economic Development and Cultural Change*, July 1965.
35. Hamid Mowlana, "Capital Formation in the Middle East: A Study of Human Factors in Economic Development," *Tennessee Survey of Business*, Center for Business and Econonic Research, University of Tennessee, Vol. III, No. 1, September 1967, pp. 1–8.
36. Simon Kuznets, *Modern Economic Growth*, New York, Oxford University Press, 1966.
37. Irma Adelman and Cynthia Morris, "Who Benefits from Economic Growth?" Unpublished manuscript—paper prepared for the World Bank, 1972. See also their *Economic Growth and Social Equity in Developing Countries*, Stanford, CA, Stanford University Press, 1973; and Irma Adelman, "Development Economics: A Reassessment of Goals," *The American Economic Review*, LXV, May 1975, p. 302.
38. Rostow, *Politics and the Stages of Growth*; see also Hollis Chenery, Montek S. Ahluwalia, C. L. G. Bell, John H. Duloy, and Richard Jolly, *Redistribution with Growth*, London, Oxford University Press, 1974.
39. Address to the Board of Governors of the World Bank Group, International Bank of Reconstruction and Development, Washington, DC, September 25, 1972, p. 19.
40. George M. Foster, *Traditional Culture and the Impact of Technological Change*, New York, Harper & Row, 1962, p. 267.
41. Everett E. Hagen, *On the Theory of Social Change: How Economic Growth Begins*, Homewood, IL, Dorsey Press, 1962.
42. Ibid., p. 86.
43. Ibid., p. 88.

44. See Erik Erikson, *Childhood and Society,* New York, Norton, 1950.
45. McClelland, *The Achieving Society;* see also, David McClelland and David Winter, *Motivating Economic Achievement,* New York, Free Press, 1971.
46. Ibid., p. 54.
47. For a survey of theories of imperialism, see Wolfgang J. Mommsen, *Theories of Imperialism,* Chicago, University of Chicago Press, 1977.
48. J. A. Hobson, *Imperialism: A Study,* Ann Arbor, University of Michigan Press, 1965; the earliest version was published in 1902 in London.
49. Joseph Schumpeter, *Imperialism and Social Classes,* Oxford, England, Oxford University Press, 1951.
50. Rudolf Hilferding, *Das Finanzkapital,* London, Routledge and Kegan Paul, 1981; for a summary of his views see Mommsen, *Theories of Imperialism*, pp. 36–39.
51. Rosa Luxemburg, *The Accumulation of Capital,* New York, Monthly Review Press, 1964.
52. V. I. Lenin, *Selected Works in Three Volumes,* Moscow, Progress Publishers, 1967.
53. Karl Kautsky, *The Dictatorship of the Proletariat,* Ann Arbor, University of Michigan Press, 1964.
54. Herbert Luthy, "Colonialism and the Making of Mankind," *Journal of Economic History*, 21, 1961.
55. Ronald Robinson and J. Gallagher, "The Imperialism of Free Trade," *Economic History Review*, 6, 1953.
56. David K. Fieldhouse, *Economics and Empire, 1830–1914*, Ithaca, NY: Cornell University Press, 1973.
57. Paul Baran and Paul Sweezy, *Monopoly Capital,* New York, Monthly Review Press, 1966.
58. Harry Magdoff, *The Age of Imperialism: The Economics of U.S. Foreign Policy*, New York, Monthly Review Press, 1969.
59. Paul A. Baran, *The Political Economy of Growth,* New York, Monthly Review Press, 1957; and Kwame Nkrumah, *Neo-Colonialism: The Last Stage of Capitalism*, New York, International Publishers, 1965.
60. See Theotonio Dos Santos, "The Structure of Dependency," *American Economic Review,* LX, May 1970, pp. 231–236; Fernando Henrique Cardoso, "Dependency and Development in Latin America," *New Left Review,* July–August 1974, pp. 83–95; Celso Furtado, *Economic Growth of Brazil: A Survey from Colonial to Modern Times,* Berkeley, University of California Press, 1963; and his *Development and Underdevelopment,* Berkeley, University of California Press, 1964; Osvaldo Sernkel, "Big Business and 'Dependencia,' " *Foreign Affairs,* April 1972, pp. 517–531. For a review of the literature on dependency theory, see Ronald H. Chilcote, "Dependency: A Critical Synthesis of the Literature," *Latin American Perspectives I*, Fall 1974, pp. 4–29.
61. André Gunder Frank, "The Development of Underdevelopment," *Monthly Review*, Vol. 18, No. 4, September 1966, pp. 17–31; and his *Capitalism and Underdevelopment in Latin America: Historical Studies of Chile and Brazil*, New York, Monthly Review Press, 1967.
62. Samir Amin, *Accumulation on a World Scale: A Critique of the Theory of*

Underdevelopment, New York, Monthly Review Press, 1974; and his *Unequal Development: An Essay on the Social Transformation of Peripheral Capitalism,* New York, Monthly Review Press, 1976.

63. Johan Galtung, "A Structural Theory of Imperialism," *Journal of Peace Research,* VII: 2, 1971, pp. 81–117.
64. Immanuel Wallerstein, "Class Formation in the Capitalist World-Economy," *Politics and Society,* V: 3, 1975, pp. 367–375; and his *The Capitalist World-Economy,* Cambridge, England, Cambridge University Press, 1979.
65. Mowlana, *Global Information and World Communication,* pp. 211–222.
66. Hamid Mowlana, "Communication for Political Change: The Iranian Revolution," in George Gerbner and Marsha Siefert, eds., *World Communications: A Handbook,* White Plains, NY, Longman, 1983, pp. 294–301.
67. Robert McNamara, Address, Montreal, Quebec, May 18, 1966.
68. See, for example, S. M. Lipset, "Some Social Requisites of Democracy: Economic Development and Political Legitimacy," *American Political Science Review,* 52, March 1959, p. 69; and Donald J. McCrone and Charles F. Cnudde, "Toward a Communication Theory of Democratic Political Development," *American Political Science Review,* 61, 1967, pp. 72–79.
69. See, for example, Ernesto Laclau, *Politics and Ideology in Marxist Theory,* London, New Left Books, 1977; Arghiri Emmanuel, *Unequal Exchange: A Study of the Imperialism of Trade,* New York, Monthly Review Press, 1972; and Geoffrey Kay, *Development and Underdevelopment: A Marxist Analysis,* London, Macmillan, 1975.
70. Lerner, *The Passing of Traditional Society,* p. 46.
71. Ibid., p. 79.
72. Ibid., p. 151.
73. Wilbur Schramm, *Mass Media and National Development,* Stanford, CA, Stanford University Press, 1964, p. 36.
74. See, for example, "Modernization Revisited: An Interview with Daniel Lerner," *Communication and Development Review,* Tehran, Iran, 1: 2 and 3, Summer-Autumn, 1977, pp. 4–6; also, Everett Rogers, ed., *Communication and Development,* Beverly Hills, CA, Sage, 1976; and Huntington and Nelson, *No Easy Choice.*
75. Huntington and Nelson, *No Easy Choice,* p. 20.
76. Ibid., p. 21.
77. Ayatollah Ruhollah al-Moosani Khomeini, *Hokumat-e Islami* (Islamic Government), Teheran, 1979; his *Islam and Revolution: Extracts From the Writings and Declarations of Imam Khomeini* (translated by Hamid Algar), Berkeley, CA, Mizan Press, 1982; and his collection of speeches, *Sahifeh Noor,* 15 volumes, Teheran, 1983–1985.
78. Murtaza Mutahhari, *Jame'a va Tarikh* (Society and History: An Introduction to Islamic World View), Teheran, Sadra Publications, 1980 (for an English version see his three-part article, "Sociology of the Qur'an: The Islamic View of History," *Al-Tawhid: A Quarterly Journal of Islamic Thought and Culture,* Vol. 1, Nos. 3 & 4, 1983–1984, and Vol. II, No. 1, 1984); and his *Majmoo'a Goftarha* (Collection of Speeches), Teheran, Sadra Publications, 1983.

79. Ali Shari'ati, *On the Sociology of Islam*, Berkeley, CA, Mizan Press, 1979; and his *Marxism and Other Western Fallacies*, Berkeley, CA, Mizan Press, 1980.

80. Paulo Freire, *The Pedagogy of the Oppressed*, New York, Seabury Press, 1968; and his *Cultural Action for Freedom*, London, Penguin Books, 1970.

81. Gustavo Gutierrez Merino, "Notes for a Theology of Liberation," *Theological Studies*, 31: 2, June 1970.

82. Frantz Fanon, *The Wretched of the Earth*, Harmondsworth, England, Penguin Books, 1967; and his *Black Skin, White Marks*, London, MacGibbon and Kee, 1968.

83. Julius K. Nyerere, *Ujamaa*, Nairobi, Oxford University Press, 1968.

84. Merino, "Notes for a Theology of Liberation," p. 243.

85. Denis Goulet, *The Cruel Choice*, New York, Atheneum, 1973, p. 213.

86. Denis Goulet, "Development for What?" *Comparative Political Studies*, July 1968, p. 296.

87. Ivan Illich, "Outwitting the Developed Countries," *New York Review*, November 6, 1969.

88. Julius Nyerere, *Freedom and Development*, New York, Oxford University Press, 1973, p. 60.

89. Freire, *The Pedagogy of the Oppressed*, pp. 52–53.

90. See for example, Murtaza Mutahhari, *Sexual Ethics in Islam and in the Western World*, Teheran, Bonyad Bethat, 1982; and Ali Shari'ati, *Civilization and Modernization*, Houston, TX, Free Islamic Literature, 1979.

91. Ayatollah Ruhollah al-Moosani Khomeini Speech, *Imam*, London, Jamadee Al-Thani/Rajab 1405—March 1985, p. 7.

92. Hamid Mowlana, "Regional and International Implications of the Iranian Revolution," paper presented at the Third World Conference, Omaha, NB, October 1979.

CHAPTER 2

Beyond Developmentalism: A Framework of Analysis

COMMUNICATION, CHANGE, AND THE EVOLUTION OF SOCIETY

It is paradoxical that much of the literature dealing with communication and development contains units on the definition of *development* yet fails to make any attempt to define what is meant by the term *communication* or *communications* as currently used. Nevertheless, a survey of the literature shows that almost all the writers in this field continue to use the term as though they knew exactly what it means and that others have a similar understanding.

As early as 1955, James H. Platt noted the lack of a clear working definition of *communication* in the general literature.[1] In 1963, Lee O. Thayer also noted that problem,[2] and in 1968, Robert L. Minter wrote that there were more than 25 conceptually different definitions in the literature on communication.[3]

Minter's suggestion was that communication scholars should not seek the meaning "of" communication but rather the meaning "for" communication: one that would provide a common ground for the various disciplines. His survey of 150 members of the National Society for the Study of Communication (later renamed the International Communication Association) found that the respondents preferred the Jurgen Ruesch and Gregory Bateson definition of communication, which contained an unintentional orientation to communication theory. Ruesch and Bateson's definition (which was among a dozen definitions quoted by Minter, including those of Wilbur Schramm, George A. Miller, Colin Cherry, Warren W. Weaver, Edward Sapir, and Carl Hovland) was that "Communication does not refer to verbal explicit, and intentional transmission of messages alone. . . . The concept of communication would include all those processes by which people influence one another. . . . This definition is based upon the premise that all actions and events have communication aspects, as soon as they are perceived by a human being; it implies, furthermore, that such perception changes the information which an individual possesses and therefore influences him."[4]

It must be noted that although there have been attempts by communication scholars to arrive at a single, universally acceptable definition of communication, these efforts have been rather unsuccessful. Writers in the field have added or emphasized different dimensions of communication in their work. For example, whereas Harry Grace emphasizes the concept of confidence in a communication act,[5] Colin Cherry sees it as a process of trust and sharing.[6] Human relations have been noted by a number of writers who have suggested that a breakdown in communication inevitably means a breakdown in human relations, whether on an individual or group basis.[7]

Nevertheless, it has been the technological and quantitative dimensions of communication that have been given most emphasis by both scholars and policy makers over the last few decades. The notion that communication is a means or a process of transmitting ideas or information is based on the assumption that communication is something that one *does* rather than something that occurs.

Thus, communication has been defined and emphasized from the technological deterministic point of view, especially as it relates to culture, by such writers as Harold Innis and Marshal McLuhan, who have noted the importance of the medium over the message.[8] McLuhan's oft-quoted phrase, "the medium is the message," is one of the most popular and now largely orthodox views of the nature of social and cultural change.[9] More recently, there has been a proliferation of the notion of communication, resulting in "the current disciplinary confusion," with "textbooks exhibiting conceptual schizophrenia."[10]

Challenging these somewhat orthodox views of communication, we can speak of the so-called "information age," in which individual, group, national, and international communication are becoming viewed not only as hardware and software development but, more important, as behavioral and social development as well. The emphasis here, then, is on communication as a process and not on communications as a means.[11]

In addition, we recognize a need for a shift in emphasis from an exclusive concern with the source and content of the messages to the message distribution process. *Communication*, therefore, is defined here as social interaction by means of messages both in human and technological forms. Thus the communication act, on societal, national, or international levels, can be explained as (1) who produces and (2) who distributes (3) what (4) to whom

(5) in which channels (6) under which conditions (values) (7) with what intention (purpose) (8) in which political economy, and (9) with what effect?[12]

Communication is a human phenomenon that is facilitated by language, culture, and machines (the channels). These human and technological components rooted in human value systems are distinctive levels of analysis that have influenced profoundly the historical debates in communication research in general and "communication and development" in particular. To what extent do the machines and value systems distort or enhance the communication act? Put differently, does the *communications* revolution mean a *communication* revolution? Given these considerations, a useful distinction can be made between the communication approach and other approaches to the study of development by using the general explanation of a communication approach given some years ago by George Gerbner:

> The distinction between the "communication approach" and other approaches to the study of behavior and culture rests on the extent to which (1) messages are germane to the process studied, and (2) concern with the production, content, transmission, perception, and use of messages is central to the approach. A "communication approach" (or theory) can be distinguished from others in that it makes the nature and role of messages in life and society its central organizing concern.[13]

Extending this explanation to societal evolution, we can thus define communication not so much as the act of transmitting messages or exchanges of information, opinion, and thought but as the process in which human and societal relationships are established, maintained, changed, or even terminated through the perceived meanings of signs, symbols, and language. Communication is not something that happens between two or more persons and things; it is an integral part of what people and things are all about.

In summary, the debate of the 1970s and 1980s has made it clear that (1) communication, although vital, is a much more complex component of development than was originally thought and that it cannot be removed from its social and cultural contexts; and (2) development itself is still a somewhat unsettled concept that continues to have certain less universal and more culture-bound values attached to it. Consequently, any discussion of communication and development must begin with the question of value systems: What is meant by "development," for what, and for whom?

A FRAMEWORK OF ANALYSIS

Since World War II the concepts of development and communication have been viewed as two distinct but interrelated phenomena. In outlining a framework of analysis that can best describe the phenomenon under consideration in the post-developmental era, we intend to treat communication and development not as two distinct entities but instead as a single entity in and of itself. Our analysis, therefore, must be focused on communication and change and the evolution of society. Evolution is a complex but holistic dynamic phenomenon of a universal enfolding of order that becomes manifest as the organization of matter and energy into the organization of information and knowledge—all of which can be understood as the evolution of consciousness, or in other words, of autonomy and emancipation.

Indeed, as there is no universal agreement on the meaning of *development*, there are also differences in the definition of *communication* across cultural and linguistic frontiers if the term is used independently and in a third-party role. Although a comparative review of the definitions and meaning of *communication* in different civilizations such as Islam, Hinduism, and Buddhism are outside the scope of this chapter, the questions we seek to explore are answerable only as human communication is considered in relationship to philosophy and social systems and traditions.

In an attempt to understand the complexities of communication, we can begin with a conceptual framework in which the various dimensions of development policies and communication policies can be incorporated into the schema of both societal and individual development. However, such a schema cannot be mapped without relating these dimensions to the central question of the meaning and philosophy of development. The primary emphasis here is to draw a framework of analysis in which all the activities focused on the phenomenon of development can be satisfactorily accommodated once the phenomenon itself is clearly defined and identified. It is only after such an examination that an attempt can be made to lay a foundation for an identification and critical evaluation of major approaches, theories, concepts, and propositions. The pluralistic state of developmental studies is seen here as purposive and meaningful, as a means to dialectic synthesis. The schismogenic relationship between the constituents of development theory is a signal of the defensive posture with which these polarities are treated, not an attribute of the polarities themselves. In this framework, these polarities can be used to produce grounds for a development theory that refers to itself, and to its own development.[14]

As shown in Figure 2.1, central to the study of *development* is the meaning and the philosophy of the phenomenon itself in its fundamental, basic, and epistemological sense. Unless this question is well articulated and defined, there is bound to be confusion in the secondary and peripheral areas of both policies and strategies of development and communication. It is proposed that inherent in the meaning and philosophy of development will be the value system of any community and nation in which a variety of economic, political, social, and cultural activities are under examination. The point here is not to emphasize which values ought to be adopted at the

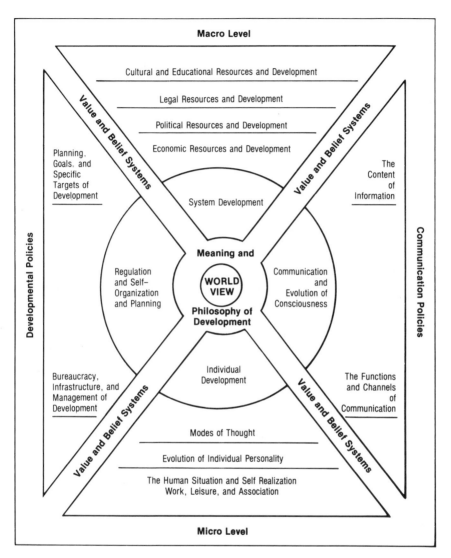

Figure 2.1. Understanding the Complexities of "Development": A Framework of Analysis.

expense of others, but rather to recognize that stability and equilibrium of any living system are directly connected to the process of value orientation and value maintenance. Thus, two axes can be created: one horizontal and one vertical. On the vertical axis, and in direct relationship to the core area of the meaning and philosophy of development, we can identify two distinct but interrelated components of change and evolution. First is the macro, or systems, level of development identified specifically with such areas as capital, labor, economic and resource development; cultural and educational development; legal development; political and institutional development; and of course, a number of other areas not necessarily identified in the figure. Second is the area dealing with micro analysis, specifically with individual development and its relationship to the evolution of society.

On the horizontal axis and equally connected to the core area of the meaning and philosophy of development, we can describe other components in two main areas: communication and regulation. Communication in both macro and micro levels will show the evolving norms in feedback relations between consciousness and reality, which in turn will determine what we perceive, what we know, what we are, and what we feel. Connected to the system and the individual levels of development, the evolving norms through communication and evolution of consciousness will be our expressions of the physical, social, and spiritual orders encountered. Regulation here is referred to as the process of movement of human life within a dynamic world and within a higher order that transcends those that are usually associated with organismic and mechanistic models. Regulation through self-organization and planning in the domain of individual and societal life may be seen as a necessary condition for autonomy as well as coordination and is indicative of co-evolution of macro and micro cosmos. It is through these processes of communication and regulation that specific developmental goals are identified; information content is formed; the functions and channels of communication are specified; and bureaucracy, infrastructure, and management are organized. Thus, development and communication policies are sets of principles that are laid out for the purpose of regulation, coordination, and interaction pertaining to a number of dimensions of human life.

The approaches to stimulating so-called "development" in a host of pre-industrial or "less industrialized" societies have largely been mechanistic, the products of optimistic schemes of economic planners. Far too often, the prescriptions did not address the maladies of the societies under examination. Today, one hopes, any analysis of a national economy's ability to withstand or put to profitable use a given development plan must include knowledge of its internal communication.

The notion of perceived human and societal progress toward a satisfactory way of life at individual, community, national, and international levels implies improved communication at these levels. It is also allied with a need to discard those parts of tradition that, having served their historical purpose, linger in the path of development until demystified. But we do not view development in the tradition-transition-modernity continuum; nor do we see all traditional authorities, institutions, and modes of communication as impediments to the process of development. Although it is easy to label the new as modern, it is naive and misleading to try to itemize traditions in the same fashion. It is in this area that communication plays its most fundamental role.

As depicted in the figure, the term *communication* is used here in a broader sense to include both its human and its technological and institutional aspects. Communication is an act of sharing and trust. Thus, we can regard society as "people in communication." It is the pressure and disorganization of communication that bring about the downfall of societies and institutions. If such powers are attributed to the communication function, a more fundamental set of questions arises, namely, how can communication serve as a positive, progressive force; and who will activate the control levers, directing this force away from disruptive, anti-developmental digressions?

It is with these questions in mind that we approach a study of the use of communication in the process of development, particularly in the less developed countries. Of necessity, we will address, generally and specifically, the philosophical issues and approaches as well as the practical application of communication in development programs in the hope that we can learn from the past and present those lessons that will positively affect the future.

It should be noted that no part of this proposed framework can be analyzed without reference and relation to the others. The point is that as a framework of analysis, such an integrative schema is needed if one wishes to identify, analyze, evaluate, and explain the phenomenon under investigation.

In a reflected manner, the field of development has mirrored the phenomenal domain of development itself. Instead of working together and managing conflict as an essential and meaningful dimension of development, interaction is devalued, conflict transformed into defensive barriers, with a regression into power politics as the final outcome. This watershed field seems to contain a culture and mythology of its own. First, it values a subordination of itself to the content level of analysis that it is addressing. Development is used to support various theories of psychology, economics, political science, and sociology. Second, the field seems to be unwilling to face the polarities and conflicts inherent in the notion of development itself. And whose development are we speaking of any way? The fragmentation and abuse of the field of development has come to serve a purpose—the purpose of being a reflection of those phenomenal problems that we are investigating. The development of development is dependent, first on the recognition of itself as a field and, second, on the application of principles of development to its own discipline.

NOTES

1. James H. Platt, "What Do We Mean 'Communication'?" *Journal of Communication,* 5: 1, Spring 1955, p. 21.
2. Lee O. Thayer, "On Theory Building in Communication: Some Conceptual Prob-

lems," *Journal of Communication,* Summer 1963, pp. 217–235.

3. Robert L. Minter, "A Denotative and Connotative Study in Communication," *Journal of Communication,* 18: 1, March 1968, p. 27.

4. Ibid.

5. Harry Grace, "Confidence, Redundancy, and the Purpose of Communication," *Journal of Communication,* 6: 1, Spring 1956, pp. 16–17.

6. Colin Cherry, *World Communication: Threat or Promise?* London, Wiley-Interscience, 1971, p. 2.

7. See, for example, Elwood Murray, "What Are the Problems of Communication in Human Relations?" *Journal of Communication,* 1: 1, May 1951, p. 24.

8. See Harold Innis, *The Bias of Communication,* Oxford, England, Oxford University Press, 1950; and Marshal McLuhan, *Understanding Media,* New York, McGraw-Hill, 1964.

9. For a critique of this and other schools of thought, see Hamid Mowlana, "Mass Media and Culture: Toward an Integrated Theory," in William B. Gudykunst, ed., *Intercultural Communication Theory: Current Perspectives,* Beverly Hills, CA, Sage, 1983, pp. 149–170.

10. See Frank E. X. Dance, "Disciplinary Confusion," *Journal of Communication,* 37: 1, Winter 1987, pp. 118–124.

11. See Hamid Mowlana, *Global Information and World Communication: New Frontiers in International Relations,* White Plains, NY, Longman, 1985, especially chapters 1, 9, 11, and 12; also, Hamid Mowlana, *International Flow of Information: A Global Report and Analysis,* Reports and Papers on Mass Communication, No. 99, Paris, UNESCO, 1985.

12. Mowlana, "Mass Media and Culture," p. 163.

13. George Gerbner, "Mass Media and Human Communication Theory," in Frank E. X. Dance, ed., *Human Communication Theory: Original Essays,* New York, Holt, Rinehart, and Winston, 1967, p. 43.

14. Hamid Mowlana, "Development: A Field in Search of Itself," *Occasional Papers,* No. 2, Leicester, England, International Association for Mass Communication Research, 1987.

CHAPTER 3

Contending Theories and Approaches to Communication and Development

VIEWS OF COMMUNICATION AND DEVELOPMENT

In tracing the evolution of communication and development, we can cite three categories of writings or approaches that have dominated the field since the 1950s. The first approach, prevalent in the 1950s and 1960s, is to view communication and development as a cause-effect relationship. This approach is based on the premise of causal relationships between the components of communication and the entire process of development. It is characterized by debate over which occurs first or causes the other: Is communication a prerequisite for development, or does development precede the establishment of communication? Since the answer to this question is largely contingent on definitions of communication and development, contenders in this approach are easily ensnared in the definitional problems addressed in the previous chapter.

The second approach deals primarily with what might be called cost-benefit analysis, or utilitarianism. Here, the role of a specific media or communication strategy in the service of development and social change is basic to the overall approach. The third approach in the literature deals primarily with infrastructural analysis. Political economy, cultural identity, and value systems are linked with communication and development by examining the structure of existing communication, economic, political, and cultural systems at all levels: national, international, and global.

Causal Approaches to Communication and Development

Under the heading of communication as a cause of development, a range of writers have advanced various theories and models, most of which are based on Max Weber's theories of social and economic change. Writing mostly in the late 1950s and early 1960s, the adherents to this school of thought used a macro level of analysis that tried to employ communication as a concept to better understand social change. Classical and neo-classical economic thinkers saw communication as a necessary factor for economic development and growth.

In the United States, various causal models correspond roughly with this theoretical perspective, including the works of such writers as Daniel Lerner, Everett Hagen, David McClelland, and a number of other theoreticians associated with the school of modernization. Often, these models were stage theories such as those proposed by Walter W. Rostow, who wrote primarily on economic history and growth, and Daniel Lerner, whose communication analysis of modernization and development became a classic in the literature of the West.

This liberal/causal approach to communication and development has been criticized on the grounds of being ethnocentric and of helping to expand the capitalist world system. Furthermore, this type of literature has been under attack for stressing the economic and historical legacy of the colonial era, maintaining the imbalance of the center-to-periphery flow economically and culturally.

Lerner's causal model suggests a sequence of institutional development leading to self-sustaining growth and modernization: urbanization, literacy, extension of the mass media, higher per capita income, and political participation.[1] Lerner contends that growth in one of these areas listed sequentially stimulates growth in the others, and that the process moves society toward modernization. Lerner further maintains that a society must develop empathy—the ability of a person to imagine significant positive change in his or her own status—in order to proceed to modernity. In explaining an individual's progression from traditional to transitional to a modern way of life, Lerner advances the notions that (1) modernization in developing societies will follow the historical model of Western development; (2) the key factors to modernization are physical, social, and psychological mobilities, which express themselves in the concept of empathy; and (3) this entire process is facilitated by the mass media, which act as an agent and index of change.

According to the model of modernization, the change from traditional to transitional and then to modern society was always accompanied by a change from oral communication systems to mass communication systems. The change was always unidirectional from traditional systems to modern systems, never the reverse. The difference between these two systems is, according to Lerner, that traditional interpersonal communication enforces traditional attitudes and mores, whereas mass communication teaches new skills, attitudes, and behavior. Mass media are, therefore, a "mobility multiplier"; that is, they have the capacity to communicate both the character and the possibility of change to a growing audience.[2] Lerner asserts that an interactive relationship exists between the media index of modernization and other social institutions.[3] The closest correlational growth of urbanization and literacy happens after take-off at 10 percent urbanization and ends at 25 percent urbanization. After this point, literacy growth correlates most highly with mass media growth. Significantly, Lerner's proposition that access to mass media is a precondition for participation in modern society and that mass media directly affect personal attitudes and behavior has been challenged not only by the critics of the orthodox models but also by the proponents of some of the liberal/capitalist theories of communication and development. For example, whereas Lucian Pye asserted that all aspects of communication, rather than the mass media by themselves, are important agents of political participation, Ithiel de Sola Pool was skeptical about whether the media have the same direct effect on changes in attitudes and skills.[4]

Another area of contention was Lerner's correlation growth hypothesis. Seymour Martin Lipset, who used a similar model in his study on political participation, was among the early writers of modernization who cautioned that the functional interdependence of urbanization, literacy, and media exposure and political participation may not be as well established as Lerner's data showed.[5] Although a few studies on mass media exposure and modernization partially confirmed Lerner's correlation hypothesis,[6] there were others that could not verify the basic chain of interaction in which urbanization, literacy, media participation, and political participation increase in direct relationship to one another.

For example, Wilbur Schramm and W. Lee Ruggles's study concluded that in 1961, urbanization was no longer as basic to the growth of literacy and mass media as Lerner had assumed several years earlier.[7] Their suggestion was that the spread of modern electronic technology (especially radio), coupled with roads and rapid transportation into villages, had made urbanization less essential to the process of development and the general growth in education. It was found that the monotonic relationship of growth stopped at substantially lower levels of urbanization than those proposed by Lerner.

Examples of causal models dealing with communication and development on the individual level include those of David C. McClelland and Everett Hagen. McClelland's work included elaborate studies on the relationship between personality and innovational activity.[8] In his study, McClelland attempted to measure the degree of achievement motivation present in various countries at various periods in history and to correlate it with economic advance in those countries. He concluded that the need for achievement (*n* achievement), which he equates with entrepreneurial activity, is a precursor of economic growth, not only in Western capitalist countries but also in economies controlled and fostered largely by the state. Thus socialization, communication in the early stages of life, plays a crucial role in the process.

Everett Hagen, also a causal model theorist, agreed with McClelland that social and economic growth are basically functions of personality and psychological motivation and are related to childhood patterns of communication and socialization. Both agreed, also, that changes in motives and values can occur in adulthood. But Hagen's model viewed the traditional society as a system in stable equilibrium that is not easily altered.[9] Changes come about when some historical accidents cause a change in behavior of the top elites, causing middle-level or lower elite groups to feel that their performance in the society is being curbed. This is what Hagen referred to as withdrawal of status respect. This loss of status causes some members of the group ultimately to reject some of the society's traditional values and eventually results in an increase in initiative in future generations. Hagen's study was based on data from England, Japan, Columbia, Indonesia, and in the colonial case, Burma and Sioux Indian reservations.

The whole social process explained in both Lerner's macro-level analysis and McClelland and Hagen's micro-level studies fits well with the theory of Max Weber, who argued that the Protestant reformists were responsible for the development of the spirit of capitalism and consequently of economic growth. In terms of politics and nation building, Karl W. Deutsch's study illustrates a macro-level model in which social communication, mobilization, and assimilation play crucial roles in the development of a nation.[10]

The causal models of communication and development, both on the macro and micro level, are equally as prevalent in Marxist and non-Marxist but revolutionary theories of social change. The difference, however, is that for the non-Weberian revolutionary theorists, the basic change in one's power and personality arises not so much in early socialization but through a continuous process of action itself. It is the revolutionary spirit, the belief system, and the act in its general form that are believed to transform the personality.

In fact, it is here that the non-Western theories of development and communication, such as Islam, differ significantly from those of Weberian and even Marxist traditions. Whereas personality as a Western concept is rooted in individualism, some non-Western views (including Islam) see personality as a central ingredient in the human mode of existence: man's relationship with God, with other people, and with nature. Anthropologist Francis K. Hsu, using the concepts of psychological homeostasis and "jen" instead of personality, designed a framework "to extricate our subdiscipline" from what he called "this intellectual prison."[11] Hsu, by reviewing China, the United States, and Japan, showed "the process whereby the human individual tends to seek certain kinds of affective involvement with some of his fellow humans."[12] Comparable analyses, previously mentioned in Chapter 1, by Murtaza Mutahhari and Ali Shari'ati show the differences between the personality and socialization models in the West and those in Islam.

Utilitarian/Cost-Benefit Approaches to Communication and Development

Present from the early part of this century but expanded rapidly during the 1940s and popularized thereafter, the utilitarian, or cost-benefit, approach examines the relationship between communication technology and developmental policies. This approach is much more practical than theoretical, and it attempts to analyze the relationship between the cost of investing in technology for development and the benefits that might be gained from such an investment. For example, will Indonesia's investment in a domestic satellite system—*Palapa*—bring benefits that will outweigh the enormous costs, or will the benefits be too few in comparison with too great a cost?

The notion of communication in development has varied over the years, fluctuating to fit the different notions of development itself, the geographical emphasis, and the availability and level of development of communication technology. This second set of approaches to communication and development contains divergent themes that have become popular in the literature and can be classified as (1) diffusion models, (2) mobilization theories, (3) technology assessments and transfer theories, (4) development communication approaches, and (5) general systems approaches and analyses.

The diffusion model, one of the most well-publicized, well-cited, and dominant approaches to the role of communication in development, reached the pinnacle of its popularity in the 1960s, partially through the publication of the synthesizing work of Everett Rogers and his associates and partially because of the planning and execution of numerous well-financed projects by the U.S. Agency for International Development (USAID) in which diffusion models were tested in Latin America, Asia, and Africa.[13] The USAID communication and development projects, carried out under the direction of a number of scholars at Michigan State University, University of Wisconsin, Stanford University, and Massachusetts Institute of Technology (MIT) in the 1950s and 1960s, were more or less in line with this tradition. Diffusion research is, at the most abstract level, an approach to understanding the process of social change. Social change, the process by which alteration occurs in the structure and function of a social system, may in Rogers's view, be either imminent change—stimulated from within a social system—or contact change—the result of an external stimulus. It can be understood as a process of three sequential stages: "(1) invention, the process by which new ideas are created or developed; (2) diffusion, the process by which these new ideas are communicated to the members of a given social system; and (3) consequences, the changes that occur within the social system as a result of the adoption or rejection of the innovation."[14] Rogers and his associates thus place themselves among those social scientists who assert that social change (and in this case the entire process of development) may best be understood as a communication process: Social change is seen as an effect of communication, and diffusion research is regarded as a subset of communication research dealing with the transfer of ideas.

The emergence of diffusion research as a single integrated body of concepts and generalization was very much facilitated as a result of its application to a variety of developmental ideas since the 1950s. The earliest of these traditions of diffusion research was very much rooted in anthropology, where *diffusionism* came to stand for the point of view that explained change in one society as a result of introduction from another society. Sociology was another discipline in which diffusion research occurred. The French sociologist Gabriel Torde, for example, in the beginning of this century was among the first who suggested that the adoption of a new idea can be an S-shaped curve: A small number of individuals initially adopt the innovation, followed by a rapid rate of adoption and then a diminution as the last members of the system finally adopt. Some of the classic studies were conducted in the field of rural sociology, which dates from the study conducted by the U.S. Department of Agriculture in the 1920s of campaigns carried out by county extension agents to introduce new agricultural practices. In the 1940s, a study on the diffusion of hybrid seed corn in Iowa investigated the social characteristics of innovators and the functions of various communication channels in the innovation-decision-making process.[15] Other fields that have produced diffusion research of importance are education, marketing, journalism, and medical sociology, in which studies have sought to understand the pattern and the pace by which new ideas are diffused within and among the different strata of society.

Many scholars who have been critical of developmental models as being applicable only to the West have also criticized communication models as being too Western and unresponsive to the needs and circumstances of developing countries. For example, it has been said that communication models employed by the West in the analysis of developmental phenomenon are basically Aristotelian, emphasizing the four components of the communication act: the communicator, the message, the receiver, and the objective. Critics see this emphasis as necessarily subordinate to media manipulation. Little attention was paid to the cultural and social structure in which the communication system operates. In case of Latin America, Luis Ramiro Beltran is concerned with the negative effects of the uncritical transferral of the conceptual framework and methodological patterns of the United States to a Latin American context.[16] Criticizing the traditional diffusion model and its use in the Latin American context, another researcher, Juan Diaz Bordenave, calls for the merger of the classical model of diffusion with that of Paulo Freire's conceptualization of *conscientiazation,* which proposed the elimination of the "transmission mentality" in education and communication and its replacement with a more emancipatory type of communication education that would contain more dialogue and would be more receiver-centered and aware of the social structure surrounding it.[17]

Indeed, there are some hidden assumptions in the communication and diffusion model: the idea that communication by itself can generate development regardless of socio-economic and political conditions; the idea that increased production and consumption of goods and services represents the essence of development and that a fair distribution will follow in time; and the idea that the key to increased productivity is technological innovation, no matter who benefits or who is harmed. It can be said that these orthodox theories of communication and development did not pay attention to the many powerful moral and ethical questions that were inherently involved in efforts to change the way people live. Although some of the main religious and cultural factors that were barriers to this type of "development" were recognized and illustrated, the writers often neglected the ethical dimension of the induced social change.

An area of convergence between communication theories and development planning is in the diffusion of technology, or the transfer of technology and know-how from the developed industrial countries to the less industrial developing nations. It has been demonstrated that this process of import-export involves not only the desired expertise and technology but values as well. That technology is, in fact, politically and culturally neutral is a myth.[18]

New diffusionists and new liberals who are now among the critics of the orthodox theories have admitted flaws in diffusion theory, modernization theory, and the traditional communication models that carry their imprint. Yet a close scrutiny of recent writings shows that, although critical of the pitfalls of past experience, they are basically loyal to the underlying tenets of the dominant paradigms of both communication and development. In the last two decades, the research and interest in the area of development communication and the use of different communication strategies and technologies for developmental programs have increased considerably. These topics are discussed in some detail in chapters 6 through 9; it is enough to say here that countries and communities throughout the world face the interrelated problems of deciding how best to use modern technology while minimizing any negative impact on indigenous cultures. Although it has been demonstrated that the various forms of mass media have considerable potential for use in developing countries, traditional forms and channels of communication and their integration with modern communication systems have been found to be most effective in generating desired results with minimal negative impacts.[19]

Communication and diffusion research in the United States had found mass media channels to be relatively more important in the information and "knowledge" function, whereas interpersonal channels were relatively more important in the persuasion function of the decision-making process in general and in the innovation-decision-making process in particular.[20] Two "important" concepts were thus identified by these studies, the "two-step flow" of mass communication ideas and the "opinion leadership" notion, in which the flow of information in the first step was from source to opinion leaders and in the second step from opinion leaders to their followers.[21] This discovery in the United States, though negating some of the earlier notions of direct influence of mass media messages on the public, was hardly a new finding for non-Western and less industrially developed countries, where modern mass media systems were not yet dominant. Nevertheless, because the development of these societies along prescribed Western lines required the spread of modern mass media technologies, for some time, especially in the 1950s and 1960s, the "two-step flow" notion was replicated to the developmental projects in the Third World, with emphasis given to the spread of centralized communication technologies. It was only in the 1970s and as a result of a number of socio-cultural analyses, coupled with the drastic changes in political, economic, and social systems of many developing countries, that the function and role of traditional communication systems (such as religious meeting places and marketplaces) as independent and fully integrated systems of their own were realized.

Structural Approaches to Communication and Development

This political economy and cultural approach to development and communication examines the present infrastructure of the world communication system to determine whether it impedes or promotes development on all levels. This approach is characterized by a number of movements, such as the call for a new international economic order and the debate over a new world information/communication order, which advocate an examination and critique of the structure of the system on both international and national levels. The report of the International Commission for the Study of Communication Problems (The MacBride Commission), for example, calls for structural changes to equalize and balance the communication structure.[22] Such balance is necessary, according to the proponents of the new order, if development—economically, politically, socially, and culturally—is to be effectively promoted. This approach sees communication as the infrastructure of and precondition for economic growth, and thus, development.

As one of the major documents looking structurally at communication and development, the MacBride Commission report notes that certain countries were able to improve national growth rates, material living standards, and educational levels and also to achieve cultural, scientific, and technological progress either through the market mechanism or through state planning. These countries may be considered developed in these respects; however, these achievements have been at the expense of economic and social equity or of political freedom. The report points out that today a more holistic approach to development is emerging, an approach that places weight on political and social reforms, including democratization of communication and increased popular participation in decision making.

The structural approach or infrastructural analysis of communication and development is relatively new when compared with the literature on causal and utilitarian approaches. Not only does it cover the traditional political economy approach to communication but it also includes a number of well-articulated works dealing with the social and cultural dimensions of communication systems, both on national and on international levels. Firmly grounded in economics, political science, or sociology, the contributors in this area come from a variety of epistemological and methodological schools of thought, but almost all adopt critical analysis in their study of communication and development theories, and many use the tradition of the Frankfurt school of critical theory. Although a good number of studies in this area are oriented toward the Marxist and neo-Marxist theories of development, a substantial portion of the work, especially in the 1980s, has been carried out by non-Marxists whose views of development most approximate those of what we have called monistic/emancipatory models.

Third World and European scholars form the core of contributors, although a number of leading scholars from the United States have been among the pioneers. In most cases, they represent the new generation of communication specialists who have challenged the dominant traditional paradigm(s) of the past. Examples of research and writings in this area include Dallas W. Smythe's work on communication, capitalism, and the "dependency road" in Canada;[23] Herbert I. Schiller's critical examination of the structure of the American communication system from political and economic perspectives;[24] Armand Mattelart's research on the role of transnational actors and cultural industry;[25] Hamid Mowlana's analysis of the international flow of information and his integrative approach to communication and developmental processes;[26] Cees J. Hamelink's writings on self-reliance, cultural autonomy, and national and international communication policies;[27] Kaarle Nordenstreng and Tapio Varis' research on the international flow of television programs and the international implications of communication policies;[28] Thomas H. Guback's examination of the transnationals and the international film industry;[29] Luis Ramiro Beltran and Elizabeth Fox de Cardona's structural perspectives on communication and development in Latin America;[30] Jeremy Tunstall's comparative communication policy studies of the United States, Britain, and a number of Western European countries;[31] and Tamas Szecsko's work on Eastern European socialist systems of communication.[32]

Popularizing what was rapidly becoming a primary concern of developing countries, Schiller in the late 1960s cited the powerful union of electronics and economics as the impetus for American business expansion abroad, noting that the colonial system as an institution was rapidly disappearing, only to be replaced by "an intricate web of economic, political, and cultural dependencies."[33] Schiller focused on the increasing role of the multinational corporations in the international market, naming it "the international extension of the domestic behemoth."[34] Thus, a new notion of "imperialism" or "empire" was being conceptualized that had a communication and cultural component and consisted of functions rather than of territory.

A more liberal view was that American expansion is characterized by penetration, not acquisition, and is more clearly seen in terms of the deployment of American personnel and resources rather than the explicit control of foreign peoples and resources. Some went even further, viewing American expansion as pluralistic and consisting of a variety of transnational organizations. These formulations necessitate a reassessment of claims of American expansion. However, the importance of the information sector in the industrial countries' domestic economy, such as in the United States, was being revealed by the fact that close to half of the American labor force in the mid-1970s was employed in the information sector, which also accounted for at least 20 percent of the nation's gross national products and was rapidly increasing.[35]

In 1971, Mowlana's research on international communication, which encompassed a span of 120 years beginning in 1850, found that more than half of the studies coded—52 percent—were written between 1960 and 1969; research on the role of mass media in national development, particularly as it related to the less industrialized countries, had reached considerable proportions, with three times as many studies published in the decade after 1960 as in the preceding 30 years. Of all aspects in the impressive accumulations of data in international communication by American scholars, studies of communication and national development, including studies in communication and socio-political development as well as communication and the diffusion of innovation, topped the list of available literature in the 1960s. Research emphasis on developing nations usually stressed how to communicate Western ideas and models *to* these countries, not how to communicate *with* them. Therefore, it was not unusual to find that studies in specific cultural and geographical areas have corresponded roughly to the United States involvement in those areas. Mowlana's study concluded that "This factor of involvement seems to have influenced heavily what domestic studies have been undertaken and what foreign works translated" and that "United States interests and involvements in world events generate scholarly studies as much as methodological and research development.[36]

Using Mowlana's data of U.S. research as an example, Schiller does not hesitate to use the terms *cultural imperialism* and *cultural domination* to describe the industrial capitalist world, especially U.S. involvement in the world economic system. He maintains that cultural imperialism develops in a world system, similar to that described by Emanuel Wallerstein, "within which there is a single market, and their terms and character of production are determined in the core of that market and radiate outward."[37] The cultural-communication sector of the world system necessarily develops in accordance with and facilitates the aim and objectives of the general system.

Hamelink prefers the term *cultural synchronization* to *cultural imperialism*. In his view, cultural imperialism is the most frequent, but not exclusive, form in which cultural synchronization takes place.[38] The solution for Hamelink, therefore, is dissociation, a principle he borrowed from Dieter Senghass. To be successful, Hamelink maintains, dissociation has to combine resistance to external synchronization with internal equality and self-reliance.

The notion of self-reliance also preoccupies the attention of several other scholars, including Armand Mattelart, who have examined the structure of the political economy of information. For Mattelart, self-reliance constitutes the realization and affirmation of the failure of a particular aspect of development—recognizing the value of solidarity, the demand for cultural diversity and identity, "refusal of an instrumentalist conception of technology," and "invitation to developed countries to reconsider their own growth schemes" and negative spillover.[39] Examining the transnational systems in whose web nation-states exist, Mattelart traces the developmental models that he thinks are being imposed on the Third World. The major goal for the New World Communication and Information Order, according to him, should be to "re-equilibriate an international flow of information marked by an unequal exchange."[40]

The structural analysis of communication and development deals not only with the questions of the political economy of information but also with a set of cultural and social indicators relevant to communication and society in general. For example, an integrated framework for comparative communication systems has been proposed in which emphasis is given to the process of both message production and distribution and intent rather than to the atomistic notion of content and effects.[41] The distribution stage of communication systems, long neglected, has been singled out and emphasized, and a number of indicators have been identified that focus on the linkages among society's cultural, economic, political, and communication institutions. In short, this integrative approach to communication and development policies and planning not only considers such variables as ownership, production, and distribution but equally takes into account the "perceived" and "actual" control in communication systems and pays attention to such variables as capital, income disposition, bureaucracy, and message use.

The structural approach rejects the argument of the liberal/capitalist theorists that communication brings about structural change by first creating socio-demographic conditions or by changing individual psychological characteristics. Acknowledging the importance of the individual level of communication and change, it takes the position that structural change is a precondition for any successful developmental objectives.

MODELS OF COMMUNICATION AND DEVELOPMENT

Considering the different politico-philosophical and socio-economic orientations assigned to the terms *development* and *communication* throughout history, and after examining the variety of writings on the relationships between communication and development outlined above, we can identify three major categories of models that have been the subject of scholarly, professional, and policy debate, especially since the 1950s: (1) liberal/capitalist models, (2) Marxist/socialist models, and (3) monistic/emancipatory models. We use the term *models* in the plural sense since there are variations in each of the three major schools of thought outlined here.

Liberal/Capitalist Models

The first set of dominant models of communication and development are the liberal models, based more or less on the notion of modernization as in the West and within the capitalist economic system. This model generates primarily from the socio-economic theories of Max Weber. Weber's writings have led to "appendage theories," such as those of McClelland and Hagen on entrepreneurship.[42] In short, these theories emphasize the role of the economic elite in development while paying particular attention to the factors of information, knowledge, and innovation.

According to McClelland's theory, the rise of capitalism was not the direct result of Protestantism, but rather was due to the fact that Protestantism in the form of a religious and ethical framework promoted the need for achievement among its followers. This in turn helped to promote entrepreneurship, which resulted in economic growth. The need achievement (*n* achievement) in this context refers to an individual's motivation to establish himself or herself without the need for power and affiliation and to meet the demanding standards of excellence that exist. McClelland's theory maintains that the need for achievement strongly relates to economic growth and development; in fact, by injecting need achievement into society through its communication infrastructure and through socialization and education, economic development can be stimulated. In short, changes in the need for achievement are causally related to the rate of economic growth.

Hagen's theory of entrepreneurship holds that social structure and economic growth are primarily functions of personality and psychological motivation, an assumption shared also by McClelland. Hagen believed that economic growth can occur only when there is a definite change from the traditionally oriented personality, associated with self-centeredness, low esteem, and authoritarian overtones, to a more modern, open, and innovative personality structure. Hagen believed that this change can come about primarily through changes in the home environment and child-rearing practices. Thus communication behavior within the family structure and early socialization are the most important aspects of this phenomenon.

The dominant liberal/capitalist model of development, as was discussed in Chapter 1, is essentially a model of growth and is made up of the following four main elements: (1) economic growth through industrialization and accompanying urbanization; (2) capital-intensive technology mainly imported from the more developed nations; (3) centralized planning, mainly by economists and financial experts, to guide and speed up the process of development; and (4) assertion that the causes of underdevelopment lay mainly within developing countries themselves. The implication for the role of communication in such a model was obvious: to transfer technological innovations from industrially developed countries and agencies to their clients and to create an appetite for change by raising a "climate for modernization" among the public in the industrially less developed nations. The classical diffusion models of communication as well as the orthodox theories of communication and modernization were indeed compatible with this macro-level model of development.

From philosophical and political points of view, the liberal/capitalist models have their base in the liberal thinking of such theorists as John Stuart Locke, Thomas Hobbes, Adam Smith, David Ricardo, and a host of intellectuals arising out of the French and American revolutions, such as Jean Jacques Rousseau, Thomas Jefferson, and James Madison. The 16th century provided the roots for the liberal democratic experience, the 17th century saw the development of its economic and political principles, and the 18th and 19th centuries witnessed its practice and growth. By the beginning of the 20th century, liberal democratic ideas had been extended to many parts of the world.

One of the characteristics of these types of models is that they are generally less concerned with the traditional form of communication and infrastructure, emphasizing rational bureaucracy, formal institutions, and modern Western governmental systems. Mass media and mass communication are recognized as fundamental organizing powers, and such models of communication and culture as the triple M theory (mass media, mass culture, and mass society) and the technological determinist approach are the outcome of this process.

The liberal/capitalist models of development are based on the fundamental concepts of individual freedom; universal rights of suffrage; popular sovereignty; a free marketplace of ideas and commodities; and the separation of legislative, judicial, and executive powers, with the public media becoming the Fourth Estate. Democracy is identified with individual liberty, popular participation, private ownership of the means of production and distribution, and freedom of enterprise. Secularization of thought, separation of church and state, and division of religion from politics are some of the historical outcomes of these models over the last few centuries. The ideological and economic underpinnings of liberal/capitalist models as they relate to the communication industry is most obvious: Consumers' economic self-interest, taking into account the cost/demand attributes, will determine the success and the growth of technologies and services.

Often cited as "the dominant model," the liberal/capitalist approach to communication and development is best illustrated in the theoretical, conceptual, and methodological works of such writers as Daniel Lerner, David Riesman, Harold Lasswell, Paul Lazarsfeld, Karl W. Deutsch, Lucian W. Pye, Ithiel de Sola Pool, Frederick W. Frey, Wilbur Schramm, David C. McClelland, Everett Hagen, Everett M. Rogers, and a number of their colleagues and students whose research and contributions dominated the field between the 1950s and the 1960s.[43]

Following the line of Ibn Khaldun in the 14th century, who had distinguished two distinct patterns of society—elementary, which was rural, and complex, which tended to be urban—Western social scientists from Ferdinand Tonnies to Karl W. Deutsch had applied the stage theory to explain the current pattern of mobilization and social integration. Tönnies had identified *Gemeinschaft* and *Gesellschaft,* meaning simple community and complex society, and Deutsch had distinguised between two stages of tribal and nation-state systems.[44] Lerner changed this dual typology into a three-stage model—traditional, transitional, and modern. Transitional came to constitute a special stage in social development. Thus, the stage was set in an unfolding process of theorizing when David Riesman, in an introduction to Lerner's *The Passing of Traditional Society*, identified the new breed as such:

> The Transitionals are the men in motion, variously proportioned in the different countries, who listen to American jazz in Beirut, to the trusted BBC even in Cairo, to the Voice of the Arabs and Radio Moscow in Damascus. Many of them don't live in a city—yet. But, already encouraged by the media into ecological window-shopping, they can imagine living in one—even in one outside their native land.[45]

Transitional society, according to these writers, characterizes many developing countries. Lucian Pye described transitional society as a dual society in which modern and traditional sectors exist side by side. The two sectors are likely to be physically separated—urban and rural producing two distinct cultures in some countries. Yet the separation cannot remain long. Slowly, according to Pye, the modern sector penetrates the traditional. Everett Hagen divided transitional society into three cultures: elite, peasants, and what he called "great traders." The traders play a vital modernizing role, essentially a communication function, of bridging the modern and traditional sectors.

Traditional society is characterized as having a subsistence economy without industrialization, investment being low or non-existent. Politically, traditional society, according to these models, is authoritarian and highly decentralized. Traditional peoples are rural, illiterate, uneducated, fatalistic about life, and not mobile. Typified by "the subculture of peasantry," traditional society to Everett Rogers had ten central elements:

> . . . (1) mutual distrust in interpersonal relations, (2) perceived limited good, (3) hostility toward government authority, (4) familialism, (5) lack of innovativeness, (6) fatalism, (7) limited aspiration, (8) lack of the ability to offer gratification, (9) limited view of the world, and (10) low empathy.[46]

On the other hand, the modern society is highly urban, literate, and educated and has extensive mass media. The modern person is secular, educated, and literate and is mobile physically and psychologically, according to Lerner. Traditional and modern societies communicate quite differently as well. Traditional societies, viewed from the perspective of liberal/capitalist models, rely entirely on face-to-face communication. They seek information to confirm their role and status. Modern societies, on the other hand, rely on mass media as well as face-to-face communication. People seek information for a variety of utilitarian reasons, including economic gain and political and social mobility.

Lerner used a communication framework to characterize the traditional/modern difference. Modern society to him was the "media system." Within the media system, the channel of communication is the "broadcast," the audience is "heterogeneous" (mass), the content of the message is "descriptive" (news), and the source is "professional" (skilled). In the oral system, the channel is the person, the audience is "primary" (small group), the content is "prescriptive" (rules), and the source is "hierarchial" (status-oriented).[47]

In Pye's view, traditional and modern opinion leaders face quite different problems of handling information. In traditional society, the opinion leader puts together information handed down from past generations in order to tell a story with a moral to the community. In modern society, opinion leaders must select information that their group and they believe is significant and screen out a great deal of extraneous information.[48] Rogers labels opinion leadership in traditional societies "polymorphic" (one gives advice on many topics) and "monomorphic" in modern societies (different people are opinion leaders on different topics).[49]

It is indeed striking to see not only the ethnocentric and Western-oriented concepts and propositions in these analyses but also almost a total lack of understanding and appreciation of the complex social structures and communication systems that have characterized many of these "traditional" societies in the Middle East and Latin America. Not only is "tradition" posed as the opposite of modernity and "enlightenment," but there is no assurance that there could be a light at the end of the tunnel. Riesman puts it this way: "Thus, while we can prefigure the end of tradition, it is hard to envisage the beginning of enlightenment."[50] Riesman refers to Lerner's book as a story of pseudo-participants, of mobs on the streets of Cairo or Tehran who have been brought into the political process—though they lack the skills needed to make their new slogans come more nearly true.[51] With the "modernization" model underway, the Islamic revolution in Iran and the events in Lebanon in the 1980s showed only the futility and the naiveté of that observation. Yet Riesman in 1958 was willing to assert that "it is to the credit of American empathy and generosity, as well as to our naiveté, that we have been willing to promote that theory, and to stand throughout the world as apostles of modernity."[52]

Lerner thought that for the purpose of creating a new identity in the traditional society, a national spokesperson is needed. The spokesperson may be a great national leader like Ataturk, who promoted Western secularism in Turkey in the 1920s and 1930s, or a modernizing elite. New ways of life must be presented to the peasantry. Lerner assigned this task primarily to the mass media.

In somewhat similar fashion, Pye wrote in 1964 that

> It was the pressure of communication which brought about the downfall of traditional societies. And in the future, it will be the creation of new channels of communication and the ready acceptance of new content of communication which will be decisive in determining the prospects of nation building. . . . Similarly, the process by which the modern world has impinged upon traditional societies, producing both cosmopolitan leaders and xenophobic nationalists, is in essence a communication process.[53]

Although the views of Pye, Lerner, Frey, and Pool on political development and modernization differ slightly from each other, they basically agree that political development involves some type of change in the political system, which is usually caused by modernization of the system through communication. Pool viewed political development as a modernization process in which the mass media play the principal role. He especially noted four policy issues that most nations in "transition" must resolve: (1) how much of their scarce resources should be invested in mass media, (2) what roles should be assigned to the public and private sectors, (3) how much freedom should be imposed, and (4) at what level the cultural pitch should be for the media output.[54] Clearly, Pool viewed political development exclusively from the mass media standpoint and formal modern institutions, with little attention to other types of communication possibilities including the traditional channels that were used so effectively in the Islamic revolution in Iran.[55]

It should be noted that the communication-development models such as those of Lerner, McClelland, and Hagen—founded primarily in this economic realization—found their social realization counterpart in the work of Rogers and Pool. Rogers defined the role of communication as providing the channels for passage of development information; and he proposed that since mass communication exists in advanced societies, developing countries should consider these same infrastructural ideas in their societies. Pool carried the psychological weight of communications structure further by suggesting that only changes in the latent structures of communication will change attitudes of the systems' users toward modernization.

Lerner's hypothesis that the spread of mediated experience through mass communication brings about empathy fails confirmation in several studies. For example, as James N. Mosel, in the case of Thailand, and Hamid Mowlana, in the case of Iran, have demonstrated, as an agent of political socialization, communication systems in these countries have in many respects strengthened and accommodated the process of cultural continuity and persistence.[56] In fact, if the pattern and strategy of the Islamic revolution in Iran were news, so too was the recognition that, in older societies such as Iran, control of modern communication media does not guarantee political control. For modern media to be effective, they must integrate themselves into the complex system of traditional communication channels. The Iranian case underlines the importance of understanding and appreciating the total communication system of a culture when explaining past events or predicting the future.

As the foregoing analysis shows, within the larger framework of liberal/capitalist models of communication and development, three perspectives have been central in attempts to explain the role of communication in development: (1) the correlation role of simple association of such variables as income, literacy, urbanization, and indices of media distribution; (2) the empathy-psychological role, in which change is perceived as requiring new attitudes and values among individual members of the society; and (3) the diffusion-exogenous role, in which development is a type of social change and new ideas are introduced into a social system to produce higher per capita incomes and levels of living through modern production methods and improved social organization.

These approaches are all grounded in psychological theories of change, which conceive of development as a process of individual enlightenment, an aggregate of personality adjustments producing new types of people. They also display an ethnocentric Western bias, ignoring the dimensions of cultural relativity and displaying lack of knowledge and awareness about culture, tradition, and history. As adeptly criticized by Peter Golding, the search for universal functional psychological prerequisites is condemned by its own results, although its influence is pervasive.[57] Golding's critique entails a discussion of market-oriented, quantitative, and thereby ethnocentric mind-sets prevalent in the communication and development theories in the liberal/capitalist category. In criticizing these theories, Golding implied that communication strategies necessarily adhere to liberal democratic theory's goals by creating an environment in the developing countries that is conducive to "liberal theories of progress" and "idealist theories of history."

Marxist/Socialist Models

The second set of dominant models to be examined in the field of communication and development is the Marxist/socialist models. Communication is seen in these formulations as an integral part of the entire political theory and ideology and an essential element of the development process. The Marxist/socialist model emphasizes propaganda, agitation, organization, mobilization, and self-criticism as essential and primarily functions of communication channels, especially the mass media. It also views a high level of interpersonal and group communication, especially through the political party apparatus, as prerequisite to the formation and implementation of developmental plans, objectives, and strategies.

The Marxist/socialist perspective is an economic determinist model that claims that political participation first will lead to economic growth later. It assumes that the growth of media participation is a result of awareness, social change, and revolution. There are some similarities between the liberal/capitalist and Marxist/socialist models despite the political and ideological contrasts that divide them. The two models emphasize, to a high degree, economic growth and materialism, but they differ on how they should be accomplished. This material determinism can also be seen in the way economic development is measured in aggregate terms such as GNP and per capita income. Former United Nations Secretary General U Thant's definition that development equaled economic growth plus social change can be seen in both models in general terms. Both models are secular in nature, both hold science as a key paradigm in their development, and both are oriented toward the modern nation-state system.

Marxists and neo-Marxists alike are strong believers in the causal role of communication in development. They see communication as a set of ideological formations that usually follow the patterns of material production in society, contributing a factor of dynamism to the process. In the liberal/ capitalist model of communication and development, the media of communications are the parents of mass culture; mass culture is the child of mass communication; and mass media were born out of urban, industrial mass society. The Marxist/socialist models view the process from below, where through an elaborate feedback of political and economic machinery, the masses can participate in the production and distribution of cultural messages. Consequently, communication can generate awareness and help to organize and mobilize the masses for political change leading to economic and social development. Political figures such as Lenin and Mao, as well as Marxist and neo-Marxist scholars, generally treat communications as an instrument of action or a concept within which to implement social liberation. There have been sharp differences among them, however, especially in the 1960s and 1970s, concerning the role of the state and the party in the process of communication policies and control in society. Communications also provide the service of legitimization for the Marxists, a concept important to most social systems but fully embodied as vital for the theoretical proliferation of Marxist ideas.[58]

The Marxist/socialist perspective on communication and development is not only an eastern European, Soviet, or Chinese perspective. It is a view that has found adherents in several Latin American, Asian, and African countries as well. This perspective has found expression outside the socialist world through the works of those scholars in the United States, and especially in Europe, who take a more or less Marxist or neo-Marxist view of development:

> The struggles of the oppressed classes are the living foundation on which is built the communication process. . . . Communication is nothing more, nor nothing less, than the articulation of the social relations between people. In a profound sense, communication is one of the most unique products—and producers—of society's development.[59]

Marx and Engels stated, "The ideas of the ruling class are in every epoch the ruling ideas."[60] The technology and means of communication thus help the ruling class disseminate their ideas, which will in turn determine the direction of communication in society.

Whereas the individual theory of communication depends on the freedom of the individual from social constraints, the revolutionary theories of communication depend on total commitment of the individual and the system to the revolutionary movement. It is here that from the perspective of Marxism and Leninism, communication and any developmental processes cannot be separated from each other. Indeed, as was articulated by Lenin, the function of the media in socialist societies can be termed propaganda and agitation, mobilization and organization, education and self-criticism.[61] The major task of a communication system is to focus on problems of national integration, economic productivity, political maturity, and social equality. As with all the means of production, communication systems have also to be nationalized.

The elevation of the state as representative of the party and the working class and as the ultimate source of all authority, and its task in controlling all the channels of communication, has been criticized by the neo-Marxists in that "a socialist perspective which does not go beyond attacking existing property relationships is limited."[62] Communications under the Marxist/socialist models have tended to be centralized, with major emphasis on both the modern communication technologies and the group and interpersonal communication at the party and local levels. Beyond this, the structure, functions, and strategy of communication and development in Marxist/socialist systems have varied, depending on their cultural, ethnic, geographical, and leadership traditions as they are illustrated in Yugoslavia, the People's Republic of China, Albania, and Hungary.

Yugoslav researcher Matko Mestrovic suggests that when information systems are technically expanded, special consideration must be given to the social implications.[63] He is echoed by Hungarian Zoltan Jakab, who states that "the type of society desired in a developing country should shape the choice of media."[64] The media should not shape society. Jakab suggests that developing countries must assess their communication and information needs on local, national, individual, and institutional levels and then select appropriate technologies.

What should be the content of communication when developmental stages are considered? The choice of programs and the contents reflect the choice of society. For example, under socialism, entertainment is not separated from work and learning. According to Tamas Szecsko, a Hungarian communication researcher, in the first years of building socialism there was disapproval of any program that did not contribute to learning or was not directly linked with the domain of work.[65] As socialist society developed, a broader concept of entertainment was allowed. Unlike the liberal/capitalist model, in which there is a division between elite and mass culture, program policy in the socialist models, according to Szecsko, seeks to lift the individual out of everyday life and bring him or her to the level of science and society.[66]

Monistic/Emancipatory Models

The third set of models, which emerged during the 1970s and 1980s and is now beginning to occupy a central position, is in many ways a response to both the liberal/capitalist and the Marxist/socialist models. This approach, which we call the monistic/emancipatory model, is basically a revolutionary, humanistic, and spiritual movement that emphasizes "quality" over "quantity" and calls for equality and balance in the international system. Although there are variations of this general model that might be tailored to fit the specific cultural and social setting of different societies, all the writings in this area "promote self-determination, and have their roots in more humane, ethical, traditionalist, anti-bloc, self-reliance theories of social development."[67]

The concept of monism must be carefully examined because, through time, its meaning has become ambiguous and subject to conflicting definitions. Here, monism in its general philosophical meaning, can be traced back to world views which are centuries old and even originate, as shown by Collum, in the beginning of civilization in Mesopotamia.[68] As defined by Sir Oliver Lodge:

> "Monism" should apply to any philosophic system which assumes and attempts to formulate the essential simplicity and "oneness" of all the apparent diversity of sensual impression and consciousness, any system which seeks to exhibit all the complexities of existence, both material and mental—the whole of phenomena, both objective and subjective—as modes of manifestation of one fundamental reality.[69]

Lodge continues to show different schools of monistic theory that have been born from this basic philosophy, not the least of which (but perhaps the most misleading) has been a purely physical formulation which can be best described as monistic materialism.

Pure monistic philosophy rejects this largely physical view as incomplete and as elevating physical, observable phenomenon above the less tangible beliefs, cultural systems, thoughts, and behavior which are the very essence of humanness. It is upon this conception of monism that the monistic/emancipatory approach to development is based. The monistic portion of the model implies a unity of life, an interconnectedness of all things.

The concept of *emancipation* applied herein is subtly different from the concept of *liberation* as it has been employed by a number of scholars including Paulo Freire and Denis Goulet. Liberation simply means to set free and is associated with the concept of freedom in its political, economic, and social context. The term emancipation used here implies release from personal bondage, liberation occurring within the individual.

Advocates of this approach maintain that both inter- and intra-personal communication should be a concern of development planners. They also emphasize the importance of traditional channels of communication as well as modern technology. They do not see economic and political development as the most important developmental goals, nor do they reject them; they merely emphasize the importance if not the dominance of cultural, social, and individual development as well. They also place more importance on qualitative growth and the way in which change processes might take place.

The major thinkers and proponents of these models, mostly in the Third World and the Islamic countries as well as those in small communities in the West, went unnoticed in the literature in the United States and Europe, partly because they were predominantly writing in non-European languages and partly because of the ethnocentricity and lack of knowledge and appreciation of others in this field.

Further, many of those actually involved in efforts based on monistic/emancipatory philosophies refused to participate in the discussions and arguments over "development" that would have given them academic and political legitimization because they deemed such activity and legitimization counter-productive and compromising. Because of the Western tradition of separation of religious thought—and thus anything spiritual—from "knowledge and intelligence," which was deemed scientific and secular, obtaining legitimization would have meant abandoning the propositions that formed the very basis of the underlying philosophy in the first place.

In the United States, echoing the opinion of many, Denis Goulet in the early 1970s criticized the developmental models as elitist, unbalanced, and discriminatory. Under the banner of "liberation," he called for a new definition of development. In his words, "liberation implies the suppression of elitism by a populace which assumes control over its own change processes."[70] Success to him did not mean quantitative measurement. He wrote, "Visible benefits are no doubt sought, but the decisive test of success is that, in obtaining them, a society will have fostered great popular autonomy in a non-elitist mode, social creativity instead of limitation, and control over forces of change instead of mere adjustment to them."[71] Although Goulet and others did not offer any specific models of development, their critical view of the prevailing models attracted the attention of many Western writers to the alternative models, which we have identified in this study as monistic/emancipatory models.

We have used *monism* and *emancipation* in their general philosophical and epistemological terms. Monistic/emancipatory models view development within the context of particular cultural values, which lend it specific purpose and mold its path. Strategies that attempt to modify values and behavior are checked against the unified and monistic core of societal value and world view so that the cultural base of society can be preserved. In short, change must not proceed in ignorance of the cultural, religious, and traditional core values of the system. Knowing the core value and belief system, the people are encouraged to become agents in their own development. Social change and development in society cannot be based on accident or dualism and disharmony. For this school of thought, there is only one, ultimately real, absolute, all-inclusive being. The problem of the nature of the unity of the universe and its relationship to the diversity and plurality of the observed world takes a different emphasis than that of liberal philosophers and Western pluralists. In liberal/capitalist and, to a great extent, in Marxist/socialist conceptions, development manifests itself in the notion of the state, bureaucracy, rational behavior, stages of growth, and strategies set up to enable the system to move toward economic development, political change, and ecological and environmental manipulation and control.

In this model, in contrast, the values and concepts within communication are taken to be prime movers in social change. Any communication affects one or more of four targets: society, the individual, subgroups, and the cultural system. Within society, communication increases social cohesion, allows for common norms and experiences, and continues education, whereas for the individual, communication aids in integration and helps reduce anomie. Communication extends power to subgroups and works as an agent for socialization while standardizing and maintaining the cultural consensus for the cultural system.[72]

Monistic/emancipatory models of communication and development argue that freedom of expression is being threatened through a gradual process of cultural homogenization, in part the by-product of global transportation and communication systems. Present growth strategies have minimized the degree of cultural freedom. As the countries are subject to cultural invasion, they come to perceive reality with the outlook of the so-called "invaders" rather than with their own; their ability to formulate localized and relevant development goals and strategies thus becomes more impoverished, even in the midst of increasing wealth. One must realize the importance of culture and the goals of the society, for development is not just economic but a stage in the unfolding of each society's cultural potential.

There are growing numbers of writers both in the developed and developing countries who see the present educational system as detrimental, not so much because of the pathological behavior it might promote but because of its deliberate use by those in authority (the oppressors) to keep the populace (the oppressed) in a dehumanized state.[73] The "banking system of education," which is an international phenomenon, views students as objects—vessels to receive deposits of value and attitude-laden information. Creativity, according to these writers, thus has no part in this system.[74] The ingested information dictates the accepted socio-cultural structure of the elite *vis-à-vis* the masses.

By this system, the "oppressed" are denied the right of "praxis," of becoming fully human; the "oppressors" (equally victims of their distorted, stratified view of society as static) are also victims. This is the point that Paulo Freire, Ali Shari'ati, and a number of other writers emphasize. Monistic/emancipatory models offer a number of solutions in which both the elite and the masses (the "oppressed") become learners. In communication terminology, the new system must be receiver-centered (rather than sender-centered), contain true two-way flow (dialogue), and take the context (social structure) into account. The emphasis is on *communication* rather than *communications*:

> The communications revolution has meant the spread of technology, systems innovation, and the speed and quantity of messages. The real revolution, however, has been the *communication* revolution, explained in terms of a quest for satisfactory human interaction, rather than a communications revolution viewed through the lens of technological and institutional spread and growth. In other words, the cultural components of international and human relations have been overshadowed by the political, economic, and technological aspects of the field. This is unfortunate, for modern political development, social rebellion, religious resurgence, and contemporary revolutionary movements in both the industrially developed and the less industrialized societies can be better understood if we look at them from the perspective of human interaction (i.e., from a communication analysis), rather than from a purely politico-economic or technological perspective.[75]

The "transmission" mentality emphasizes one-way vertical communication in which *true* communication is prohibited.[76] A truly liberating education and communication are horizontal and humanizing: Both sender and receiver grow and change through the experience. It has been pointed out that "revolutions" that have been or are unaccompanied by this quest for dialogue do not result in freedom. If anything, the so-called revolutions of the past have led to ever increasing alienation of the individual and his or her reduction into "roles." The incredible growth in communications technology has been equally, if not more, debilitating. Increased contact has not been paralleled by a growth in true communication (sharing and trust).[77]

Monistic/emancipatory models of communication and development always emphasize the importance of dialogue. Dialogue imposes itself as the way by which men and women achieve significance as human beings, so communication is an existential necessity. Dialogue requires both an intense faith in the individual and his or her ability to be creative. Dialogue is the encounter between persons attempting to name the world, and in order to do so, they must perceive the world in the same manner, having the equal right to name the world by speaking. When one group dominates the right to use words and name the world, imposing this named world on the others, dialogue stops and one-way communication in the form of monologue begins. To impede communication is to reduce individuals to the status of objects—which is what oppressors do. That is the difference between an authentic revolution and a take-over by a coup.

Development in the monistic/emancipatory form is the all-inclusive social unity. The emphasis is on the community rather than on the nation-state, on monistic universalism rather than on nationalism, on spiritualism rather than on secular humanism, on dialogue rather than on monologue, and on emancipation rather than on alienation. The quest for community development in Africa, the theology of liberation movements in Latin America, the various religio-political currents in Europe and other industrial countries, and most visable of all, the new wave of movements of the Islamic world emphasizing an Islamic *ummah* (community) and world view are all manifestations of this third category of models that we have called monistic/emancipatory.[78]

NOTES

1. Daniel Lerner, *The Passing of Traditional Society: Modernizing the Middle East,* Glencoe, IL, Free Press, 1958, pp. 19–107.
2. Ibid., pp. 52–54.
3. Ibid., p. 62.
4. See Lucian W. Pye, *Communication and Political Development,* Princeton, NJ, Princeton University Press, 1963, p. 3; and Ithiel de Sola Pool, "The Mass Media and Politics in the Modernization Process," in Pye, *Communication and Political Development,* p. 251.
5. Seymour Martin Lipset, "Some Social Requisites of Democracy: Economic Development and Political Legitimacy," in the Bobbs-Merrill Reprint Series in the Social Sciences, reprinted by permission of the *American Political Science Review,* Vol. LIII, March 1959, p. 82.
6. See for example, R. Vincent Farace, "Study of Mass Communication and National Development," *Journalism Quarterly,* 43: 305-313, Summer 1966.
7. Wilbur Schramm and W. Lee Ruggles, "How Mass Media Systems Grow," in Daniel Lerner and Wilbur Schramm, eds., *Communication and Change in Developing Countries,* Honolulu, University of Hawaii Press, 1967.
8. David L. McClelland, *The Achieving Society,* Princeton, NJ, Van Nostrand, 1961; see also David L. McClelland and David Winter, *Motivating Economic Achievement,* New York, Free Press, 1971.
9. Everett E. Hagen, *On the Theory of Social Change: How Economic Growth Begins,* Homewood, IL, Dorsey Press, 1962.
10. Karl W. Deutsch, *Nationalism and Social Communication,* Cambridge, MA, MIT Press, 1953.
11. Francis K. Hsu, "Psychological Homeostasis and Jen: Conceptual Tools for Advancing Psychological Anthropology," *American Anthropologist,* 73, 1971, pp. 23–44.
12. Ibid., p. 23.
13. Everett M. Rogers, ed., *Communication and Development: Critical Perspectives,* Beverly Hills, CA, Sage, 1976; see also Everett M. Rogers and F. F. Shoemaker, *Communication of Innovations: A Cross-Cultural Approach,* New York, Free Press, 1971.

14. Rogers and Shoemaker, *Communication of Innovations*, p. 38.
15. Bryce Ryan and Neal C. Gross, "The Diffusion of Hybrid Seed Corn in Two Iowa Communities," *Rural Sociology*, 8, 1953, pp. 15–24.
16. See Luis Ramiro Beltran, "Alien Premises, Objects, and Methods in Latin American Communication Research," in Rogers, ed., *Communication and Development*, pp. 15–42.
17. Juan Diaz Bordenave, "Communication of Agricultural Innovations in Latin America: The Need for New Models," in Rogers, ed., *Communication and Development*, pp. 43–46.
18. See Hamid Mowlana, "The Multinational Corporation and the Diffusion of Technology," in Abdul A. Said and Luiz R. Simmons, eds., *The New Sovereigns: Multinational Corporations as World Powers*, Englewood Cliffs, NJ, Prentice-Hall, 1975, pp. 77–90; and his "Political and Social Implications of Communication Satellite Applications in Developed and Developing Countries," in Joseph N. Pelton and Marcellus S. Snow, eds., *Economics and Policy Problems in Satellite Communications*, New York, Praeger, 1977, pp. 124–142.
19. Hamid Mowlana, "Technology Versus Tradition: Communication in the Iranian Revolution," *Journal of Communication*, 29: 3, Summer 1979, pp. 107–112; Hamid Mowlana, "Communication for Political Change: The Iranian Revolution," and Kusum J. Singh, "Mass Line Communication: Liberation Movements in China and India," in George Gerbner and Marsha Siefert, eds., *World Communications: A Handbook*, White Plains, NY, Longman, 1983, pp. 294–301 and 302–308, respectively; Godwin C. Chu, ed., *Popular Media in China: Shaping New Cultural Patterns*, Honolulu, University of Hawaii Press, 1978.
20. Rogers and Shoemaker, *Communication of Innovations*, p. 255.
21. Elihu Katz, "The Two-Step Flow of Communication," *Public Opinion Quarterly*, Vol. XXI, Spring 1957.
22. International Commission for the Study of Communication Problems, *Many Voices, One World*, London, Kogan Page, 1980.
23. Dallas W. Smythe, *Dependency Road: Communication, Capitalism, Consciousness and Canada*, Norwood, NJ, Ablex Publishing, 1981.
24. Herbert I. Schiller, *Mass Communication and American Empire*, New York, Kelly, 1970; and his *Who Knows: Information in the Age of the Fortune 500*, Norwood, NJ, Ablex Publishing, 1981; and *Information and the Crisis Economy*, Norwood, NJ, Ablex Publishing, 1984.
25. Armand Mattelart, *Multinational Corporations and the Control of Culture*, Atlantic Highlands, NJ, Humanities Press, 1979; and his *Transnationals and the Third World: The Struggle for Culture*, South Hadley, MA, Bergin and Garvey Publishers, 1983.
26. Hamid Mowlana, *Global Information and World Communication: New Frontiers in International Relations*, White Plains, NY, Longman, 1985; and his "A Paradigm for Comparative Mass Media Analysis," in H. D. Fischer and J. C. Merrill, eds., *International and Intercultural Communication*, New York, Hastings House, 1976; and "Mass Media and Culture: Toward an Integrated Theory," in William B. Gudykunst, ed., *Intercultural Communication: Current Perspectives*, Beverly Hills, CA, Sage, 1983; also his *International Flow of Information: A Global Report and Analysis*, Reports and Papers on Mass Communication, No. 99, Paris, UNESCO, 1985.

27. Cees J. Hamelink, *Cultural Autonomy in Global Communication*, White Plains, NY, Longman, 1983.
28. Kaarle Nordenstreng and Tapio Varis, *Television Traffic: A One-Way Street?* Reports and Papers on Mass Communication, No. 70, Paris, UNESCO, 1974.
29. Thomas H. Guback, *The International Film Industry*, Bloomington, Indiana University Press, 1969; and Thomas H. Guback and Tapio Varis, *Transnational Communication and Cultural Industry*, Reports and Papers on Mass Communication, No. 2, 92, Paris, UNESCO, 1982.
30. Luis Ramiro Beltran and Elizabeth Fox de Cardona, "Latin America and the United States: Flaws in the Free Flow of Information," in Kaarle Nordenstreng and Herbert I. Schiller, eds., *National Sovereignty and International Communication*, Norwood, NJ, Ablex Publishing, 1979, pp. 99–111.
31. Jeremy Tunstall, *The Media Are American*, New York, Columbia University Press, 1977.
32. Tamas Szecsko, "The Development of a Socialist Communication Theory," in George Gerbner, ed., *Mass Media Policies in Changing Cultures*, New York, John Widen, 1977, pp. 223–234.
33. Schiller, *Mass Communications and American Empire*, p. 84.
34. Herbert I. Schiller, *The Mind Managers*, Boston, Beacon Press, 1973, p. 125.
35. A. G. Dettinger et al., "Foreign Policy Choices for the 1970s and 1980s," Program on Information Technologies and Public Policy, Cambridge, MA, Harvard University, 1976.
36. Hamid Mowlana, "Trends in Research on International Communication in the United States," *Gazette: International Journal for Mass Communication Studies*, 19: 2, 1973, pp. 79–90.
37. Herbert I. Schiller, *Communication and Cultural Domination*, New York, International Arts and Sciences Press, 1978.
38. Hamelink, *Cultural Autonomy in Global Communication*, pp. 4–5.
39. Mattelart, *Transnationals and the Third World*, p. 25.
40. Ibid., p. 130.
41. Mowlana, "A Paradigm for Comparative Mass Media Analysis."
42. See Everett E. Hagen, *On the Theory of Social Change: How Economic Growth Begins*, Homewood, IL, Dorsey Press, 1962; and David McClelland, *The Achieving Society*, Princeton, NJ, Van Nostrand, 1961.
43. For references to the works of these authors, see their entries in Chapter 1, especially Lerner's *The Passing of Traditional Society;* Pye's *Communication and Political Development*; and Wilbur Schramm's *Mass Media and National Development*, Stanford, CA, Stanford University Press, 1964.
44. See Ferdinand Tönnies, "On Gemeinschaft and Gesellschaft," in Marcello Truzzi, ed., *Sociology*, New York, Random House, 1971, pp. 146–154; and Karl W. Deutsch, "The Growth of Nations: Some Recurrent Patterns of Political and Social Integration," *World Politics*, 1953, pp. 168–195.
45. Lerner, *The Passing of Traditional Society*, p. 13.
46. Everett M. Rogers, *Modernization Among Peasants: The Impact of Communication*, New York, Holt, Rinehart, and Winston, 1969, p. 25.
47. Lerner, *The Passing of Traditional Society*, pp. 55–57.
48. Lucian Pye, *Aspects of Political Development*, Boston, Little, Brown, 1966, pp. 59–60.

49. Rogers, *Modernization Among Peasants*, pp. 225–227.
50. Preface to Lerner's, *The Passing of Traditional Society,* p. 7.
51. Ibid., p. 5.
52. Ibid., p. 10.
53. Pye, *Communication and Political Development*, pp. 8–9.
54. Ithiel de Sola Pool, "The Mass Media and Politics in the Modernization Process," in Pye, *Communication and Political Development*, pp. 234–235. See also, Frederick W. Frey, "Political Development, Power, and Communication in Turkey," in Pye, *Communication and Political Development*, pp. 298–326.
55. Hamid Mowlana, "Technology Versus Tradition: Communication in the Iranian Revolution," *Journal of Communication*, 29: 3, Summer 1979, pp. 107–112.
56. James N. Mosel, "Communication Patterns and Political Socialization in Transitional Thailand," in Pye, *Communication and Political Development*, pp. 184–233; and Hamid Mowlana, "Communication for Political Change: The Iranian Revolution," in Gerbner and Siefert, eds., *World Communications*, pp. 294–301; and Mowlana, "Technology Versus Tradition."
57. Peter Golding, "Media Role in National Development: Critique of Theoretical Orthodoxy," *Journal of Communication*, 24: 3, Summer 1974, pp. 39–52.
58. Seth Siegelaub, "A Communication on Communication," preface to Armand Mattelart and Seth Siegelaub, eds., *Communication and Class Struggle, Vol. I: Capitalism, Imperialism*, New York, International General, 1971. For a sample of writings on the socialist models of communication, see Szecsko, "The Development of a Socialist Communication Theory."
59. Siegelaub, "A Communication on Communication," p. 11.
60. Karl Marx and Friedrich Engels, "Ruling Class and Ruling Ideas," in Mattelart and Siegelaub, eds., *Communication and Class Struggle*, p. 98. (Reprinted in part from C. J. Clark, ed., *The German Ideology*, London, Lawrence and Wishart, 1970.)
61. See V. I. Lenin, *What Is to Be Done?* Moscow, Progress Publishers, 1947.
62. Hans Magnus Enzensberger, "Constituents of a Theory of the Media," in Denis McQuail, ed., *Sociology of Mass Communication*, London, Penguin, 1972, p. 104.
63. Matko Mestrovic, "The Class Conditionality and the New Communications Technology," in *Der Anteil der Massmedien Heider Herausbildung des Bewusstseins in der Sich Wandelden Welt* (Proceedings of the International Association of Mass Communication Researchers Conference), Leipzig, Karl Marx University, August 17–21, 1974, p. 189.
64. Zoltan Jakab, "The New World Information Order: An Eastern European Perspective," in Gerbner and Siefert, *World Communication*, p. 46.
65. Tamas Szecsko, "Comenius' Whistle," translated by Jeno Farago, in *Radio es Television Zzemle—Recent Studies 1976–1977*, Budapest, Mass Communication Research Centre, 1978, pp. 35–36.
66. For a sample of additional writings on the socialist models of communication, see Szecsko, "The Development of a Socialist Communication Theory"; Dallas Smythe, "Realism in the Arts and Sciences: A Systemic Overview of Capitalism and Socialism," in Nordenstreng and Schiller, eds., *National Sovereignty and International Communication*, pp. 99–111; Chu, *Popular Media in China;* Alan P. L.

Liu, *Communication and National Integration in Communist China*, Berkeley, University of California Press, 1971; and Mark W. Hopkins, *Mass Media in the Soviet Union*, New York, Pegasus, 1970.

67. Hamid Mowlana, "Communication, World Order, and the Human Potential," in Andrew Arno and Wimal Dissanayake, eds., *The News Media in National and International Conflict*, Boulder, CO, Westview Press, 1984, pp. 27–35; and Mowlana, *Global Information and World Communication*, p. 212. See Paulo Freire, *The Pedagogy of the Oppressed*, New York, Seabury Press, 1968.

68. Vera Christine Chute Collum, *Manifold Unity: The Ancient World's Perception of the Divine Pattern of Harmony and Compassion*, London, John Murray, 1940.

69. Sir Oliver Lodge, *Life and Matter: A Criticism of Professor Haeckel's "Riddle of the Universe"*, New York, Putnam, 1905, p. 6.

70. Denis Goulet, "Development or Liberation?" *International Development Review*, XIII: 3, 1971/3, p. 7.

71. Ibid.

72. Hamid Mowlana and Elizabeth Ann Robinson, "Ethnic Mobilization and Communication Theory," in Abdul A. Said and Luis R. Simmons, eds., *Ethnicity in an International Context*, New Brunswick, NJ, Transaction Books, 1976, pp. 48–63.

73. See Freire, *The Pedagogy of the Oppressed;* Sarah McCarthy, "Why Johnny Can't Disobey," *The Magazine for Creative Learning*, 9: 4, September 1980, pp. 2–3; and Mowlana, *Global Information and World Communication*, pp. 213–214.

74. See for example, Freire, *The Pedagogy of the Oppressed*, p. 58.

75. Hamid Mowlana, "Communication, World Order and the Human Potential: Toward an Ethical Framework," in Andrew Arno and Wimal Dissanayake, eds., *The News Media in National and International Conflict*, Boulder, CO, Westview Press, 1984, p. 29; see also Mowlana, *Global Information and World Communication*, p. 211.

76. See Goulet, "Development or Liberation?"

77. Mowlana, *Global Information and World Communication*, pp. 211–222; see also chapters 7, 9, 10.

78. Hamid Mowlana, "Toward a New Perspective in Communication and Development," paper prepared for the Annual Conference of the International Communication Association, May 23–27, 1985, Honolulu, HI.

CHAPTER 4

Culture, Society, and Communication

Several important concepts, problems, and processes of communication and culture have been receiving overwhelming attention in the world of mass media theorists, especially during the 1980s. A larger proportion of the literature falls normally under the headings of mass culture, mass media and society, cultural integrity, communication and cultural domination, cultural dependency, and cultural pluralism.

At the same time, these subjects are assuming great importance in the broader disciplines of sociology, economics, political science, and anthropology, as well as in the areas of development and regional studies. As a result, interdisciplinary approaches have become more frequent. As the phenomena under examination are highly complex and cover a wide spectrum of social reality, any attempt at a global interpretation necessarily transcends the limits of a given discipline. Consequently, the study of mass media and culture must involve cross-disciplinary frontiers, making a holistic as opposed to a specialized, compartmentalized approach to social science imperative.

The emphasis of this chapter is on the theoretical and analytical bases of mass media and culture. After an examination of the range and definition of this subject, an attempt will be made to lay a foundation for an identification, classification, and critical evaluation of major approaches, theories, concepts, and propositions, paying particular attention to problems of analytical integration and interdisciplinary contributions and coherence. Finally, a framework of analysis, or integrative theory of mass media and culture, will be outlined.

There is a considerable body of speculation and generalization concerning the relationship of the mass media of communication to culture. Among a wide variety of assertions on this topic, there are three positions of prominence that approximate some provocative, if not necessarily clear, "theoretical" statements. The word *theoretical* is placed in quotation marks to indicate that the statements of the proponents do not in fact constitute a set of interrelated propositions of sufficient coherence to justify the label of a theory. Nevertheless, the following theoretical positions—by virtue of their popularity, provocativeness, articulateness of their supporters, and prevalence among the students of mass media—must be taken as the point of departure in the discussion of mass media and culture.

THE TRIPLE M THEORY

Perhaps the most discussed of these three schools of thought in the Western world is the theory of mass society. Its articulation by the students of mass media and culture has created a triangle labeled "triple M theory"—mass society, mass media, and mass culture (see Figure 4.1). The essentials of the theory are rather familiar.[1] *Society* refers to a relational system of interaction between individuals or groups; and *culture*, to the pattern of values, norms, ideas, and other symbols that shape the individual's behavior. Thus, *mass society* refers to a type of society in which the relationships among individuals have assumed a mass character. As the mass of the population has become incorporated into society, the central institutions and the central value systems guiding and legitimizing these institutions have extended their boundaries. Mass society, furthermore, is an industrial society. The division of labor has made its members more interdependent. Mores and morals are in constant flux; relations between individuals are tangential and compartmentalized rather than organic. With successive technological advances, especially in communication, the economics of mass media and the polity of such societies demand that a successively broader audience be reached and, hence, the level of performance be directed more and more toward a common denominator of taste. One result of this process, as the proponents of this theory assert, is the origin of mass culture, or popular culture. As individuals lose a coherent sense of self in such societies, their anxieties increase. They search for new faiths to provide anchors.

Mass culture represents the cultural correlates of mass society and mass media.[2] With the rise of industrialization and urbanization, the traditional monopoly of culture by the aristocracy is broken. Whereas folk culture was the outcome of community and is centered on community, mass culture emerges when the community—that is, the different groups and individuals linked to each other by concrete values and interests—is eroded. Mass culture is distinguished thus by its standard mass production and marketability.

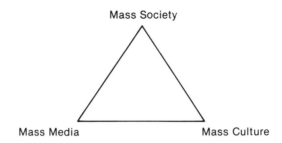

Mass Society

Mass Media   Mass Culture

Figure 4.1. Triple M Model.

Culture under the triple M theory has often been divided into a series of discriminatory categories such as high culture and popular culture, highbrow and lowbrow, avant-garde and kitsch. The term *mass culture* is often used to mark a distinction between authentic, long-lasting art and mass-produced commodity culture such as popular music and soap operas.

In its early days, the growth of mass culture, or what has been termed *commodity culture* by the critics of capitalism, led to strong dissenting movements and a wide appeal in the industrialized West for discrimination and taste. Some of its best-known critics included Mathew Arnold[3] in England, Friedrich Nietzsche[4] and Karl Mannheim[5] in Germany, Charles Baudelaire[6] in France, Ortega y Gasset[7] in Spain, and C. Wright Mills[8] in the United States.

Following the early elitist critics were those who not only denounced the mass media but also attempted to explain the division of cultures into various categories. There are considerable differences—moral, political, scientific— among these writers, but all came from the Western industrial-capitalist economy, especially the United States and England, where features of mass society and mass media were well developed. Among them were sociologists such as Ernest Van den Haag,[9] Daniel Bell,[10] David Reisman,[11] Bernard Rosenberg,[12] Edward Shils,[13] and many others; the social scientists and philosophers of the Frankfurt school such as Theodore W. Adorno,[14] Leo Lowenthal,[15] Walter Benjamin,[16] Herbert Marcuse,[17] and Max Horkheimer;[18] and finally, culturalist and media critics such as T. S. Eliot,[19] Dwight Mac-Donald,[20] Irving Howe,[21] Clement Greenberg,[22] Q.D. Leavis,[23] Raymond Williams,[24] Denys Thompson,[25] and a host of others.[26]

Rejection or dispute over mass culture and mass media implies concern for the cultural deprivation suffered by individuals and not a rejection of the masses. Perhaps the only common ground for those involved in the debate over the role of mass media and the merits of mass culture is the general consensus that the major concern is with the artists and individuals and their relationship to the society and culture. It is the business of defining what that relationship is and should be that generates disagreement.

The debate falls into two very broad, and often overlapping categories of opinion. It involves those who discern something positive in the development of mass culture and those who do not. Within these categories, of course, there are differing hypotheses, qualifications, and projections. Critics on both sides may have similar insights in the structures of their viewpoints but differ radically in their conclusions.

TECHNOLOGICAL DETERMINISM

A second set of propositions concerning mass media and culture is that of technological determinism (see Figure 4.2). It is one of the most popular and now largely orthodox views of the nature of social and cultural change: Modern civilization is the history of new technological inventions. The steam engine, printing press, television, and automobile have created for modern humanity these new conditions. Research and development, which have set conditions for modern technology and thus for cultural and social change, are self-generating. One of its most quoted advocates, Harold Innis,[27] suggested that historically, fundamental breakthroughs in technology are first applied to the process of communication. The printing press created the age of mechanics, and the telegraph opened the age of electronics. The forms of social organization and the stages of society and the characteristics of culture were all determined by the medium of the time. In fact, the development of Western civilization can be best analyzed and understood in terms of a competition for dominance among media of communication.

Innis argued that any given medium will bias social organization. For example, time and space took on cultural meanings: Time meant the sacred, the moral emphasis on religion and hierarchy; space meant the present and future emphasis on state, technical and secular development. The bias of the media in favor of one institution meant the ensurance of its cultural characteristics. On the cultural level of time and space, this principal contrast could be seen between oral and written traditions. Whereas oral culture tended to be time-binding, with limited capacity for technical change, written tradition led to space-binding, and consequently favored the growth of political authority.

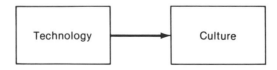

Figure 4.2. Technological Determinism Model.

In debate over the mass media and culture, this technological determinist school of thought made its popular appearance in the writings of Marshall McLuhan[28] in the 1960s—first in North America and then in western Europe. Extending on the work of Innis, McLuhan argued that "the things on which words were written down count more than the words themselves." He sharpened Innis's thesis; that is, the medium is the message. Whereas Innis and McLuhan assumed the centrality of communication media in their argument, they differed concerning the way the medium affects the individual and the culture. Whereas Innis saw the medium of communication principally affecting social organization, McLuhan found its principal effect on sensory organization and thought. Art and technology become extensions of humanity: stone axe for hand, wheel for foot, glasses for eyes, radio for voice and ears, and money for storing energy. His theme throughout his writing is that the West has lost its balance primarily because with writing and then with print, it allowed sight to take precedence over the other senses. On the other hand, tribal people, that is, the non-Westerners who rely on speech more than anything else, live in a more vivid world, using more of their senses than the people in the West, and therefore are in balance with their environment. In terms of the media, radio thus becomes a hot medium and the telephone, cool; movies are hot, television cool. Hot media extend one single sense in high definition, the state of being well filled with data.

The technological determinist school of mass media and culture, especially the ideas and methodologies associated with Marshall McLuhan, has come under attack and criticism by both culturalist and media theorists in the West and the neo-Marxists elsewhere.

Less determinist than the pure technological determinist school is the view of symptomatic technology. Emphasizing other causal factors in social change, it views particular technologies as symptoms of change of some other kind; but like pure technological determinism, it assumes that research and development are self-steering, except in a more marginal way. This margin, however, is being used in the total service of the system.

The theory of technological determinism, as it relates to the mass media and culture, suffers from two inherent weaknesses. First, it views only one aspect of a medium—its material or technological form—as its essential defining and determining characteristic. In short, theory can be seen to depend on the isolation of technology, that the dominant technology of communication increasingly shapes the rest of the culture. Or to put it simply, it does not really matter how and to what purpose the medium is used, just that it *is* used. From this point of view, to diversify video necessitates only an expansion in the number of channels and a further expansion and proliferation of the technology. Second, much of the technological determinist view is based on the historical evidence, with no dynamic of its own, and also entirely on Western experience. The generalization begins to suffer.

POLITICAL ECONOMY THEORY

The third théory of mass media and culture is a political economy theory. Among its many proponents are neo-Marxists, the New Left, or just simply those with socialist views of society. In essence and in a general sense, the political economy theory is a socialist strategy. But like the students of the mass society theory and technological determinism school, the writers of this tradition, too, are varied.

In the triple M theory, the triangle of mass culture, mass media, and mass society is closed; the media of mass communication are the parents of mass culture, mass culture is the child of mass communication, and mass media were born out of mass society. The political economy theory questions this closed   circle and substantiates the supposition that the media of mass communications are not so much a cause of mass culture as a tool to shape it. They serve as channels to convey cultural contents, which have already filled—and independently of those media—the cells of a social structure that has assumed a "mass" character. As the Polish scholar Zygmunt Baumann[29] writes, "for culture to become 'mass' it is not enough to set up a television station." Certain conditions of life and social situations first become standardized, providing the right chemistry and the right conditions for the reception of uniform mass media messages. The following are the components involved in this process: Component one is *dependence on the market*, "where a man placed in the macro-social situation of the circulation of commodities is exposed to the culture-forming influence of the market." Component two is *dependence on organization* that "is supra-personal rather than non-personal—absolutely and without exception." And finally, component three is *dependence on technology*. Dependence on technology generates disorientations and anxiety, and humanity cannot bypass technology in the complex modern society it has generated. But how can we strive to end the isolation of the individual participants from the social learning and production process so entangled by these three dependent factors? This is the political core of the political economy theory. It is over this point that socialist concepts differ from the triple M theorists and technological determinists.

If the image of mass society that the triple M theorists portray is drawn from the *laissez-faire* doctrine of economics (if not totally from the Protestant view of society), the political economy theorists draw most of their ideas from the Marxist view of production.[30] An exception, however, is Jurgen Habermas, who in the tradition of the Frankfurt school of critical theory approaches these tasks through a combination of conceptual analyses, systematic reflection, and critical reconstructions of such thinkers as Marx, Weber, Durkheim, and Adorno. By and large, the triple M theory is one of social control from above even though it is based on the need to make concessions to mass tastes in order to control the masses most effectively. The political economy theorists view the process from below, where through an elaborate feedback of political and economic machinery, the masses can participate in the production and distribution of cultural messages (see Figure 4.3). Furthermore, whereas the so-called theory of mass society is a statement of alienation from contemporary society, the political economy theory views the process on a more positive ground.

Most proponents of this school of thought assume that humanity is essentially good and that social forces are responsible for its corruption. From this point of view, cultural standards are not seen as problematical but as epiphenomena of social conditions. If favorable social conditions and the right economic and political institutions are created, desirable cultural standards will blossom. Erich Fromm,[31] as one of the leading spokespersons of this school, argued that because of the unfavorable conditions of a mass society, humanity becomes so alienated that it is unable to resist mass culture. It loses its consumer sovereignty and is compelled to buy whatever supply of culture is at hand. Dwight MacDonald's metaphor of Gresham's law gives support to the theorists of political economy.[32] For him, the market is purely one of runaway inflation that cannot be checked because standards are continually falling. Low-grade demand stimulates low-grade supply and vice versa.

One of the first political-economic analyses of the media and culture within the total context of capitalist society was made by the Frankfurt school. This group included Walter Benjamin, who studied the interconnection between technological advances and culture forms; Leo Lowenthal, who examined the popular literary cultures; Theordore Adorno, who wrote on radio music and jazz; and Herbert Marcuse, whose theory of the effect of the rationalizing process of capitalism on language and culture became the basic assumption of many media and culture critics, especially those of the New Left in the 1960s and 1970s. Like the triple M theorists, these, too, included both optimistic and pessimistic views.

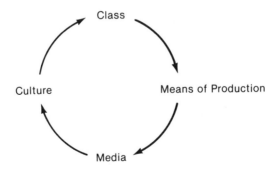

Figure 4.3. Political Economy Model.

For example, whereas Henri Lefèbvre[33] emphasized the disappearance of a general code of communication and the conversion of daily life into a spectacle, and Jean Baudrillard[34] spoke of the implication of this change in which objects are transformed to signs, Hans Magnus Enzensberger[35] took a more optimistic view, arguing that the new media of socialism could democratize culture once it had been taken out of the hands of the bourgeois intellectuals.

During the 1980s, a growing number of media theorists and writers taking another view of political economy analyzed the specific conditions of cultural production in colonial and dependent countries. Such writers as Ludovico Silva,[36] Antonio Pasquali,[37] Evelina Dagnino,[38] Armand Mattelart,[39] Herbert Schiller,[40] and others, drawing their ideas heavily from the studies of the dependency theorists, advanced the notion of cultural imperialism and cultural domination to show how media have been used to homogenize culture and create a market mentality.

To summarize, the political economy theorists base their analysis of the media and culture on the notion that the dominant ideas in a society are those of the dominant class and that the class that is the dominant material power of the society is also the dominant cultural and spiritual power. Thus, they concentrate on the basic structural and economic foundations of society. It is in these foundations that the political economy determinists perceive the fundamental reason for the increasing preponderance of those elements in the culture of the entire society that have become macro-social universals over those that are still subject to subcultural diversification.

CULTURAL STUDIES AND POSTMODERNISM

From a different angle, a number of political economy and neo-Marxist writers have approached the phenomenon of communication and culture using concepts ranging from cultural anthropology, classical hermeneutics, semiotics, aesthetics, to literary criticism. Representatives of this tradition, known as the British school of culture studies, are Raymond Williams[41] and Stuart Hall[42] who have combined cultural studies with critical research perspectives.

Hall and his colleagues at the Center for Contemporary Cultural Studies at the University of Birmingham define communication not as products explicitly for or by the media, but rather as including a wide variety of cultural expressions and the ritual forum of everyday life—education, religion, colloquial conversation, and sports. The focus is on lived culture, especially aspects of working-class (mass) culture, in contrast to the critical school's early focus of writers such as Adorno, Horkheimer, and Benjamin on elite (high) culture. This perspective laid the framework for a cultural interpretation of the role of communication technology and the media systems, especially in the 1970s. In Hall's view, mass media are the most important instruments of twentieth-century capitalism for maintaining ideological hegemony, as they provide the framework of mass culture.

Other perspectives on communication and culture within the European radical sociology can be found in the works of German philosopher and sociologist Jurgen Habermas[43] and Italian writer and political activist Antonio Gramsci.[44] Habermas believes that Marx's attempt to recover the object from Hegel's philosophy of identity led to a reduction of self-reflection of the instrumental quality of labor. This reduction degrades both social interaction and the emancipatory quality of knowledge. In response, as with Horkheimer, Habermas calls for the recovery of the cultural dimension of social interaction.

In recapturing the cultural dimension of social interaction, Habermas focuses on the role of language in attributing historical circumstances to the world in particular. The basis for Habermas's communication theory of society is to re-establish the dialectic interaction of emancipative knowledge from the internal and external constraints of nature. The two moments of this dialectic are *communication praxis* and *productive activity*. Here Habermas's critique of Marx becomes clear. Habermas believes that Marx relegated the meaning of inter-subjective communication and symbolic interaction as an epiphenomenon of universal laws pertaining to the material interaction of man and nature in the instrumentality of social labor. Habermas attaches equal importance to the material infrastructure and the cultural superstructure of Marx, synthesizing them in the purposive-rational action of emancipatory critical interest. The action systems of instrumental-work and communication-symbolic—or man-nature—and, man-man interaction are in mutual relation, neither reducible to nor independent from one another.

Gramsci on the other hand attempts to synthesize the idealism of Hegel with the materialism of Marx. Gramsci's philosophy of *praxis* locates capitalist power and domination not only with the material dimension of economic means and relations of production, but also within the ideological hegemony which disintegrates, at an idealist socio-political level of analysis, collective consciousness to class consciousness. Ideological hegemony is used, according to Gramsci, by the ruling class, through institutions such as education, religion, family, and industrial organization, to legitimize power relations. Gramsci had a major influence on the thinking of a number of writers of the British school of cultural studies including Stuart Hall.

Superordinate to the triple M theory, the technological determinist school of thought, and the political economy paradigm is the theory of so-called postmodernism or poststructuralism which co-existed as a salient partner in the literature of philosophy, history, and literary criticism from the 1940s onward. The genesis of postmodernist thought lies in a re-evaluation of the limits of existentialism and in a disenchantment with the structuralist phenomenology of critical theory and the objectively quantitative restrictions of empiricism. It is represented in the writings of such critics as Jean Baudrillard,[45] Michel Foucault,[46] Jean-François Lyotard,[47] and Gilles Deleuze and Felix Guattari.[48]

The postmodernists and poststructuralists attack the authority of reason. Not only do they criticize the rationality of the natural world and the methodological difficulties of conquering it, but they also question the concept of self as living. Their discourse circles around *becoming*. They are not concerned with the study of structures such as laws, and patterns, but with the practical historical forces that would impose or resist structure. Mostly an intellectual exercise in the French social science tradition, this postmodernist writing is based in the esoteric realm of philosophy, language, and literature. Its appeal to and acceptance by Western social scientists came much later, in the 1980s, when its tenets appeared to offer possible explanations for the unconventionality of contemporary communication issues and events. As modernism created its own forms for authority, postmodernism tended toward anarchy, in deeper complicity with things falling apart.

The postmodernist philosophy of communication and culture is developed as a response to the crisis in leftist and Marxist thought and as a means of figuring and legitimizing the proliferation of alternative identity groups. Within this tradition, there are some who claim that in today's cultural politics there is a basic opposition between a postmodernism which seeks to deconstruct modernism and resist the *status quo*, and a postmodernism which rejects modernism to celebrate the *status quo*.

TOWARD AN INTEGRATIVE THEORY

One of the most fundamental fallacies underlying the biases of the triple M theory is the assumption that mass society is an atomized system in which the relationships between individuals have become increasingly amorphous. The technological determinists fall into the same trap when they view Western society as print-oriented and linear, contrasting that designation with non-Western society. However, the quest for cultural integrity around the world and the development of political, social, and economic subcultures in both the Western and non-Western worlds, as well as in other global regions, are only recent examples of some of the pluralist societies in which—through the course of structural differentiation—an increasing variety of solidarities has been developing.

Most of the theories and discussion of the mass media and culture reviewed in the previous pages are historically biased. For example, in the triple M theory, since the effort is directed toward preserving the standards of the past, continual references to these standards usually accompany the debate. What is needed is a dynamic paradigm that can take the social, economic, political, and structural variables into account. Such a model must make a distinction between production and distribution of cultural messages.

There is a need for a shift in emphasis in the analysis of communication systems, especially mass communication systems, from an exclusive concern with the source and content of the messages toward analysis of the message distribution process.[49] Control of the distribution process is the most important index of the way in which power and values are distributed in a communication system, which may be the global community, a country, or some smaller cultural unit.[50] To prepare a documentary television program of one kind or another that will be viewed by 10 persons requires no more effort from producers and artists than to prepare one for 10 million people. The nexus is between the economics and politics of distribution and quality, not quantity.

The mass media system is viewed here as a rather complex social system consisting of actions carried out within the context of the external social conditions of the community and the society in which it operates. The operation of no one part of the mass media system and process can be fully understood without reference to the way in which the whole itself operates; or to put it more succinctly, no part of the mass media system stands alone, but each part is related to both the formation (production) and distribution processes of its messages.

To distinguish a mass communication system from other social systems, we need to identify its main units. The boundaries of a mass communication system can be defined as all those actions more or less directly related to the formation and distribution of its messages in a society.

Although "the fabric of popular culture that relates the elements of existence to one another and shapes the common consciousness of what is, what is important, what is right and what is related to what else, is now largely a manufactured product,"[51] the research on mass communication has made little effort to apply economic principles and concepts to this "manufactured product." The distribution sequence of the mass media has been one of the most neglected areas of communication research; yet this very distribution sequence has become the most critical, vital, and controversial aspect of the total mass media system.[52]

Our traditional preoccupation with the rights of individuals and groups to *produce* and *formulate* their desired messages rather than the right to *distribute* and *receive* them has been one reason for this neglect. Our assumptive framework of communication research, with emphasis on producers and consumers of messages, and the consequent social effect have been another reason. Yet the growth of communication technology, the expanding national and international market, and the creation of institutional policies and regulations all have made distribution the most important sequence in the chain of mass communication.

Mass communication, in economic terminology, is a form of indirect exchange, and the problem involved is the transfer of manufactured products or messages from the producer of form or utility to the ultimate consumer. Owing to the great size and complexity of our modern means of mass communication, this transfer is sometimes a very involved process and requires the assistance of a number of intermediate agents.

A good deal has been written in recent years, mostly by economists, about the high cost of distributing mass communication messages to the consumers.[53] It is easy enough to see that the journalists are productive agents. It is more difficult to give full credit to the telecommunication machinery that hauls their written messages and the local distributor who sells them over the counter—simply because they are not creators of messages.

But the promptness and convenience with which one may secure a news item or a newspaper depend on the services rendered by the distributor—be it the International Telecommunication Satellite Organization (INTELSAT), the Radio Corporation of America (RCA), or a given post office—as much as on the productive efforts of the journalist.

In analyzing the mass media and culture, the structural changes occurring in the media must be taken into account for they produce expansion, differentiation, and domination. One major consequence of national development is the expansion of and accessibility to cultural content by a large segment of the population. In the new societies, and especially in the so-called Third World countries, the most conspicuous example has been the expansion of education.

The second aspect of change is that of differentiation. The term *mass* media itself has been misleading, suggesting both undifferentiated content and undifferentiated audience. Although the intention here is not to discuss the definition of mass media, it is important to emphasize that it is difficult by any standard to find a modern mass medium directed at or used by the entire population. Rather, a preponderance of mass media is explicitly directed at differentiated segments of the population. In fact, the trend in some highly industrialized countries like the United States is toward specialized and class media.[54] Henceforth, then, the term *mass* media should be redefined to include those impersonal channels—old and new—that are intended for, and made available to, anyone who is a potential user of them within distributive limits.[55]

The third aspect of change is domination. With differentiation and specialization, functional capacity in the communication system increases with the consequences of domination. Not only can one medium become dominant over another, but such dominance can also lead to changes in content. That is, one system's method and content can become dominant over the other. The consequence of this interaction will determine the cultural level of that society or that system.

Another aspect of the integrative theory is the concept and phenomenon of cultural pluralism.[56] Although the notions of cultural pluralism and multi-culturalism are recent, the phenomenon they express is not. The birth of nations from the 1950s through the 1970s and the upheavals and changes occurring in the old nations, are not simply the result of drastic changes in demographic or economic sectors. They also indicate an important development on the intellectual level. Advances in communications and transportation have helped to lessen cultural isolationism. These advances in technology also tend to increase the cultural awareness of minorities by making them more conscious of the distinctions between themselves and other groups. The individual becomes more aware of alien ethnic groups as well as those who share his or her identity. Communication plays a pervasive role not only in social mobility and nation building but also in strengthening ethnic consciousness.[57]

Previous theories of communication and culture fail to explain both the historical incidence of ethnic states and solidarities outside the context of social and economic modernization (such as the Germanic states and the medieval political community of western Europe) and instances in which societies emerge from the experience of modernization without an ethnically defined political identity, and thus are unable to assume a dual identity. This identity depends on the distribution of ethnic and cultural characteristics and a congruity among such components as language, religion, cultural heritage, and physical proximity. Where this congruity exists a particularistic identity and pattern of solidarity is also likely to exist. Conversely, where there are significant incongruities in these components, the mobilized individual will opt for an ethnically neutral, universalistic political identity. When cultural consciousness precedes political consciousness and presupposes an awareness of other cultures, increased antagonisms are likely to occur. Assimilation is even more of a natural foe to self-determination than the multi-national state because of the emotional power of ethnic consciousness.

Thus, significant diversification of the mass media requires not only better and varied technologies but also new conceptions of cultural functions and new patterns of initiation and audience. "However much [television] may be contributing to social stability and unity in American society," John C. Cawelti[58] of the University of Chicago has stated, "the medium of commercial television is not contributing much to enhance the pluralism of American society." He suggests that "initiators would have to be responsible to the traditions of the subculture rather than to their success in getting more undifferentiated people to watch their programming." Expounding on the concept of the new media, Cawelti downplays the elements of "the vehicle (representing the technology or craft which is employed in the transaction)" and "the conventions (representing the genres of symbol systems involved in the process)" but emphasizes two remaining elements in the communication process, the initiator (generally, the sender of the message) and the audience:

> In this medium, the initiator would be a particular subcultural group and the audience would be defined as members of various other subcultural groups. The genres of this medium would grow out of the purpose of enabling one subculture to project its values, styles, and traditions to other groups, or conversely enabling members of a particular subculture to see themselves as other groups see them.[59]

Finally, central to the integrative theory of the mass media and culture is the role of the state, with its own special and unique image of itself and the role it perceives it should play.[60] This is one of the most neglected aspects of the media and culture phenomenon as discussed by the triple M theory and the technological determinism theorists. A centralized system of mass communication tends to emphasize the instrumental use of the media more than the authentic side of the arts and culture. Such a central system, whether capitalist or socialist, reinforces and reproduces existing relations of production and distribution. The main task of the media becomes the programming of ideology in forms of mass culture, popular culture, and people's culture.

Writing on radio and television as art forms in the Soviet Union, Nikolai Shanin considers successful programs as those that "tend toward the journalistic style and belong to the 'document-art' genre." It stems, he continues, "from the specific nature of television art which is permeated with documentary and journalistic aspects that create a *feeling of immediacy of experience*" (emphasis added).

> On account of its immense audience appeal, television art is the most democratic vehicle to carry out the ideological tasks assigned to it. It enters television programs during the peak evening hours, in the actual leisure time of the working-man.[61]

The similarity of perception of the capitalist and certain socialist countries on the role of mass media, especially television, *vis-à-vis* the mass or working person has not gone unnoticed. Enzensberger has advanced the line of left-wing criticism from the point at which the mass society theorists left off:

> A socialist perspective which does not go beyond attacking existing property relationships is limited. The expropriation of Springer is a desirable goal but it would be good to know to whom the media should be handed over. The Party? To judge by all experience of that solution, it is not a

possible alternative. It is perhaps no accident that the Left has not yet produced an analysis of the pattern of manipulation in countries with socialist regimes.[62]

The following is a summary of the factors underlying the urgency for an integrative theory of the media and culture:

1. Emergence of a global culture based on science and technology
2. Development of world economy and a new division of labor
3. Revival of religion and the quest for new cultural orders
4. Appearance of transnational actors
5. The role of nation-states in national development
6. Development of information and communication technologies

Such a theory will encompass the following major variables:

1. Technology
2. Production process
3. Distribution process
4. Cultural message
5. Political and economic system
6. Cultural and value system

The relationship between the mass media and culture and the dissemination of cultural messages in a national system, when this distinction is made, may then be presented in rudimentary terms, as in Figure 4.4, which depicts the media and culture cycle at work. Stage A, representing production and technology lines, is the core of the media hardware; the production of radio and TV sets would be an example of the associated technologies. Stage B represents the distribution capability of the system in terms of both telecommunication and communication infrastructure. Stage C, sharing the distribution and cultural content lines, represents the marketing and management side of the process. Finally, stage D would include the programming and actual program production, completing the cycle. The process of production and reproduction of these cultural messages in all four stages is controlled by two factors: (1) cultural and value systems and (2) political and economic systems.

As identified previously, the communication act, in societal, national, or international levels, then, is comprised of *production* and *distribution* of a *message(s)* to a *receiver(s)* in a *channel(s)* under *conditions* or *value system* with a specific *intention (purpose)* under a specific *political economy* with an *effect*.

Here we can see that external interference has the ability to play a decisive role in shaping the cultural content of any system if the sovereignty in each or a combination of these four stages is lost to an outside system. This aspect of cultural dependency can be illustrated by looking at the media and culture cycle (Figure 4.4) in terms of the quadrants created by the communications technology axes. The type of communications technology that has been most frequently transferred from industrial to nonindustrial countries falls in the upper and lower right-hand quadrants, designated as stages A, B, and C, such as media hardware, television programs, and marketing. The implications of this pattern of technology and program transfer become clear when the diagram is seen as representing the components of control in a communication system, absolute control over which occurs only to the possessor of all four components. In the absence of a single actor controlling all four components, effective control of a system will fall to the possessor of certain of the components before others. For example, a country may have the most sophisticated broadcasting apparatus imaginable and the technical know-how to disseminate messages through it. But unless this country is also producing its own messages, its control over the total communication process is lost to the outsider, and hence its dependency on the outside system increases.

The Americanization of world culture, so often discussed, might be better understood as the interaction of such a message-producing and -distributing system *vis-à-vis* the media technology and cultural content components of the diagram. If American pop culture is successful around the world—and it is—it becomes so by this circular process. The software aspect of communication technology, for example, in the forms of programs, shows,

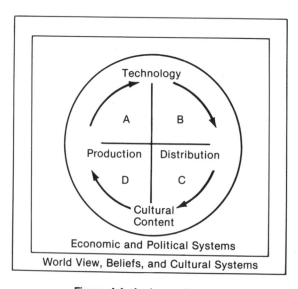

Figure 4.4. An Integrative Model.

and film, enters into a national system seeking to reflect some popular cultural tastes; the product in turn feeds back into the system and reinforces that which has already been found popular.

In the interaction of two cultural systems it is clear that external links and relationships have exercised a fundamental influence on the shaping of the structure of mass media and cultural systems, and therefore, on their functioning and outcome, as well as on the process of structural transformation. Nevertheless, the importance attached to these external links should not lead us to underestimate the existence of structures of underdevelopment internal to the system.

It is here that the pure theory of the so-called free flow of information ignores the inherent weaknesses in many dependent areas of the globe and the total lack of the structures that would seek to instill a counteracting discriminatory capacity in their citizens faced by a bombardment of messages originating in the outside system.

However, unfurling the banner of an open-door policy, the commercialist insists that the removal of all impediments—by both the strong and the weak—will contribute to the development of world culture and redound to the benefit of all concerned. Though this even-handed judgment seems admirable and even attractive in the abstract, it ignores the experience of four centuries during which the powerful imposed Ricardian free-flow trade principles on the weak, while themselves violating those principles to protect favored sectors of their economies. The irony is well-captured by economist and historian Carlo Cippola:

> It was fortunate for England that no Indian Ricardo arose to convince the English people that, according to the law of comparative cost, it would be advantageous for them to turn into shepherds and to import from India all the textiles that were needed. Instead, England passed a series of acts designed to prevent importation of Indian textiles and some "good results" were achieved.[63]

CONCLUSION

Because of the growing awareness of the importance of "culture" in national and international relations, the media and developmental theorists and policy makers have had to deal more and more frequently with questions of a cultural nature. Faced on one hand with the considerable complexity of the subject, and on the other hand with the inconsistencies and imbalances of this phenomenon in the cultural program of nations, the relations of mass media and culture have occupied a prominent and crucial role in the relations among and between nations. The integrative theory presented here is an attempt to show the complexity and the process of this phenomenon, with the hope that it might suggest certain guidelines for the students and practitioners of the mass media and culture as well as for those in policy-making positions.

The need for a new conceptual framework stems from the explicit recognition that some of the major theoretical explanations analyzed in this chapter were concerned primarily with Western historical experience—a parochialism reflected in some of the concepts employed. Such phenomena as the multiplicity of nation-states, the rise of ethnicity, the diversity of national developmental goals and needs, the incredible diffusion of technology by national and transnational actors, and the simultaneous entry of many nations into the industrial-technological as well as communication and information age have not been taken into consideration by past theorists. It is for this reason that such models of mass media and culture have proved inadequate for understanding communication problems that have arisen during the 1970s and 1980s; they are even less appropriate for the study of mass media systems in new nations.

In light of the integrative theory of mass media and culture, it is evident that the developing countries must develop their own national communication policies, striving for more control over all sectors so as to further their developmental goals, reassert their cultural sovereignty, and protect their cultural heritage.

Any communication system striving to integrate itself into a national cultural system must have its policies clear in regard to the following areas:

1. Cultural heritage and community tradition
2. Individual and human rights
3. Economic and political policies and spread of culture
4. Cultural exchange and enrichment in the field of international communication
5. Cultural diversity
6. Intelligent discrimination in the selection of communication technology, both hardware and software, and the media

For example, what are the rights of a minority group that wants to protect and develop its own cultural identity in a national or international system? Can the kind of cultural situation prevailing in the relationships between the developed and less developed countries be called, to use the popular term, *interdependent*? In the promotion of culture, worldwide, what are to be the components of an international cultural program? What should be the role of the mass media in helping to articulate and give identity to the various biological (age group), psychological, and aesthetic groupings that have begun to emerge as a result of the decline of traditional groupings in modern societies?

The old theories of communication and culture usually took a one-way view of the process—that of the impact of the media on culture. They also dismiss the factors of culture and value systems in this process by basing their argument either on political and economic systems or technological and mass phenomena. The integrative view, in contrast, introduces such variables as culture and value systems and attempts to assess the impact of culture on the media. In short, the integrative theory can help explain why such countries as the Soviet Union, the People's Republic of China, Cuba, Yugoslavia, and Tanzania might pursue different and varied media systems because of their cultural differences, although they all speak of a socialist strategy. What were the cultural factors and the communication systems that brought about the Islamic revolution in Iran? How are Muslim societies around the world responding to the dominance of Western culture and why? How should we take into account, in a country like Lebanon, the differences among the various groups playing roles in Lebanon's civil war and political structure? What will be the relationship between the Indian caste system and the conception and reception of mass media? How about the Scandinavian countries, where there are two principles that the triple M theorists consider quite contradictory: stringent economic control and a degree of political freedom and autonomy?

A given communication system might not be able immediately to find answers to these and similar questions, but taking an integrative approach will enhance that system's ability to minimize and manage them better because under this theory it becomes evident that no one system operates in isolation. By becoming aware of all the components, a given system can evolve policies to increase its effectiveness and carry out its policy objectives. Whereas the triple M theory is too narrow in scope and the political economy theory presents a monolithic picture, ignoring the importance of different cultural variables and the rise of new phenomena on the world stage, the integrative theory attempts to take a broad overview while not avoiding the importance of micro-level components. In such a framework, the communication act is not incorporated into production and work. Value systems and the communication act take the central role in the evolution of society. In short, communication and culture, instead of becoming subservient to the mode of production, are viewed as super-structure itself.

NOTES

1. Daniel Bell, "The Theory of Mass Society," *Commentary 22*, July 1956, pp. 75–83; and *The End of Ideology*, New York, Collier Books, 1961. See also W. Kornhauser, *The Politics of Mass Society*, London, Routledge & Kegan Paul, 1960.
2. Bernard Rosenberg and David Manning White, eds., *Mass Culture*, New York,

Free Press, 1957; and R. A. Bauer and Alice Bauer, "America, Mass Society, and Mass Media," *Journal of Social Issues*, 16, 1960, pp. 3–6.

3. Mathew Arnold, *Culture and Anarchy*, Cambridge, England, Cambridge University Press, 1960.

4. Friedrich Nietzsche, *The Will to Power*, in *Complete Works*, London, Russell & Russell, 1910, Vol. 2, pp. 265–266; and *Human All-Too-Human: A Book for Free Spirits*, Vol. 7, Lincoln, NE, The University of Nebraska Press, 1984, p. 277.

5. Karl Mannheim, *Essays on the Sociology of Culture*, London, Routledge & Kegan Paul, 1956; and *Man and Society in an Age of Reconstruction*, London, Routledge & Kegan Paul, Trench & Trubner, 1940.

6. Charles Baudelaire, *A Lyric Poet in the Era of High Capitalism*, London, New Left Books, 1973.

7. José Ortega y Gasset, *The Revolt of the Masses*, London, Unwin Books, 1932.

8. C. Wright Mills, *The Power Elite*, New York, Oxford University Press, 1956; and *White Collar: The American Middle Classes*, New York, Oxford University Press, 1951.

9. Ernest Van den Haag, "Of Happiness and of Despair We Have No Measure," in Rosenberg and White, eds., *Mass Culture*, pp. 504–536.

10. Bell, "The Theory of Mass Society." See also his *The Coming of Post Industrial Society*, New York, Basic Books, 1973.

11. David Riesman, "Listening to Popular Music," *American Quarterly*, 2, 1950, pp. 359–371; and his *The Lonely Crowd*, New Haven, CT, Yale University Press, 1950. See also David Riesman and Michael Maccaby, "The American Crisis," *Commentary*, 29, June 1960, pp. 461–472.

12. Bernard Rosenberg, "Mass Culture in America," in Rosenberg and White, eds., *Mass Culture*, pp. 3–12.

13. Edward Shils, "Mass Society and Its Culture," in Norman Jacobs, ed., *Culture for the Millions?* Boston, Beacon Press, 1964, pp. 1–27.

14. Theodore W. Adorno, "Television and the Patterns of Mass Culture," in Rosenberg and White, eds., *Mass Culture*, pp. 474–488.

15. Leo Lowenthal, "Historical Perspectives of Popular Culture," *American Journal of Sociology*, 55, 1950, pp. 323–332; and *Literature, Popular Culture and Society*, Englewood Cliffs, NJ, Prentice–Hall, 1961; also "An Historical Preface to the Popular Culture Debate," in Jacobs, ed., *Culture for the Millions?* pp. 28–42.

16. Walter Benjamin, "The Work of Art in the Age of Mechanical Reproduction," in Hannah Arendt, ed., *Illumination*, London, Jonathan Cape, 1970, pp. 219–253.

17. Herbert Marcuse, *One Dimensional Man*, Boston, Beacon Press, 1962; and *Counterrevolution and Revolt*, Boston, Beacon Press, 1972.

18. Max Horkheimer, "Art and Mass Culture," *Studies in Philosophy and Social Science*, 9, 1941.

19. T.S. Eliot, *Notes Toward a Definition of Culture*, London, Faber & Faber, 1948.

20. Dwight MacDonald, "A Theory of Mass Culture," *Diogenes*, 3, Summer 1953, pp. 1–7; reprinted in Rosenberg and White, eds., *Mass Culture*, pp. 59–73. See also his "Masscult and Midcult," *Partisan Review*, 27, Spring 1960, pp. 203–233.

21. Irving Howe, "Notes on Mass Culture," in Rosenberg and White, eds., *Mass Culture*, pp. 496–503.

22. Clement Greenberg, "Avant-Garde and Kitsch," in Rosenberg and White, eds., *Mass Culture,* pp. 98–107; see also his *Art and Culture*, Boston, Beacon Press, 1961, pp. 3–21.

23. Q. D. Leavis, *Fiction and the Reading Public*, London, Chatto & Windus, 1932; and *Mass Civilization and Minority Culture*, Cambridge, England, Minority Press, 1930.

24. Raymond Williams, *Culture and Society*, London, Penguin, 1963; and his *Television: Technology and Cultural Form*, London, Fontana, 1974.

25. Denys Thompson, ed., *Discrimination and Popular Culture*, London, Penguin, 1964.

26. For a broad discussion of culture see A. L. Kroeber and Blyde Kluckhohn, *Culture: A Critical Review of Concepts and Definition*, New York, Vintage Press, 1952; and Louis Schneider and Charles Bonjean, eds., *The Idea of Culture in the Social Sciences*, New York, Cambridge University Press, 1973, especially chapters by Talcott Parsons, Kenneth Boulding, and Lucian Pye.

27. Harold Innis, *The Bias of Communication,* Oxford, England, Oxford University Press, 1950.

28. Marshall McLuhan, *Understanding Media*, New York, McGraw-Hill, 1964.

29. Zygmunt Baumann, "A Note on Mass Culture: An Infrastructure," in Denis McQuail, ed., *Sociology of Mass Communication,* London, Penguin, 1972, pp. 61–74.

30. Karl Marx, *Capital*, 3 vols., Moscow, Foreign Language Publishing House, 1961; see also *Marxism and the Mass Media: Towards a Basic Bibliography*, New York, International Mass Media Center, 1974. Also see Jurgen Habermas, *Communication and the Evolution of Society,* Boston, Beacon Press, 1976; and his *The Theory of Communicative Action, Volume One, Reason and the Rationalization of Society,* Boston, Beacon Press, 1981.

31. Erich Fromm, *The Sane Society*, London, Routledge & Kegan Paul, 1956; also his *Escape from Freedom*, London, Routledge & Kegan Paul, 1942; and *Man for Himself*, New York, Rinehart, 1947.

32. Dwight MacDonald, "A Theory of Mass Culture," in Rosenberg and White, eds., *Mass Culture*, pp. 59–73.

33. Henri Lefèbvre, *Critique de la Vie Quotidienne*, Paris, Gallimard, 1970.

34. Jean Baudrillard, *La Société de Consommation*, Paris, Gallimard, 1970.

35. Hans Magnus Enzensberger, "Constituents of a Theory of the Media," *New Left Review,* 64, 1970, pp. 13–36.

36. Ludovico Silva, *Theoria y Practica de la Ideologia*, Caracas, Nuestro Tiempo, 1971.

37. Antonio Pasquali, *Comunicacion y Cultura de Masos,* Caracas, MonteAvila, 1972.

38. Evelina Dagnino, "Cultural and Ideological Dependence: Building a Theoretical Framework," in Frank Bonita and R. Girling, eds., *Structures of Dependency*, Stanford, CA, Stanford University Press, 1973.

39. Armand Mattelart, "The Nature of Communications Practice in a Dependent Society," *Latin American Perspectives,* 5, Winter 1978, pp. 13–34; see also his *La Cultura como Eurpresa Multinacional*, Mexico City, Editorial ERA, 1974; *Mass Media: Ideologies et Mouvement Revolutionnaire*, Paris, Anthropos, 1974.

40. Herbert I. Schiller, *Communication and Cultural Domination*, White Plains, NY, International Arts and Sciences Press, 1976; also his *Mass Communication and American Empire*, New York, Kelly, 1969; and his *The Mind Managers*, Boston, Beacon Press, 1973.

41. Raymond Williams, *Problems in Materialism and Culture*, London, Verso, 1980.

42. Stuart Hall, "The Rediscovery of 'ideology': Return of the Repressed in Media," in Michael Gurevitch, Tony Bennett, James Curran and Janet Woollacott, eds., *Culture, Society, and the Media*, London: Methuen, 1982, pp. 56–117; and Stuart Hall, ed., *Culture, Media and Language*, London, Hutchinson, 1980.

43. Jurgen Habermas, *The Theory of Communicative Action: Reason and the Rationalization of Society*, Boston, Beacon Press, 1981.

44. See Stuart Hall, "Gramsci's Relevance for the Study of Race and Ethnicity," *Journal of Communication Inquiry*, 10: 2, Summer 1986, pp. 5–15.

45. See Jean Baudrillard, "The Ecstacy of Communication," in Hall Foster, ed., *The Anti-Aesthetic: Essays on Postmodern Culture*, Port Townsend, WA, Bay Press, 1983; and his "The Implosion of Meaning in the Media and the Implosion of the Social in the Masses," in Kathleen Woodward, ed., *The Myth of Information: Technology and Postindustrial Culture*, Madison, WI, Coda Press, 1980.

46. Michel Foucault, *Discipline and Punish: The Birth of the Prison*, New York, Vintage Press, 1979.

47. Jean-François Lyotard, *The Postmodern Condition: A Report of Knowledge*, Minneapolis, University of Minnesota Press, 1984.

48. Gilles Deleuze and Felix Guattari, *A Thousand Plateaus: Capitalism and Schizophrenia*, Minneapolis, University of Minnesota Press, 1987.

49. Hamid Mowlana, "A Paradigm for Comparative Mass Media Analysis," in Heinz-Dietrich Fischer and John C. Merrill, eds., *International and Intercultural Communication*, New York, Hastings House, 1970, pp. 474–484.

50. Hamid Mowlana, "A Paradigm for Source Analysis in Events Data Research: Mass Media and the Problems of Validity," *International Interactions*, 2, 1975, pp. 33–44.

51. George Gerbner, "Communication and Social Environment," *Scientific American*, 227: 3, September 1972, pp. 152–162.

52. Hamid Mowlana, "Political and Social Implications of Communications Satellite Applications in Developed and Developing Countries," in Joseph N. Pelton and Marcellus S. Snow, eds., *Economic and Policy Problems in Satellite Communications*, New York, Praeger, 1977, pp. 124–142.

53. Roger Noll, *Economic Aspects of TV Regulations*, Washington, DC, Brookings Institution, 1973.

54. Hamid Mowlana, "Mass Media and the 1976 Presidential Election," *Intellect*, 106, February 1977, pp. 244–245.

55. Hamid Mowlana, "Mass Communication, Elites and National System in the Middle East," in *Der Anteil der Massenmedien bei der Herausbildung des Bewusstseins in der sich Wandelnden Welt*, (Proceedings of the IXth General Assembly and Scientific Conference of the International Association for Mass Communication Research, September 17–21, 1974), Leipzig, Vol. 1, pp. 55–69.

56. Jerzy A. Wojciechowski, "Cultural Pluralism and National Identity," *Cultures*, 4, 1977, pp. 50–54.

57. Hamid Mowlana and Ann Elizabeth Robinson, "Ethnic Mobilization and Communication Theory," in A. A. Said and L. R. Simmons, eds., *Ethnicity in an International Context*, New Brunswick, NJ, Transaction Books, 1976, pp. 48–63.

58. John C. Cawelti, "Cultural Pluralism and the Media of the Future: A View from America," *Cultures*, 4, 1977, pp. 56–82.

59. Cawelti, "Cultural Pluralism and the Media of the Future," p. 70.

60. Hamid Mowlana, "Toward a Theory of Communication Systems: A Developmental Approach," *Gazette: International Journal of Mass Communication*, 17, 1971, pp. 17–28. For the role of various states in national communication policies see George Gerbner, ed., *Mass Media Policies in Changing Cultures*, New York, Wiley, 1977; and M. Teheranian, F. Hakimzadeh, and M. L. Vidale, eds., *Communications Policy for National Development: A Comparative Perspective*, London, Routledge & Kegan Paul, 1977.

61. Nikolai Shanin, "Radio and Television as Art Forms in the Soviet Union," *Cultures*, 4, 1977, pp. 83–92.

62. Hans Magnus Enzensberger, "Constituents of a Theory of the Media," in McQuail, ed., *Sociology of Mass Communication*, p. 104.

63. Quoted in Mark Selden, "Dollars and Dependence: Blue Prints for Southeast Asia," *The Nation*, April 23, 1973, p. 522. For a critical commentary on culture and imperialism see Julianne Burton and Jean Franco, "Culture and Imperialism," *Latin American Perspectives*, 5, Winter 1978, pp. 2–12.

CHAPTER 5

Communication Policies and Planning for Development

Communication is a crucial and pervasive part of society's life support system, and the opportunities for applying improved communication to both stimulate development and mitigate problems appear substantial. Yet the realm of communication policy, strategy, and planning remains a fairly new area of inquiry. Moreover, questions of effective implementation remain largely unanswered. For the most part, the role of communication as development has not been operationalized and integrated into societal communication plans. Discussion and analysis of individual countries' communication policies and planning are beyond the scope of this work; and the specific studies and experiments using communication technologies in the service of development are reserved for the next three chapters. Nevertheless, it is important to review the current state of the literature and of communication policy and planning itself, especially as it may apply to developing countries.

Recently, contributions in development planning have been significant. An emerging area of development study is, in fact, the application of planning and management to development efforts. Some specific work has been dedicated to the role of communication in development projects and in planning and strategy specifically in development communication. Although our discussion here cannot be exhaustive, it does highlight the most important elements, factors, and issues and refers the reader to more comprehensive discussions of planning and policy, key factors in the success of development communication. Further, we have outlined our own integrated approach to communication policy and planning with the hope that such a schema might incorporate the elements of the society's economic, political, and cultural communication institutions.

RESEARCH ON POLICY AND PLANNING

Communication policy and planning is still an emerging area of research. A survey by Syed Rahim of seven well-known journals of communication from 1966 through 1976 found that the terms *policy, planning,* or *strategy* appeared in titles or subtitles of only .7 percent of the total articles.[1] Further, Rahim cited his own bibliographic research in 1976, which revealed that questions of communication planning and policy were mostly raised in the narrow context of adopting a new communication technology to a development program, with sparse attention to overall concepts, theories, and methods. Although we have seen a progression of policy research and a rise in the number of national communication policies during the last decade, writings on communication strategy and planning as they relate to development remain somewhat fragmented, simplistic, bureaucratic, and market-oriented. With the exception of a dozen or so monographs and highly analytical essays, the literature seems to be a variety of "how-to" pamphlets, usually prepared under the sponsorship of agencies and organizations involved with "development communication" or "communication support" projects. This is by no means to minimize the efforts undertaken in this area, but only to alert the reader to the great profusion and variety of works that characterize communication strategy and planning.

Similarly, telecommunications policy in developing countries seems to be equally as fragmented and diverse. With the exception of a few farsighted nations such as Brazil, India, and the People's Republic of China, the developing nations of the world have little cohesive communications policy. It is generally accepted in those nations that control over information and communication resources is fundamental to sovereignty and development, yet formal telecommunications policy is rare.[2]

Defining Communication Policy and Planning

Policies, strategies, and planning are applications of theory to reality, usually in the form of social, political, economic, and cultural actions. In particular, large-scale communication action first requires a coherent and well-defined policy, and second, a well-articulated strategy and plan. The United Nations Educational, Scientific and Cultural Organization (UNESCO) has defined communication policy as "sets of principles and norms established to guide the behavior of communication systems."[3] This broad definition might include both the long-range and short-range orientation of communication objectives, which "are shaped in the context of society's general approach to communication." Accepting this general observation, we define communication policies as systematic institutionalized principles, norms, and behavior that are designed through legal and regulatory procedures and/or perceived through historical understanding to guide formation, distribution, and control of communication in both its human and technological dimensions. Furthermore, communication policies (or the perceived lack of such policies) reflect the prevailing cultural, political, and economic behavior of a given system. On the other hand, communication planning refers to both general and specific strategy and operations of given policy goals, both long range and short range, for the purpose of execution and implementation.

Institutional interest in communication policy and planning research has grown over the last 10 years. At the international level, UNESCO has published a series of studies on national communication policies, and the World Bank has conducted feasibility studies and has published a number of monographs on "communication support" planning and a book on telecommunication and economic development.[4] The United Nations Development Programme (UNDP), United Nations Centre for Transnational Corporations, and the International Telecommunications Union (ITU) have prepared regional and international telecommunication plans and studies on the economics of communication. The report of the International Commission for the Study of Communication Problems (MacBride Commission) and the declarations and deliberations of UNESCO and the International Programme for the Development of Communication (IPDC) have given further impetus to the questions and problems of communication policies. The Intergovernmental Bureau of Informatics (IBI), the International Institute of Communication (IIC), the Organization for Economic Cooperation and Development (OECD), and a number of other organizations have studied broadcasting, computers, and telecommunications interaction policy.

At the national level, both developed and developing countries have implemented studies on long-term communication policy and the impact of modern technology on culture and society. A number of development aid institutions as well as national foundations have ongoing research programs in these areas. When all the governmental as well as academic institutions engaged in policy and planning research in developed and developing countries are added to the list, the emerging field of communication policies, strategies, and planning seems to be a wide-ranging area of professional and scholarly activities.

Strategies and Approaches

Upon examination of both the literature and institutions dealing with communication policy and planning, the following different research approaches have been identified:

1. Long-range planning with policy goals toward equitable distribution of communication power in a society's future
2. Comprehensive planning examining all aspects of a communication system within the broader socio-political framework of society
3. Development support communication designed to encourage the participation of beneficiaries in a project and to ensure its execution and success
4. Technology transfer and assessment, especially innovations in such areas as satellite communication, cable television, and telecom-computer link-ups
5. Control and regulations and their legal and institutional consequences
6. Normative and goal-oriented approaches in which the information program policy plays an active role in broadening the political and cultural views of the people through alternative and critical programs
7. Information economics, determining the information sector of the economy's contribution to overall economic growth
8. An integrated approach toward a unified comprehensive methodology[5]

These strategies often must combat three major problems at institutional, national, and international levels. The first problem is that whereas freedom of communication is a highly desirable social goal at the normative level, the realities of national security and commercial and political interests too often influence and even control communication policy and planning at the programmatic level. The second problem, which stems from the process just mentioned, is the use of communication technology without regard for its effects on a people, since national communication policy and planning often are not only uncoordinated but also manipulated by commercial and political interest groups. Finally, the third problem is the fragmentary nature of communication planning and policies, which are often directed toward a single institutional goal and bureaucratic decision-making process without considering the integrated nature of communication in all spheres of societal activities: political, economic, and cultural. This last problem is one of the most crucial areas of communication planning and policy because in the process of coordination and integration, a system must deal with differing ideologies and views of people and the different attitudes and tolerances of societies toward control and manipulation.

As was observed in previous chapters, present-day models of development are expanding to include non-economic factors in the entire phenomenon of development. Although this is an important and necessary refinement of the concept of development, it renders the task of creating an operational framework for development analysis much more difficult, and consequently, communication planners and strategists often neglect these non-economic areas in their measurement. For example, communication as an investment alternative relative to other sectors such as steel and oil production is not highly rated because benefits tend to be both long term and difficult to measure.

Other strategic and policy decisions and choices that are often cited in the literature and for which the developing countries must strike a balance based on their own unique geographical, economic, cultural, and political case are (1) individualistic versus collectivistic development dimensions, (2) human versus capital-intensive developmental plans, (3) long-range versus short-range communication infrastructure, (4) control versus decentralized planning and national versus local projects, and (5) the choice and balance between urban and rural areas.

Most of the writings in communication policies and planning emphasize the notion that the role of communications technology in national development is to change the audience's attitudes and behavior. There is agreement, however, that communication is critical to the process of national integration, socio-economic mobilization, and political participation as well as the broadening of formal and informal opportunities. There are also those who promote reflective policy that educates the audience through interactive and responsive communication, but this goal is not as easily implemented as one might think. Communication policies are basically derivatives of the political and economic environments and institutions under which they operate. They tend to legitimize the existing power relations, which are not necessarily working for the best interests of the developing country.

Communication development strategies and objectives are generally set by the interaction of a number of parameters, chief among them the people's needs and expectations, the country's resource constraints and possibilities, and the quality of leadership allocating the limited resources to unlimited needs and demands in a dynamic domestic and international environment. For a variety of reasons, the leadership of a number of developing countries have not always taken into account the people's needs or the country's own possibilities for development, but instead have attempted to apply universal prerequisites for industrialization, which according to several studies, do not truly exist. There is the tendency to generalize the problems and situations of developing nations at the expense of careful consideration of their diversity and the benefits of culturally relative development strategies.[6]

It is important here to take note of some of the most recent diagnoses of communication policies and planning as they apply to the developing countries. For example, the International Commission for the Study of Communication Problems saw a need to link communication development with overall development, through the formulation of national communication policies. According to the commission, these policies should be based on an endogenous approach to development, but they should also take notice of opportunities and dangers in the extra-national environment. They should consider demographic imperatives and seek to provide appropriate communication infrastructures for each nation. Priority should be given to (1) instituting non-vertical flows of communication, (2) correcting existing structures and setting them on a course toward democratization, (3) selecting new technology and new technical means, (4) neutralizing potential disadvantages resulting from technological developments, and (5) creating training facilities.[7]

Technological and Institutional Approaches

Most of the writings, research, and prescriptions on communication policy and planning focus on those areas that are technologically mediated and/or institutionally arranged. These two orientations, however, are not mutually exclusive; those who have taken the technological point of view in their orientation often share a good deal with those who have concentrated primarily on insitutional arrangements. Further, the approaches themselves are somewhat overlapping, despite their general and specific distinctions.

This technology-mediated focus can be observed in the works of such writers as Ithiel de Sola Pool and Edwin B. Parker. To Pool, international telecommunications is vital to progress in the developing countries. As advanced countries increasingly transfer their reference materials from hardcopy libraries to computerized retrieval systems, the developing nations are faced with a choice: tap into these new information stores or fall further behind in information capacity. Since the modern world's technical and scientific culture is global, according to Pool, any country that cuts itself off from the flow of knowledge in that global enterprise "will pay a very heavy price to do so."[8] Parker, too, emphasized high technology and communication institutions in communication policy planning; however, he acknowledged that different mixes of technologies are needed in different countries and that countries must "strike a balance" when making information policy choices.[9]

The institutionally arranged focus has been emphasized by a number of diverse developmental schools of thoughts as well as individual contributors. It acknowledges that research and planning in communication and development is indeed a complex task and that the analyst must maintain a broad view of communication as a part of the larger development system, while at the same time focusing on the communication system itself and the relationship of its component parts. The institutionally arranged focus, however, often attempts to implement this task by presenting an operational planning design for research and analysis, planning, and decision-making processes. More specifically, a number of writers have attempted to delineate the parameters of planning, its constraints, and the factors it must accommodate. The central assumption is that communication planning for development is initiated on the premise that change is needed. Thus, these frameworks are intended for the practical use of planners and decision-makers.

For example, the early work in this area by Wilbur Schramm emphasized the imperatives of modern technology while attempting to describe what mass media can and cannot do in the developmental process.[10] More recently, Robert Hornik has outlined a number of "roles that communication technology play both expected or unexpected. Somewhat similar to the work of Schramm, these included communication as 'low-cost loudspeaker,' 'institutional catalyst,' 'organizer and maintainer' and as 'legitimator/ motivator.' "[11]

Alan Hancock, who initially sought to establish a wider context of the meaning of such concepts as "planning" and "policies," proposed a framework that illustrated the cyclical relationship between various activities in the planning and implementation process with applied factors for research, planning, and decision-making. His planning network accommodates activities at many different levels of organization.[12] Comparative institutional analyses on communication policy and planning have been carried out by a number of scholars, including Majid Tehranian, who have examined the role of media institutions, such as broadcasting, in national development planning.[13] Others such as John Middleton and Dan J. Wedemeyer[14] have approached problems of communication development with very specific recommendations on planning.

It is generally accepted by scholars that communication policy is the application of theory in the development of system goals. Well-defined communication policy gives direction to communication strategies and planning. As Alan Hancock has observed, "the form of planning with which we are primarily concerned is 'strategic,' as opposed to 'operational:' it is mostly concerned with the establishment of policy and its translation into objectives and strategies."[15]

In agreement is John Middleton, who argues that:

> The use of theory to guide strategy development is a crucial element of planning . . . . Yet most communication theory has been developed in western culture . . . [and is] faulty when applied across cultures. Communication planners in the Third World face the almost overwhelming task of developing theories and models within their own social image and culture.[16]

Development planners must also work with existing resources (largely determined by the policy established at the system level) or with those that can be realistically created within financial and time constraints. The availability of resources, then, becomes important as an element in shaping communication planning. Resource assessment is a critical component of the planning process and involves identification and evaluation, as well as assessments of distribution and potential redistribution or extension of resources. The communication resources available can be grouped into three categories: (1) traditional communication and interpersonal interactions, (2) conventional mass media and telecommunication, and (3) high technology and space applications.

Essentially, the contention is that communication policy and planning in any society or nation are influenced and shaped by real-world factors. The process can easily be divided into specific phases or steps, and a variety of methods have been devised to perform the task in diverse and dynamic environments. Policy making is the initial phase in which problems are recognized and specific governmental efforts are made to determine directions. As noted previously in this chapter, many nations of the developing world are lacking in cohesive and coherent communications policy. Although the need for some control or regulation of the information and communications technology industries is recognized, there is little agreement in most nations, on political and philosophical grounds, of the best approaches to take in any given situation. Consequently, policy is usually either fragmented and ineffective or altogether absent. A noteworthy exception is the People's Republic of China, which has integrated specific communications goals, particularly technologically oriented objectives, into its overall national policy and planning.

In many nations, information technology is a most powerful resource, one that is not depleted with use. Further, this resource aids in the organization and allocation of other resources. Policy making, particularly in the Third World, is unavoidably influenced by extra-national forces. More significant than the obvious politico-economic and diplomatic influences is the impact of private corporations on government policy formulation. These multi-national giants are very often the bearers of technology and innovation. Hamid Mowlana elsewhere observed that their "bargaining position is such that the host country is in a rather weak position because the supplier of technology has almost a monopoly over the know-how and is in a very strong position."[17] The result is often policy and resource application that is heavily influenced by private international businesses with agendas that must obviously differ from those of developing nations.

Following policy making, the planning phases begin. There are two: strategic and operational. The strategic planning phase is so named because it is the phase in which planners gather, organize, and assess information, determine the broad range of alternative efforts and goals, and decide which programs to implement and which strategies to follow. The information-gathering step is of prime importance. Information must be comprehensive and accurate. It should be obtained in a diversity of ways, both analytical and non-analytical, to ensure that adequate information is available to assess problems both quantitatively and qualitatively. Although analytical methods such as resource assessments, trend analyses, and cost-benefit analyses yield tangible, quantitative information about specific needs, methods such as brainstorming, case study research, and the Delphi technique yield important information about perceptions, opinions, and complex problems that are too complicated to lend themselves to quantitative assessment.[18]

Although information gathering, organization, and assessment is a critical step early in the strategic planning phase, information is required throughout the entire process of policy making, planning, and implementation. Hancock stresses that a comprehensive, well-organized data bank of information is critical to ensure accurate perceptions and rapid decision-making, as well as to identify the full range of appropriate alternatives.[19] Specific information is needed on social, political, religious, and cultural institutions; physical infrastructures; and technological developments. The type of information needed includes both quantitative data, such as statistics, historical growth rates, and quantified goals, and qualitative data identifying social norms, value systems, expections, historical background and events such as legal environments and regulatory actions, and social and political structure. Such vast amounts of information must be organized in a readily accessible data base or they are of little value, and they should be supplemented with a comprehensive assessment of needs. Possession and use of such a data bank of information is a key to the effectiveness of communication planning efforts.

Once sufficient information is available, planners can begin to consolidate the range of alternative goals and methods that must be examined. Again several tools are available to assist the planner in this exercise. Simulation, cross-impact analysis, systems analysis, flowcharting, scenario building, and cause-effect assessments are only a few of the methods that are used to study proposed options. Each alternative must be fully examined and its merits and shortcomings noted. A careful and comprehensive evaluation of alternatives in this stage will help prevent indecision and inaction later on.

The last step in the strategic planning phase is deciding which goal, which method, and which specific project to implement. If sufficient information has been collected and if an in-depth analysis of the alternatives has been performed, the projects selected for implementation will be the most beneficial in terms of policy goals and planning objectives. Often, cost-benefit analyses, simulations, and the newly developed cross-impact analyses[20] are applied at this point in the planning process to determine which of the alternatives have the highest potential for success, provide the greatest gain with the least human and monetary costs, and render the most desirable results.

At this point, planners make the transition into the operational planning phase, in which projects are organized, implemented, and coordinated. In the last few years, development literature has increasingly emphasized the management aspect of development projects.[21] Most of the literature seems to focus on the application of relatively common program management tools (such as Program Evaluation Review Technique (PERT), flowcharting, and management by objective) specifically applied to the problems of implementing development projects. It assimilates the work of communication and organizational behavior scholars such as Daniel Katz and Robert Kahn's social psychology of organizations and their open system models. Also frequently mentioned are Herbert Simon's decision theory, McGregor's theories *X* and *Y* management styles, and Blake and Mouton's Managerial Grid® identifying management styles as various mixtures of concern for people and for productivity. For the most part, these scholars take a systems approach to managing development, with the feedback loop being of primary importance.

A final step in the operational planning phase is evaluation and assessment to incorporate changes resulting from lessons that were learned in the other stages. Case study, survey research, and post-project cost-benefit analysis are all helpful tools in determining the success of a project and which functions need to be improved. It is important that this assessment be quantitative as well as qualitative. Projects need to be assessed on the basis of the ratio between greatest value and lowest cost. Obviously, this is not to say that the assessment should be entirely monetary; quite the contrary. The connotations of value and cost are not solely, or even primarily, financial. Hancock maintains that, in fact, the value of a communication resource is best assessed in terms of its adequacy, accessibility, and level of participation.[22] For the scarce resources of development, whether monetary, material, or human, to be most wisely and profitably applied, the evaluation phase must produce the most objective, informed, and accurate assessment of projects possible, and the results of this assessment must then be incorporated into the data bank of information from which both policy makers and development planners draw.

Although we have identified policy making, strategic planning, and operational planning as three separate phases, it must be recognized that they overlap and interrelate in the dynamic process of communication development. Ideally, planning follows policy formulation; but realistically, planning is often undertaken in the absence of coherent policy and can be one of the factors influencing new policy. Planning can also influence existing policy, which frequently changes because of the uncertainties inherent in rapidly advancing technological applications. Further, lessons learned in the evaluation portion of operational planning obviously must affect strategy to correct mistakes and improve procedures. Essentially, what we are describing is a cybernetic system in which feedback is used to correct the functioning of the system overall.

Obviously, however, the processes of policy making and planning do not occur in a vacuum. They are affected and influenced by several factors. Middleton[23] identifies four that are of critical importance to development planners:

1. Social image
2. System perspective

3. Communication goals
4. Communication resources

These four factors are interactive and affect one another as well as communication development policy and planning. They largely form the boundaries of the planner's frame of reference.

As indicated earlier, policy is set in particular political and economic environments. These environments, combined with social conditions and culture/value systems, form the basis for the prevailing social image. For example, policy may be set in such a way as to exclude a certain segment of the population from the benefits of development efforts, such as the landless poor, not because of a conscious effort to exclude them but because culturally and socially they have never been recognized. By the same token, certain communication resources may be rejected as desirable because they violate cultural norms. Some of these biases can be examined, worked with, and overcome to the best interest of development efforts; others must simply be considered an unalterable part of the prevailing social image that determines the shape of communication development policy and planning.

System perspective refers to the type and size of system the policy makers and planners envision they work within. Systems can be placed on a continuum from large and centralized to small and decentralized. The system perspective determines to some extent the level at which planning takes place, the goals are established, and the resources are employed. For example, planning on the village level would be less likely to involve establishing a television network than would planning on a regional or national level.

Communication goals are tremendously important in defining the resources used as well as the methods employed. It is in the realm of goals that we can trace the strongest link between communication practice and underlying theoretical notions. Lasswell and Schramm both identified three categories of overall goals within which more specific goals can be formulated: surveillance, transmission, and coordination.[24] Surveillance equates to collecting and organizing information; the purposes of transmission are to inform, to educate, and to persuade; and coordination facilitates management.

Middleton adds two additional categories of goals: dialogue and entertainment. Dialogue is a communication exchange or interaction. This exchange has been recognized by some scholars as critical in the political, economic, and social development of nations and people. The concept of dialogue has particularly been developed by South American scholar Paulo Freire as the communication link that can create the understanding that enables a society to achieve its potential.[25] Mowlana elsewhere describes this link as "dignity through dialogue"[26] and has identified it as "the quest . . . that underlines the current revolutionary movements around the world." In a less theoretical context, dialogue is, quite simply, the exchange of information, opinion, and perception. It provides the feedback that is critical in updating the planner's data bank, and which allows adjustment and refinement of the functioning of the system. It creates the cybernetic loop. Entertainment is a recently recognized goal of communication development. Although the use of valuable communication resources and infrastructure for entertainment causes some consternation among development specialists who insist that the resources should be put to more productive use in education, health, and agricultural projects, its positive contributions should not be overlooked. The desire for access to entertainment may well motivate the construction of communication infrastructure such as broadcast networks and phone systems. On individual levels, it may motivate the acquisition of communication hardware, such as televisions, radios, and telephones, that is the same hardware used in development efforts. Entertainment is a great motivator; people listen when they are entertained. Further, because a message is entertaining does not necessarily mean it will not be informative, persuasive, or educational. In fact, the categories of communication goals are all highly integrated or overlapping. Any one category of goal may be established as a primary objective that enlists any one or all of the other goal categories in practical application.

The fourth factor, availability of resources, is obviously important in communication planning since, in all practicality, development professionals must work with existing resources or with those that can be realistically created within fiscal and time constraints. As indicated previously, communication resource assessment is a critical component of the planning process. It involves resource identification and evaluation, as well as assessment of distribution and possibilities of redistribution or extension. A number of techniques, both quantitative and qualitative, by which resources can be identified, assessed, and included in communication development planning were discussed earlier; nevertheless, any methodology that does not include the needs of the users as a primary driver of planning is likely to be ineffective.

For our purposes, communication resources available to development planners and policy makers can be organized into three categories: traditional interpersonal interactions, conventional mass media and telecommunication, and space technology applications. Of course, these categories overlap, and perhaps their most effective use is in a complementary combination of two or more of the types of resources. For example, health projects in Alaska use local health aides (traditional interpersonal interaction) who rely on satellite links with professionals to help them diagnose and treat residents of sparsely populated areas. Teleconferencing, a relatively recent development, also illustrates the overlap of resource categories, in this case interpersonal interactions and telecommunication.

In Chapter 6, we will examine communication development projects that we believe are representative of efforts worldwide. The overlap of the resource categories becomes even more apparent when those projects are examined in detail. Projects are most easily categorized by the primary resource used, but the secondary resources must also be considered as key elements. The more we investigate the practical efforts of those who implement planning and policy, the more we begin to appreciate that the success of a communication development project is attributable to a combination of significant factors rather than to a single element. This fact makes the process both less and more difficult: less difficult in that success that depends on several factors is more readily achievable because the failure of any single factor will probably not cause failure of the entire project; more difficult in that implementation of a multi-faceted project is much more difficult to plan and coordinate effectively.

Middleton's model of the influences on planners and policy makers illuminates a paradox of communication development planning that has been addressed but not resolved by a number of development scholars and policy makers. Development as defined and expounded in this century does not occur unorchestrated; it requires planning, preceded ideally by policy making. Planning and policy making share at least two common characteristics:

1. They require input and action on the part of individuals and groups.
2. They require that power be bestowed on the individuals and groups that create them.

The power inherent in the functions of planning and policy making unquestionably affects the social image, perspective, and goals of communication development planners. Planners and policy makers become the "gate producers" controlling the gate keepers who control the processes of message formation and distribution. Further, since the planners select the communication resources to be employed in implementing communication development planning (which has been created from their own social image and personal agenda), the perennial questions of resource ownership, power, and distribution become issues of grave concern. In short, the paradox is that administrative incapacity hinders development overall, but strengthening administration hinders acquisition of the personal and political capacities that will sustain development efforts over the long term.

UNESCO's MacBride Commission agreed that policy improvement is an essential reform in developing nations. In the late 1960s, the preliminary research which precipitates such national policy initiation and reform was just beginning. By the 1970s and early 1980s, the research had moved into the area of communication and development.

Even more recently, studies of planning and management have increased in the field of communication and development. In the early 1970s, Robert Chambers extensively addressed the critical lack of effective management in development efforts in rural societies.[27] He analyzed the four common "diagnoses" for the failure of development efforts and labeled them excuses:

- Lack of high-level manpower;
- Poor attitudes among civil servants;
- Lack of integration and coordination; and
- Inappropriate infrastructures.

Chambers asserted that the true diagnosis of development failure in rural areas is poor management, and the only valid prescription is the improvement of management procedures. He went on to identify a sequence of planning procedures: plan formulation, budgeting, programming, implementation, monitoring, evaluation, and reformulation of the plan. It is interesting to note the cybernetic loop in Chambers's construct that requires plan reformulation based on evaluation.

Chambers expands on each step in his proposed planning process and ultimately even provides the necessary planning and programming forms and specific instructions on how to hold planning meetings and evaluation sessions. He draws on accepted Western principles of planning and management such as critical path method, management by objectives, action progress reporting, and subordinate participation in goal setting. His method emphasizes local participation and bottom-up initiative as opposed to top-down imposition. Finally, Chambers advocates a systems approach because development is a dynamic process that cannot be depicted as static or isolated from other concurrent societal processes.

This approach to planning, implementation, and evaluation of development efforts contributes significantly to the practice portion of development projects. What Chambers fails to do is to sufficiently tie theory and policy to this practical part of the equation. He begins at the point of implementation, assuming that policy and national priorities have been set in harmony with national ideology and world view. He, thus, avoids the very dilemma at the core of participation: Development cannot be participatory if it ignores the world view, values, belief systems, and priorities of the societies it is designed to develop.

Coralie Bryant and Louise White err in similar fashion in their exposition of methods for managing development.[28] After a review of historical approaches to the problem, Bryant and White redefine development as capacity-building and identify administrative incapacity as the culprit in failed programs. Again, they offer some very effective implementation suggestions based on administrative management (and organizational communication) literature such as decision theory, human relations theory (as illustrated by the Hawthorne studies), McGregor's theory X and theory Y management styles, and the Blake/Mouton managerial grid.® Bryant and White suggest progressive management techniques such as tree diagramming, logframes, and cost-benefit analysis. They do, of course, include the importance of evaluation, but the initial criterion is for meeting goals, not determining if the goals are appropriate and in keeping with the national ideology and policy.

Perhaps to those concerned with "getting the job done," this theoretical foundation seems unimportant; and certainly, these scholar/practitioners have shown their ability to effectively manage a project and meet the project goals. Nevertheless, in consideration of the importance of an individual's image and historical/ethical world view, meeting project goals to provide something, material or otherwise, which is possibly of little importance or offensive to that individual's belief system does not build capacity, enhance self-esteem, or liberate. The success of western development management techniques is measured against Western criteria of what is good and necessary; the approach is ethnocentric.

One solution is to ensure that the institutions that set policy and plan and implement development are strong enough to generate participation, yet responsive enough to be held accountable.[29] Such a solution places a burden on the entire population of a developing society in demanding participation and accountability. It requires the personal dedication of leaders and administrators to the welfare of the people, even at the expense of their own self-interest. We do not believe that such a scenario is impossible, only unlikely.

It would seen much more feasible to identify goals that are mutually beneficial, thereby consolidating development efforts rather than fragmenting them and wasting them on internal conflicts. Communication development is one area in which such goals are frequently identified. As discussed in earlier chapters, communication efforts often act to support other types of development projects. As such they are also development efforts, and meet needs on local, regional, national, and global levels. Governments use communication and communication infrastructure to support their national goals, which usually include fostering nationalism and disseminating information. At the same time, projects that develop communication resources tend also to make those resources more readily available for use by the citizenry. Particularly in the case of infrastructural development and telecommunications, government usually has a critical interest in their ownership, control, and/or regulation. Planning tends to be long range and centralized.

In short, communication planners and policy makers can better assure success in achieving development goals if such programs are based on well-organized information and comprehensive strategic and operational planning. Further, planners and policy makers are in an ideal position to integrate communication development projects so that they ensure adequate fulfillment of needs, are accessible, and foster participation.

AN INTEGRATED APPROACH
TO COMMUNICATION
POLICY AND PLANNING

An integrated approach to communication policy and planning operates in a broader area than those of technologically and institutionally focused frameworks. The need for this conceptual framework stems from the explicit recognition that a communication system as it relates to developmental processes is a rather complex social system consisting of actions carried out within the context of the internal and external social conditions of the community and society in which it operates. The operation of any one part of this complex system and process cannot be fully understood without reference to the way in which the whole itself operates; or to put it more succinctly, no part of the communication system stands alone—each is related to both the formation (production) and distribution (dissemination and use) processes of its messages. The term *integration* is used here in a broad context of societal, national, and community integration rather than in the integrative use of various communication technologies and hardware seen in some studies dealing with communication policies and planning. Thus, an integrated approach to the problems of communication policy and planning focuses on the linkages among society's economic, political, and cultural as well as communications institutions. As outlined by Mowlana,[30] this integrated approach encompasses the following points:

1. The communication process is divided into two distinct stages of production and distribution. Each of these in turn is further subdivided into two additional stages. In the production stage, the source or sources that initially feed the streams of information through institutions, groups, individuals, and other channels are analyzed. This step carries the process of production and creation of messages beyond the present level of analysis to that of the political, economic, and cultural actors that initially provide the information. In the distribution stages, communication policy and planning must consider information flow beyond its exposure stage to the recipients, and they should consider the process of absorption, internalization, and use of messages in a given population. Thus, the comprehensive study of communication and information must include a careful consideration of the factors in four stages of the process: (a) the source, (b) the process of production, (c) the process of distribution, and (d) the process of use. Distribution and use have become the most crucial areas in communication policy and planning because of the development of modern communication technology, the roles played by the nation-state system, and the growing number of transnational actors and national interest groups and individuals.

2. Eight broad factors or variables are introduced into each stage of production and distribution:

I. *Types of ownership.* In the search for non-culture bound concepts and operational definitions, each stage of formation and distribution of a given communication system is divided into three broad areas of public, private and mixed sectors, with further suitable categories for data gathering.

II. *Types of control.* In the formation and distribution of stages of a given communication system, the control aspect is by far one of the most significant variables in its complexity and measurement. Control over the system can take many forms: It comes from within the structure of a given communication system, as well as from the outside. Some controls are actual, others are perceived. (Control here is the process of deleting or limiting the content or distribution of any of the media of communication.)

Although the process of perceived control has become more organized and consciously applied during the past four centuries, it has existed as an informal check in all societies. This control of the communication system is applied not only by authoritarian, legal, or economic restrictions, but also by the individual's and the organization's mental processes, as well as modeled by values and cultural systems of society. In psychoanalysis, of course, the idea of thought control has been developed whereby the dominant consciousness limits the admission of certain materials to conscious attention. In individual development, standards and values are learned from the general culture, and also developed in ways that are individually unique.

These standards, existing in the conscious mind, reject alien and dangerous subjects. For example, a newspaper reporter or a broadcaster, having observed the standard of his employer or organization or culture, limits his observation to what he should do, see, and write, and after a time may be quite unaware of the limitations put upon his observation. This informal or perceived control in the interest of the social system or of folk values is pervasive and insidious. In many countries and societies this form of control is far more effective than the formal control of a ruler or a hierarchy. Thus, in the paradigm we distinguish four types of control for any communication system:

A. *Internal actual control.* These are specific rules and regulations such as education, professional qualification, internal rules, and hierarchy created and institutionalized formally by the communication system itself, to which members in a communication system subject themselves.

B. *Internal perceived control.* Social control in the communication system, peer group pressure, perceived gatekeeping functions, and unwritten but understood internal rules of the organization are examples of perceived control. These are the so-called "rules of the game," and consist of all those arrangements that regulate the way members of the communication system must behave within the perceived institutional boundaries of the unit they work in.

C. *External actual control.* Direct censorship, licensing and any other external legal, professional, governmental, or external institutionalized factors form this category. Further subcategories can be established here to divide external actual control into such areas as the constitutional, legal, economic, and political sectors.

D. *External perceived control.* In every society there are such systems as culture, personality, social structure, and economic and political elites. Each of these can constitute a major set of variables in the process of demands entering a communication system. Not all demands and influencing factors have their major locus inside the institutional system of communication. Important factors in determining the outcome of both the production and distribution stages of a system stem from constraints and unwritten rules of the environment. Predispositions and wants of readers and audiences, reactions to perceived political preferences and idiosyncrasies, and pressures exercised by elites and organizations in the society are examples of this type of control.

III. *Sources of operation.* Primarily an index of the communication system's dependence upon capital and income, this variable is at times inversely proportional to the size of a given communication system as a whole. For example, categories of sales, advertising, public subsidy, private subsidy, and licensing can accommodate a variety of income sources in different systems and media.

IV. *Disposition of income and capital.* Fiscal policies and priorities which affect the ways in which income and capital are spent and invested are influencing factors in both the formation and distribution stages of the message. The fierce competition among the media and the high cost of technology and labor make it almost imperative to invest in the continuing improvement of the product.

V. *Complexity of media bureaucracy.* The bureaucracy of a communication system can be defined as a hierarchy of non-hereditary positions subject to the authority of the executive. In organizations in which dependence upon the government is rather extensive, study of the bureaucracy is a prerequisite to the proper evaluation of the degree of autonomy or even reliability of message-gathering and distributing levels of the institution. Two subcategories are important here: *monopoly* and *change*.

Monopoly refers to the network or the organization as a whole, its subsidiaries, its subdivisions, its sister organizations, its organization chart and the concentration of ownership. *Change* is the capacity of the system to adapt itself to international and external environments. Job mobility, the degree of turnover, promotional policies, the movement of information in the system itself—in short, the infrastructure of bureaucracy—are important elements that ensure efficient and timely output in the formation and distribution of messages.

VI. *Perceived purpose*. In different countries and in different political economies, a newspaper, a broadcasting station, or a mass media system as a whole may define and perceive its role and purpose in different ways. Here we are concerned with the perceived purpose of a communication system as a larger unit in both the formation and distribution stages. Purposes often include power, prestige, profit, education, and mobilization, and may at times be illusive or overlap; but the overwhelming importance of one or two of these factors in the operation of the system cannot be denied.

VII. *Messages*. Messages refer to the number of media in the system under study. For example, units per medium in the formation stage stands for the number of newspapers for the written press, and for the number of radio and television stations in broadcasting. In the distribution stage only the number of exposures, the frequency with which the same message is distributed and repeated over time is considered. In the formation stages of the message, this could be indicated by redundancy. Here the researcher can gather data on such aspects of the media as uniformity and group reading, readership and audience data. Within the more common orbit of communication policy and planning, the planner is interested in developing a cross-cultural or cross-national index of readership and will toy with the idea of using statistics on newspaper or magazine circulation. Obviously, this would not be a valid index in countries where group readership is uniform or in a political system where the population is exposed to intensive pressures by the authorities or a political party to subscribe to newspapers or other publications.

VIII. *Types of content*. This last category is an obvious variable and is dictated by the cultural, political, and economic systems of the country, as well as by specific development objectives.

3. Modern communication channels that are technologically mediated are not divorced from traditional and indigenous communication channels rooted in the culture and society. On the contrary, instead of traditional communication infrastructure being seen as an auxiliary to mass media and modern information technology, it has been recognized in many societies as an independent system of its own, capable of fulfilling the many functions of modern communication systems in addition to its own special functions. Thus, traditional infrastructure and communications institutions are treated as being adaptable to modern technological development, but the relationship of the two is an integrated one, with emphasis given to whatever mixture provides the best grounds for the implementation of developmental objectives.

4. Viewing the communication process as an integrated whole challenges the technological determinism that has underlined much communication policy and planning. Still, this view considers the importance of modern technological innovation in terms of developmental objectives and communication needs and the distribution of political, cultural, and economic benefits to society. In short, from the perspective of an integrated approach, the connection of different societies and different countries or systems to different aspects of communication technology is diffuse rather than direct. Thus, a given society or a country on both individual and national levels may reflect features of any combination of traditions of communication systems and technology, and some may be stronger and more dominant than others at any given time and at any given level (individual and national) depending on social, cultural, political, and economic conditions. Aspects of this integrated approach to communication policy and planning have been emphasized by a number of scholars and planners since 1980.

NOTES

1. Syed A. Rahim, "Introduction: The Scope of Communication Policy and Planning Research," in Syed A. Rahim and John Middleton, eds., *Perspectives in Communication Policy and Planning*, Honolulu, East-West Center, Communication Monographs Number 3, September 1977, p. 5.
2. See Laurie J. Wilson and Ibrahim Al-Muhanna, "The Political Economy of Information: The Impact of Transborder Data Flows," *The Journal of Peace Research*, Vol. 22, No. 4, 1985.
3. "Reports of the Meeting of Experts on Communication Policies and Planning," Paris, UNESCO, 1972.
4. R. J. Saunders, J. J. Warford, and B. Wellenius, *Telecommunications and Economic Development*, Baltimore, MD, Johns Hopkins University Press, 1983.
5. Rahim, "Introduction: The Scope of Communication Policy and Planning Research," pp. 12–17.
6. Hamid Mowlana, "Toward a Theory of Communication Systems: A Developmental Approach," *Gazette: International Journal for Mass Communication Studies*, XVII: 42, 1971, pp. 17–28.
7. International Commission for the Study of Communication Problems, *Many Voices One World*, London, Kogan Page, 1980, pp. 137–199.
8. Ithiel de Sola Pool, "The Influence of International Communication on Development," in Rahim and Middleton, eds., *Perspectives in Communication Policy and Planning*, p. 105.
9. Edwin B. Parker, "Planning Communication Technologies and Institutions for Development," in Rahim and Middleton, eds., *Perspectives in Communication Policy and Planning*, pp. 43–74.
10. Wilbur Schramm, *Mass Media and National Development*, Stanford, CA, UNESCO and Stanford University Press, 1964.

11. Robert Hornik, "Communication as Complement in Development," *Journal of Communication*, 30: 2, Spring 1980, pp. 10–24.
12. Alan Hancock, *Communication Planning for Development: An Operational Framework*, Paris, UNESCO, 1981.
13. Majid Tehranian, Farhad Hakimzadeh, and Marcello L. Vidale, eds., *Communications Policy for National Development*, London, Routledge & Kegan Paul, 1977.
14. John Middleton and Dan J. Wedemeyer, eds., *Methods of Communication Planning*, Paris, UNESCO, 1985.
15. Alan Hancock, *Communication Planning for Development: An Operational Framework*, p. 37.
16. John Middleton, "Communication Planning Defined," in John Middleton and Dan J. Wedemeyer, eds., *Methods of Communication Planning*, p. 35.
17. Hamid Mowlana, "The Multinational Corporation and the Diffusion of Technology," in A. A. Said and L. R. Simmons, eds., *The New Sovereigns*, Englewood Cliffs, NJ, Prentice-Hall, 1975.
18. For an interesting and enlightening description of a variety of planning methods and their application to the various steps in strategic and operational planning, see Middleton and Wedemeyer, eds., *Methods of Communication Planning*.
19. Alan Hancock, "Resource Assessment," in Middleton and Wedemeyer, eds., *Methods of Communication Planning*, pp. 97–117.
20. For a detailed discussion of cross-impact analysis that combines the advantages of simulation and the Delphi technique, see Dan J. Wedemeyer, "Cross-impact Analysis," in Middleton and Wedemeyer, eds., *Methods of Communication Planning*, pp. 202–220.
21. See, for example, Coralie Bryant and Louise W. White, *Managing Development in the Third World*, Boulder, CO, Westview Press, 1982; and Robert Chambers, *Managing Rural Development: Ideas and Experiences from East Africa*, New York, Africana Publishing Company, 1974.
22. Hancock, "Resource Assessment," pp. 97–117.
23. Middleton, "Communication Planning Defined," in Middleton and Wedemeyer, eds., *Methods of Communication Planning*, pp. 19–36.
24. Wilbur Schramm, *Man, Messages, and Media*, New York, Harper & Row, 1973.
25. Paulo Freire, *The Pedagogy of the Oppressed*, New York, Seabury Press, 1968.
26. Hamid Mowlana, "Communication in Intercultural and International Relations: Toward a New Framework," in *Cultures: Dialogue Between Peoples of the World*, Paris, UNESCO, 1983.
27. See Chambers, *Managing Rural Development: Ideas and Experiences from East Africa*.
28. See Bryant and White, *Managing Development in the Third World*.
29. Ibid.
30. Hamid Mowlana, "A Paradigm for Comparative Mass Media Analysis," in H. D. Fischer and J. C. Merrill, eds., *International and Intercultural Communication*, New York, Hastings House, 1976, pp. 474–484; and his *Global Information and World Communication*, White Plains, NY, Longman, 1985, pp. 160–173; see also his "Toward a Theory of Communication Systems."

CHAPTER 6

Communication Technologies and Development: For Whom and for What?

Conventional uses of mass media and telecommunications technologies in the development of nations and peoples is by no means a new phenomenon. Since its invention in the 1920s, radio has been used to educate as well as entertain. In the 1930s, for example, the "Farm Forum," instituted in England and spreading to Canada and India, was used to disseminate agricultural information and advice to farmers.[1] By the 1960s, radio was a primary component of U.S. foreign assistance programs. Further, many of the development paradigms proposed in the initial "development decade" of the 1950s were based on communication and information.

The theoretical models, however, fell short in practice in developing countries, and in spite of the commitment of UNESCO—which began devoting a large percentage or its resources to mass media and development in the early 1950s—and the efforts of other nations and organizations, the knowledge about the practical use of modern technology in development remained incomplete. The criticisms of the modernization paradigm are many, but the experiences of the era are equally as important. Through the evaluation and review of past development efforts, the nature of the problem itself is now better understood. In the 1980s, more attention has been devoted to "reaching and improving the lot of the rural poor."[2] Preliminary research and field studies in the late 1960s and 1970s raised questions about the cost of technology and its various applications in education, health, nutrition, agriculture, family planning, development planning, and rural economics. Researchers began to be aware of information as a resource and its unequal distribution to those already in more socially and economically beneficial positions.[3] The myth of information as the great equalizer was exposed as studies on the international flow of information and news pointed to patterns that reinforced those of economic disadvantage. Yet typical research often stopped at questions of exposure, not addressing the deeper and more important questions of impact and influence. More important, researchers and planners may have rejected the Western model of modernization, but they did not reject Western thinking. They have been unable to put themselves into any of the thought patterns of non-Western cultures, and therefore have had limited success in adapting development efforts to fulfill conscious as well as subconscious social and cultural standards and needs.

Probably the most important conclusion of the research and pilot studies and projects of communication in development is that the role of information and communication in the process of change is more complex than previously thought. There is still much to be learned, and much can be learned from the practical application of mass media and telecommunications technology in the development programs and projects of the last decade. As was concluded by the International Commission for the Study of Communications Problems,[4] communication is a major resource for development and equity, and we must heighten our understanding of its complexities and discover its most appropriate and beneficial applications.

MACRO- AND MICRO-LEVEL PROJECT ORIENTATIONS

Development projects involving communications fall into two distinct but interrelated categories. Macro-level development programs are established on a national or regional level by central government or provincial authorities. They are generally large in scale and based on national development objectives, at the same time often implemented only after pretesting on the micro level. By the same token, development projects at the community or local level are usually experimental in nature. Most of the projects reviewed in this chapter are experimental and were initiated at the micro level, but through replication they have become tied to the macro level and therefore are rather well integrated in national planning. Characteristically, they are frequently discussed in the context of communication and development and commonly are sectoral applications.

A crucial factor in successful development project planning is determining the level of orientation or the scope of the project. Different methods and resources are employed to establish a national satellite broadcasting system than to organize farmers in a single village to combat a localized crop disease. A number of factors are involved in the planning, including determining the target group, the organizations to be used, and the funding requirements. In other words, the approach largely depends on the level and scope of the project.

Macro-level projects are usually those involving national plans with large amounts of money and equipment and numerous project personnel and local participants. As we shall see in subsequent case studies, national, governmental, and/or political commitment is often a key to the success of development projects at this level. Organizational communication and interaction become a very real concern as many organizations, some with conflicting goals, become involved and bureaucratic administration emerges as a potential obstacle. Macro-level projects are often infrastructural in nature and establish national networks, which are important to the success of micro-level development projects as well.

Cross-nationally, most macro-level communication and development projects are undertaken in socialist countries, such as China and Cuba, or in highly mobilized but well-planned national systems where internal economic, political, and social priorities are clearly spelled out. In non-socialist developing countries, the macro-level projects in which communication plays a vital role are minimal. Most of the research and communication and development experiments outside the socialist and a few Third World countries are implemented on a community, local, or at most, regional level, with the hope that they will generate feedback for national planning. Characteristically, such projects are implemented by donors or development assistance agencies such as USAID and the World Bank.

Micro-level projects are targeted more specifically at a smaller group of people, usually in rural areas, and as a rule, are much less expensive than macro-level projects. They rely on local participation, emphasizing the worker-participant interaction as well as the notion of self-help. Commonly, local volunteers are trained to perform as discussion leaders and change agents to encourage local participation and commitment. Communication networks of radio, television, or teleconferencing may be used in these types of projects; however, the projects are not based on developing infrastructure. Rather, they attempt to change individual behavior and develop individual capacity. As such they are often referred to as capacity-building or self-help projects. A fairly recent approach to capacity building is Integrated Rural Development (IRD), a term originating in the 1960s, when it became apparent that a more holistic approach was necessary. Early analyses found that economic, political, social, and cultural changes were often concurrently required to accomplish a single development objective. The process of development itself, as well as the role of communication in development, was seen to be much more complex than previously imagined. Planners began to design rural development projects in an integrated fashion, simultaneously affecting agricultural, social, and educational sectors. In fact, IRD has been formalized as policy in many organizations. The Integrated Family Life Education Project in Ethiopia is a prime example.[5] The project employed a local educator as a group leader and, in many cases, translator. It was designed to enhance local human resources as well as to achieve certain educational and development goals. Fortunately, evaluation was built into the project, and pre- and post-tests showed increases in (1) literacy/numeracy (to 89 percent), (2) the construction of pit toilets, (3) the number of people receiving vaccinations, and (4) participation in self-help projects. Further, these gains were realized at substantial cost savings because of local participation.

Organizational involvement in communication and development generally corresponds to the macro and micro division of projects. Governments and international agencies are usually involved at the macro level, interacting with the government departments in developing nations. Private organizations, on the other hand, tend to become involved on a micro or project level.

A number of nations in the industrialized world include development communications in their development assistance programs. It is logical that those most involved in such efforts are nations with already highly developed communications industries, such as the United States, the Federal Republic of Germany, France, England, Japan, and the Scandanavian countries. Some Arab countries such as Kuwait and Qatar have occasionally contributed hardware to developing Third World communication sectors. Canada is also heavily involved in supporting international development communications through its International Development Research Center (IDRC) as well as through the Canadian International Development Agency (CIDA). Further, a number of international organizations, such as UNESCO and the International Telecommunications Union (ITU), have specific policies supporting development communications.

In the United States, most efforts in development communications are coordinated through three government agencies: USAID, U.S. Information Agency (USIA), and the Export-Import Bank. More recently, the involvement of USAID has been largely project-oriented, and it has been the single most influential U.S. government agency in communication development.

The USIA's efforts are limited to some media skills training within a restricted $2 million budget and a visitor's program that is strictly for the purpose of exposure. The Export-Import Bank, on the other hand, is involved in the hardware aspect, financing large-scale telecommunications systems. Another U.S. government agency active in development communications projects is the Federal Communications Commission (FCC), which sponsors private training in the United States for 30 to 40 Third World technical media professionals every year under fellowships from the ITU. A number of other agencies are deeply involved in providing space communications technology to developing countries.

Nevertheless, assistance from the industrialized world is largely fragmented, emergency-oriented, politically tied, and evolutionary-reformist. It is also technology-oriented and reinforces the status quo. For this reason, developing nations often find it inadequate and off target.

Because the micro- and macro-level projects are so closely related, the former often serving as a pre-test or proving ground for the latter, it is difficult to separate the roles and purposes of each. In fact, closer examination reveals the roles to be essentially the same, with the primary differences being degree or scope and media application. Let us briefly examine seven roles or purposes of communication and development and relate them to both the macro and micro levels.

1. Communication and development on the macro level are most often identified as facilitators for national economic, political, and cultural goals, as well as for social integration. On the micro level, they can be seen as achieving similar objectives in the community.

2. Mobilization, assimilation, and participation are also generally spoken of in terms of national structures; however, these phenomena are as crucial, and perhaps more manageable and effective, at local levels.

3. Economic growth is usually considered in terms of national planning. Increasingly though, applications of communication at the micro level are revealing rational peasants and farmers who are eminently capable of planning for individual and community economic growth as well.

4. At the national level, development of communications, particularly infrastructure, is an assumed prerequisite to sovereignty and security. Such a capability ensures national self-reliance and fosters a sense of security, real or imagined, in matters of national defense. The same impressions can be developed on a village level as communications becomes a tie that binds local people together, engendering community self-reliance.

5. Cultural participation and autonomy are other results of communication and development that reflect its duality of purpose. Cultural integration or cooperation in the midst of cultural diversity is a macro-level phenomenon; nevertheless, cultural participation is facilitated at all levels through projects employing communication technology and techniques.

6. The infrastructure of communication has obvious benefit to the bureaucracy and administration of governmental organizations and development projects. At the same time, local administration of both government and development projects is facilitated by similar techniques adapted to fill micro-level needs as well.

7. Finally, social planning and project implementation in education, health, and welfare at both macro and micro levels are facilitated by communication.

This dualism of roles and purposes reinforces the previously observed interrelationships of the two levels of communication and development. Were it not extant, the pilot projects at community levels would have little impact on national planning. In fact, they provide feedback, pre-test, and organization, which are invaluable in national development planning and project implementation.[6]

COMMUNICATIONS MEDIA AND SELECTED CASE STUDIES OF DEVELOPMENT APPLICATIONS

With this integrated understanding, we will now examine case studies at community and national levels categorized by the type of media involved. Such studies of the applications of communication demonstrate that most campaigns are multi-media approaches. In 1982, of 85 projects surveyed by the Academy for Educational Development, all used more than one media source. Several media are used to disseminate and reinforce information, and the appropriate selection of a medium is crucial. It must be geared to the message, the audience, and the society. For example, a typical radio or television broadcast campaign may include follow-up audio or video cassettes, posters and printed materials, and personal visits to reinforce and even extend the initial message. Such applications point to the flexibility of communication media and to the advantageous application of specific media in specific ways to support and reinforce other media applications.

Nevertheless, unless the message is designed for the audience to which it is targeted, it cannot be effective. For example, the Tarahumara Radio Schools in Mexico were designed to increase the social and employment opportunities of Tarahumara Indians while reinforcing their cultural identity.[7] The project, funded and operated by the Jesuits, broadcasted programs in Spanish to schools; but very few Tarahumara Indians speak Spanish and very few finish their educational programs. The project helped Spanish-speaking children in schools in the area but did not reach those for whom it was intended.

Projects may fail or enjoy limited success for a number of other reasons as well. There are administrative and technical problems such as equipment failure or non-availability. Requisite printed material may be delayed or lost. Structural constraints hamper efforts, such as the lack of capital for implementation or the inability to act on messages because of the lack of other resources like land. Of course, problems and difficulties cannot be eliminated entirely, but many could be avoided with careful planning and prior research that will result in appropriately targeted messages and availability of necessary material.

Case studies of the application of communication media are beneficial in two major ways. First, case research normally proceeds with a set of stated or assumed hypotheses that are tested situationally. The subsequent practical information becomes the basis for refining or redefining development communications applications. Second, successful cases may provide a model for replication in similar circumstances, and failures or problems encountered may serve as lessons for future planning efforts. Critical examination is thus beneficial not only theoretically but practically as well. Although "armchair critique" often sounds unduly harsh, the intent is to glean beneficial, practical information from previous projects, and not to belittle the commitment and effort of those who were involved.

We have categorized this review of communication applications to development by types of media, recognizing that the categories are not mutually exclusive and that development projects usually employ a combination of media that transcend the boundaries of these categories. This chapter will address a diversity of media. Print media are initially discussed, including the news media. Subsequently we address telephonic technology, computers, video and audio cassettes, film, and folk media. We might view this variety as being commonly connected through its mobility. Whereas the traditional broadcast media, radio and television (addressed in Chapter 8), generally require more infrastructure and centralization, the media we first turn our attention to are undeniably conducive to more local participation and widespread usage.

Journalism and Print Media

Leaflets, Graphics, and Printed Material. Most communication and development efforts rely heavily on printed material. Usually referred to in development communication models as supplementary or support media, printed material is used primarily to reinforce messages delivered by broadcasts, experts visiting an area, or leaders of small group discussions. Flyers, brochures, and even bumper stickers deliver short reminders to vast numbers of people over vast geographical areas at comparatively minimal cost. For example, the Tanzanian "Man is Health" campaign used posters in villages as a constant visual reminder of the goals the citizens were working toward and the necessary behavior to achieve them.

In an effort to combat high rates of infant and child mortality resulting from a high incidence of diarrhea among that age group, a mass media and health campaign was launched in Honduras using printed material and village health care workers, whose message was confirmed by radio broadcast. The workers were taught to mix and administer ORT salts to treat diarrhea. Their subsequent instruction to mothers in the village was reinforced by a media campaign. In one year's time, infant mortality in the project areas dropped from 47.5 percent to 25 percent. Further, evaluation showed a significant increase in the knowledge of diarrhea and treatment, particularly noting that almost all mothers using ORT salts were administering them properly.[8]

In an experimental nutrition project in Brazil, posters, pictures, and flannelboards were used to stimulate dialogue in an attempt to organize community action.[9] One person was chosen for every 10 families to coordinate action in emergencies. In seeming confirmation of Paulo Freire's assertions about the effectiveness of dialogue, the project appears to have increased the sense of community and engendered a transition in villagers who previously perceived themselves to be helpless and controlled by fate. This result is of significant importance to the project planners, who sought to stimulate community interaction and self-reliance.

Virtually all development campaigns are multi-media campaigns.[10] Visual messages are much more effective than those unaccompanied by such stimuli. Recognizing this fact, development planners have implemented a wide spectrum of visual and participatory aids. Reinforcing graphic and printed material is commonplace in nearly all development projects. That the constant visual reminders are an inexpensive method of disseminating a message to a diverse and sometimes scattered population is undeniable. Further, print lends credibility. These media, although most often and most properly placed in a supporting role, are nonetheless crucial to the success of a campaign.

The News Media. The early focus on communication was based on the need to provide information to and persuade the public. Nevertheless, the dissemination of information has come to be nearly synonomous with journalism and broadcast news. The tradition of the Western world, and particularly the United States, is to view journalism primarily as an instrument for news dissemination and current affairs coverage. For this reason, the development of news media and journalistic communication in the developing nations of the world has not generally been supported through the agencies or channels of bilateral aid. Further, journalistic communication is not normally considered an integral component of development projects. Most development efforts in this sector result from the attention of specific communications agencies and organizations and have resulted, among other things, in the formation of regional news services and broadcast institutes established to train media personnel. The outcome of the separation of development in the broadcast and print media from development in other sectors is a lack of coordination and cooperation between the media and development planners. Rather than relying on those media personnel whose business is the assimilation, production, and distribution of information, developers themselves attempt to organize and produce the communication aspects of development programs and projects (such as television and radio training programs). Since government ministries contain few specialists as skilled in the art of disseminating information as those in the mass media, such projects reduce even further the quality of this crucial element of development.

A number of projects have been aimed specifically at developing media and media professionals to increase their effectiveness in developmental efforts.[11] On international and regional levels, such projects have been sponsored by UNESCO since the 1960s, and more recently by the International Programme for the Development of Communication (IPDC) as well.

Telephonic and Associated Technologies

The greatest difficulty faced in providing telephonic services in developing nations has been the establishment of infrastructure. Terrestrial transmission lines are expensive and time-consuming to erect and maintain. Further, the demand for such services has increased far more rapidly than the technology can accommodate. As noted previously, the infrastructure has, necessarily and practically, been concentrated in urban areas. With the advent of satellite technology, however, telephonic services have become more sophisticated, expandable, and reliable and are increasingly available in rural areas.

Telephone and Narrow Band Technology. Although somewhat neglected in the research on development and communication technology, the telephone has been termed a "social mobilizer" in that it facilitates dialogue that leads to change.[12] The telephone medium has been applied in development projects for decades and has been an important tool, particularly in the realm of economic development, which was often the primary goal of most development projects in the 1950s. In the late 1960s and early 1970s, developing nations made large investments in telecommunications to establish the infrastructure to provide increased and improved telephone service to rural areas.

The Inter-American Development Bank (IDB) has been particularly active in supporting such infrastructural projects in pursuing its policy of promoting economic and social development among the lowest income groups.[13] It began funding rural telephone projects in 1976. Although for financial reasons much of its emphasis has been on urban telecommunications, IDB has funded rural telecommunication projects throughout Latin America, including "a $52 million loan to Argentina in 1984 to finance new telephone exchanges in small towns; a $13.7 million loan to Panama in 1979 to finance the construction of 32 telephone exchanges, 28 line concentrators, and 210 public telephones in rural communities; a $12.2 million loan to Costa Rica in 1977 to finance construction of 56 telephone exchanges and 1300 public telephones in rural areas; and most recently, an $18 million loan to Guatemala to finance the installation of 7600 telephones in rural areas. Rural projects have also been funded in Colombia and Ecuador."[14]

Through its Economic Support Fund, USAID has provided concessional loans and grants to establish a microwave link between Nigeria and Chad and develop a telephone plant in Liberia. Over a five-year period, USAID provided $400 million to Egypt for telephone equipment, and Lebanon received $11.7 million to reconstruct a telephone plant.[15]

As a result of these and similar efforts, "the number of telephones in Africa, Asia, and Latin America more than doubled from 33.8 million to 78.0 million" between 1968 and 1976[16] and continues to grow. Nevertheless, the urban bias is still evident. Figures comparing urban-rural telephone distribution in 1980 show the average urban population in industrialized countries to be 39.8 percent of the total population with 51.2 percent of the telephones, whereas 14.9 percent of the population in developing countries was urban with 70.4 percent of the telephones.[17] Third World countries have 7 percent of all the world's telephones for a population of 2 billion. Even within the Third World there are inequities: In 1982, Argentina had 8.1 telephones for every 100 inhabitants, whereas Upper Volta had .03 per 100 inhabitants.[18]

The infrastructure established by widespread telephone service can be effectively used in other ways to aid in development.[19] For example, facsimile is a narrow band technology that uses the established telephone infrastructure to transmit electronic reproductions of printed material. Such methods can be used to quickly send necessary printed information to remote areas in support of development projects and project personnel. Another example is the teleconferencing previously mentioned. This versatile medium has great potential for developing areas, but until recently, such projects had a low priority. It has been the policy of most financial and development institutions that such projects should be self-supporting, indicating a lack of understanding of their tremendous impact on other development projects and efforts.

The 1979 ENTEL pilot project, co-sponsored by USAID and the National Telecommunications Corporation in Peru, was designed for evaluation of the utility and feasibility of establishing telecommunication links, specifically telephones, in depressed rural areas.[20] Because of geographic barriers, cost restrictions, and other limitations of terrestrial, microwave, and radiotelephone systems, a satellite system was chosen for the project. (The Peru Satellite Project Proposal, "Technical Analysis," reported that a terrestrial system would require cable connections throughout the service area, a microwave system would require receiving towers approximately every 30 miles, and radiotelephone transmission would be hindered by the mountainous terrain.) A satellite system is more reliable than terrestrial systems and insensitive to distance. It provides expandable capacity and does not entirely break down when one of the links fails. It is much less susceptible to geography and weather than the alternatives, and consequently is actually more cost-effective.

The satellite link of the ENTEL project was designed to extend existing telephone systems to rural areas. It also provided a channel to transmit information on seismic activity, a network for inter-community exchange of local news, and a teleconferencing capability for government training efforts. In the agricultural sector, the system was geared to ordering and monitoring the delivery of supplies and equipment, as well as to providing teleconferencing for training and information exchange. In education, the goals were coordinated curriculum, better teacher training, and better school administration. The health sector seemed to have the most to gain: Networking of health posts and health centers in rural areas with doctors and specialists at hospitals in urban areas would greatly improve health care. Teleconferencing would further ensure open discussion and dialogue, as well as public health forums and professional training.

Project evaluation is currently in progress by USAID and ENTEL, as well as by the Learning Systems Institute at Florida State University and by Human Resources Management, a private corporation. Usage evaluation is divided into two categories: public use (for agriculture, education, and health), and private or commercial and personal use. Usage logs and personal interviews are being used to determine (1) system usage, (2) system performance, (3) usage rates, (4) user characteristics, (5) alternatives to system use, and (6) results of use.[21]

The evaluation was designed to be concurrent with project implementation but has suffered from bureaucratic misunderstanding of responsibility and strategy, thus being less reliable and enlightening than was hoped. Nevertheless, some conclusions have been drawn that may be of benefit in the future of the ENTEL project, as well as in the implementation of similar projects.

Although the project has had some difficulty with the hardware because the fragile technology was placed in such a hostile environment and is behind schedule in installation as well as program delivery, it has had some success in both the health and education sectors. Doctors have frequently consulted with their patients, and educational teleconferencing sessions have been standardized. Agricultural teleconferencing has been less successful because the farmers are scattered and it is difficult to convene meetings. The telephone system, however, has probably been best received because previously people had to ride four to five hours on the bus to get to the nearest telephone and wait in line to use it. They then had to wait until the next day to catch a bus home.

Results of the evaluations seem to be mixed. Although many positive changes have occurred, unexpected costs and equipment failures have caused some difficulty. The system has, however, shown some flexibility and adaptability in dealing with obstacles. This telecommunications system has provided a method for some people of rural Peru to participate in their own development.

Heather Hudson has documented a number of other applications of the telephone in developing and/or remote areas.[22] Telecommunication is used in areas of difficult transport, like the South Pacific and Alaska, to increase transportation efficiency and to substitute for transportation. It is used to coordinate and plan shipping schedules and quantities. For the University of the South Pacific, teleconferencing is a cost-effective alternative to the travel and time previously expended for regional meetings and coordination. In Alaska, telecommunications is used for audioconferencing in the health care industry, saving both transportation and hospital costs, and possibly lives. In the same area, legislative conferencing enables participation in government, and use of the ATS–1 satellite has substantially improved rural school administration.

Computers. Computers are also becoming more commonplace in development efforts, particularly as a planning and management tool. The technological developments in this arena of communications are so rapid that policy makers have been unable to address them adequately. For example, videotext is a home retrieval system in which the merger of reception, transmission, and computer processing is complete.[23] It is continuously transmitted on unused portions of television transmissions, either one way, so the receiver enters a code to receive the desired transmission, or interactively, in which case the user's computer terminal is linked by cable or telephone to a central information bank. As the electronic data retrieval business grows, it becomes a potentially powerful tool in development efforts.

The advances in computer and communication technology are staggering and take us far beyond conventional media and development. These innovations in space technology and telematics are addressed in detail in Chapter 7; nevertheless, some examples of the application of the microcomputer as a communication tool in development efforts are useful here.

The microcomputer and hand-held calculator are becoming increasingly common tools of development specialists. They are used in a diversity of ways, from planning and evaluation to computer-aided instruction, and in a variety of development sectors.[24]

In agriculture, farmers can use computers to forecast trends, predict and control pest infestations, and manage operations. In Australia, engineers are devising an automated method of shearing sheep that will not nick the animal.[25] In Bolivia, automated systems of range management are in effect, projecting herds and crop yields; and in Kenya, computers are used to monitor cattle dips.

Computer applications in the business community have perhaps had the greatest success. Professionals, such as doctors and architects, use them for record storage, graphics, planning, word processing, billing, inventory, electronic mail, and design. In the People's Republic of China, the Computer

Information Centre in Beijing was established to expand the nation's economic data processing capabilities.[26] Examples of its contribution include a business management information system for the Beijing Municipal Auto Spare Parts Company that has enabled computerized inventory management and thereby reduced stock on hand by $6 million. Some 3000 programmers and users have been trained under the five-year project.

An application of particular importance in development projects is in statistical storage, computation, and analysis. The U.S. Census Bureau reports a number of such applications all over the world, including several in Africa and Latin America.[27] For example, computers are being used to process data in a labor usage survey in Egypt, in an economic census in Puerto Rico, and in a comprehensive economic survey in Bangladesh. Agricultural surveys have been taken in Jamaica, Ecuador, Morocco, Tunisia, Sierra Leone, the Philippines, Liberia, and the Sudan. The United Nations processes national censuses of housing and population in selected areas. Such statistical work indicates the tremendous value of computers in research and development as well. As has been evident in most surveys of development projects, research and evaluation are the weak link. When properly applied, they can drive development projects and assure effectiveness, but research and evaluation are too often inadequate or nonexistent. Computers are extremely useful in storing, processing, and analyzing data and in laboratory or field experimental design and modeling. It is important, however, to remember the crucial role of people and inter-personal communication. Data gathering is an extremely valuable tool for development planners, but it is only a tool and a part of the progression toward the goal, which is necessarily human-oriented.

In education, computer-assisted instruction is becoming commonplace. At the University of the South Pacific, it was an outgrowth of administration, and computers are now used for electronic mail and instruction as well.[28] Special programs are designed to teach math, language, or any other subject. The Texas Instruments' "Speak & Spell" toys are examples of microcomputers that can be used for simple drill with an oral response. Such "toys" are easily adapted to diverse learning situations from primary school levels through adult education.[29]

Computers have applications in several other areas as well, among them engineering, government, industry, and personal use. A crucial sector of application is health care. In September 1985, 20 health clinics in Chad were provided with microcomputers that respond with diagnoses and treatment when symptoms are entered. They are part of a newly designed health care delivery system created by the Centre Mondial de l'Informatique in Paris.[30] Health care workers will be able to use the computers to learn new treatment techniques.

In Tunisia, Indonesia, and Thailand, computers are used to process and store data on "clinical trials and maternity" and to study methods of delivering vitamin A to preschool children in Indonesia to prevent blinding eye disease.[31] Obviously, this newest technological development—although not yet widespread—has tremendous potential in the planning, implementation, and evaluation of development projects.

Mobile Audio/Visual Media

Mobile audio/visual media, including cassettes and film, are increasingly being used in development projects because of their versatility, mobility, and adaptability. Further, such media are becoming less and less expensive as technologies become more and more sophisticated. Mobile media can be specifically targeted to local situations and are easily reproduced and distributed. They lend themselves well to discussion groups and to repetition, yet carry the credibility of the electronic media and the excitement and liveliness of oral communication.[32] Further, such media are participatory and can be produced by those they are designed to reach as well as consumed by them.

Video and Audio Cassettes. The uses of video and audio cassettes are increasingly becoming known as the revolution in consumer electronics sweeps the world. In India, for example, there are a half million video cassette recorders now in use, both domestic and imported. Communal viewing halls are common sights. The boom in this industry in India came about when duties were relaxed during the 1982 Asiatic games so that sports fans could record sporting events for later viewing. Recently, sales of these media have burgeoned, and they are becoming an extremely popular, though still somewhat expensive, medium, particularly for entertainment and commercial use.

The use of these mobile technologies for development purposes, however, is of more interest here. In Tanzania, audio cassette listening forums have been implemented to train women in the skills necessary to improve their families' daily lives.[33] The educational and open-ended style has been extremely effective in changing attitudes of both literate and illiterate participants. Further, evaluation showed participation rates of 73 percent in one group and 63 percent in another. The project was successful in reaching far more people than field workers alone could have reached.

The Integrated Rural Project in Education, Health, and Family Planning targeted at farm workers (*campesinos*) in Honduras made creative use of audio cassettes to improve literacy and encourage family planning. A trained village worker organized discussion "circles," where participants listened to open-ended audio dramatizations that they would discuss and conclude. The participants would also tape stories of their own and exchange tapes with other circles. Evaluation of the project noted a number of positive behavioral changes, including an increase in functional literacy and community action in improving sanitation.

In Kenya, the Kipsigis Homesteads cattle-dip management program used audio cassettes to assimilate an oral history of area farms and to record farmers' meetings for later listening. Cassettes were also used to provide native language narration of slide presentations in which the slides themselves were subtitled in Swahili, Kenya's official national language.

Audio cassettes have been used to transcend the language barrier in a number of other projects as well. In Senegal, adult education radio broadcasts are recorded in several native languages including Wolof, Peul, and Malinke. The broadcasts have encouraged responses from farmers and have resulted in a variety of governmental policy changes, including standardizing prices for groundnuts, Senegal's largest cash crop.

Video and audio cassettes are frequently used to record commercials or sports shorts for airing over radio and television stations. In the Soybean Promotion Campaign in Bolivia, audio cassettes were used for radio, and video cassettes, combined with film and slides, were used by demonstration teams.[34] The teams demonstrated the preparation and use of soybeans as a protein food in the diets of peasants in the state of Cochabamba, especially for infants, children, pregnant women, and nursing mothers. The project was evaluated and modified for a second campaign, in which the number of recipes demonstrated was reduced and emphasis placed on three basic soya recipes. A third stage was implemented after changes were made in the radio announcements so that they were better targeted to the listening audience. Evaluation showed that soybean sales increased 10 times over the course of the project, and although initially 81 percent of the people surveyed knew nothing about soya, by the end of the campaign, only 9.8 percent had not heard of it and 62.7 percent had eaten it.[35]

In Peru, the Video-based Training for Rural Development project centered its efforts on interpersonal communication, videotape, and print media aimed at educating the rural farmers (*campesinos*) for agrarian reform. Funded by the United Nations Development Programme (UNDP) and assisted technically by the Food and Agriculture Organization (FAO), in 1974 the project established a video production center in Lima and five regional production centers to meet the specific needs of different areas. Initial efforts were to train production teams who researched, wrote, recorded, edited, and evaluated the curriculum. Each day, 18-minute videos are presented at a local extension unit followed by a discussion accompanied by a review of supplementary printed material. Sessions last about two hours and feedback plays a critical role.

Although there was some criticism that the local selection of courses is made without consulting the *campesinos* themselves, by November 1981, the project "had made more than 600 18-minute video lessons, trained over 140 video producers, and reached some 102,000 *campesinos* with video-based training."[36] Evaluation has shown that the audiovisual nature of this medium eliminates the illiteracy barriers frequently found in rural areas. Training in video production ensures local participation and input into subject matter. As a result of the success of this project, several smaller efforts have begun in Mexico, Honduras, Paraguay, and Brazil, and the FAO has been requested by Latin American extension directors to "promote video-based farmer training methodology throughout the region."[37]

A number of education and literacy projects use videocassettes and video production studios, although primarily as support media; they do not take a major role in the overall project. Examples are the MOBRAL Adult Literacy Experiment in Brazil and the Universidad Estatal a Distancia in Costa Rica. The latter employs a distance teaching program similar to that developed in the University of the South Pacific (USP) based in Fiji.[38] The USP is well known for its pioneering and innovative use of satellite and telecommunication to provide education services to a scattered island area. The university has a video production studio, and each extension center has a videocassette recorder and monitor.

A recent project that is now in a fully developmental stage is the Village Video Network.[39] Inspired by Martha Stuart Communications and co-sponsored by the United Nations University, this network is a non-profit organization consisting of several developing nations, including Mali, Zimbabwe, Egypt, Antigua, China, India, Jamaica, Nigeria, Guyana, Japan, Indonesia, and Gambia. The American Indian nations also participate in its activities.

The Village Video Network has purchased videotape production equipment and provides training in its use. It solicits funding for and consults in the preparation and production of videotape materials for developmental purposes. Although videos are produced within countries for their own specific development purposes, the cross-national organization facilitates an exchange of ideas and cultures. Women are a primary target and beneficiary of Village Video Network activities, and women's groups (such as the Self Employed Women's Association of Ahmedabad, India) are active participants in the workshops and exchanges made possible by the network.

Such participation by women in both the production and use aspects of video technology is encouraging in light of assessments that show the role of women in developmental efforts to be unacceptably passive.[40] The worldwide division of labor is such that in developing nations, women are more often than not excluded from opportunities to learn and use the technology of development.

Audiocassettes appear to have been integrated into development projects far more effectively than videocassettes, partially because of the smaller, less expensive equipment required. Although videocassettes have been used to some degree, particularly in education and training, such as in the projects discussed previously, the medium is largely considered an entertainment medium in most nations.[41] Nevertheless, its very presence in dwellings throughout the world indicates its potential reach. It is becoming a familiar and accepted medium; such favorable estimation increases its potential for use in development.

Film. Film has the advantages of mobility and flexibility, which the broadcast media alone do not possess. Although frequently used in conjunction with broadcast technology such as television, film can also be used independently in local gatherings or for project training purposes. In fact, the necessity of a community gathering to see a film is one of the benefits of this medium; subsequent discussion and peer reinforcement are valuable in achieving the purposes of projects. Film is also widely applicable in education projects.

Some fear educational use of films will lessen as the medium succumbs to demands for entertainment. In India, for example, it is not unusual for people to travel several miles to attend movie screenings. Often, commercial film industries in developing countries produce films largely patterned after Western productions, thus portraying Western values. In India, domestic films are usually "trendy," although a few are now addressing social issues such as police brutality and the dowry system.

Their use as an entertainment medium is not necessarily a problem, however, as demonstrated by two separate projects: *My Brother's Children* in Nigeria, and *Batingaw* in the Philippines.[42] In both cases, the entertainment orientation of the medium was exploited, and popular actors and film artists were recruited to produce well-scripted and entertaining films carrying important social messages.

In the former case, the film was shown in family planning centers, followed by discussion sessions. Although well produced, this film neglected consideration of tradition and culture and depicted a distortion of Nigerian life. The social message was not readily accepted because the film was a departure from reality.

On the other hand, *Batingaw*, extensively researched and pre-tested, was distributed like a commercial film and subject to public criticism and review. Formal evaluation found that a majority of respondents perceived the underlying theme of family planning as well as several secondary themes of social relevance.

In projects that use film in a more explicitly developmental manner and context, the medium usually takes more of a supporting role. In such projects, care must be exercised to plan appropriate facilities. Indeed, some projects, such as the Barani project in Pakistan and Project Poshak in India, found film difficult or impossible to use because of the lack of electrical infrastructure. Projects that are implemented in areas with a minimal amount of infrastructure, however, will usually use a regional or community center that is equipped for film viewing.

For example, the Plan Puebla project in Mexico was designed to help *campesinos* increase their productivity.[43] Although several media were used throughout the project, including posters, handbills, and radio, in the third year of the project *campesinos* were recruited as actors in three films on increasing corn yields, agricultural credit, and savings accounts. This participation is considered one of the factors underlying the project's success. Another factor is the built-in evaluation and feedback, which cause project planners to modify the project so that it is most effective. Although increased awareness of new agricultural techniques and technology is considered an important result of Plan Puebla, more tangible results are a 33 percent increase in corn yields, income gains, and improved living conditions. The project emphasizes labor-intensive practices and has been replicated in Peru, Colombia, and Honduras.[44]

The Integrated Family Life Education (IFLE) project in Ethiopia, designed to encourage self-reliance, integrated "literacy and numeracy classes with practical education in health, agriculture, civics, and family planning."[45] An educated group leader was selected by the community and trained for two weeks, after which time the leader used visual media, including films, to disseminate messages on nutrition, family planning, and other social development topics. Follow-up evaluation measured gains in literacy and numeracy, assessed attitude changes, and identified improvements in social and health practices. Increases in such skills were dramatic: At three centers, literacy increased to 89 percent, and in one case, to nearly 100 percent of the participants. Knowledge of family planning techniques also increased tremendously.

As noted, the projects employing film of some kind are numerous. This medium has great potential not only because it is mobile but because it is participatory as well.

Folk and Traditional Media

With research and increased awareness of the importance and sensitivity of cultural and traditional structures, more attention is being given to the role of folk and traditional media in development. The Islamic revolution in Iran drew world attention to the marriage of traditional communication channels and technology. The successful use of these channels in mobilizing an enormous population through the traditional structures of the mosque and the marketplace drew attention to the strength of traditional media in developing countries.[46] Since 1979, the Islamic Republic of Iran has successfully used the traditional systems of social communication in its community and national development projects, especially in social mobilization and as a system for delivery.

In Egypt, we again have an example of technology being merged with traditional media. Audiocassette recorders are popular, particularly to listen to recordings of local folk reciters and imams. Also, traditional ceremonies, feasts, and gatherings have been incorporated into the Danfa Comprehensive Rural Health and Family Planning project, which recruits local health aides and trains midwives in modern childbirth techniques. The success of the clinics is partially attributed to observance of local customs and tradition.

National government commitment and the traditional *ujamaa* was a major factor in the success of a multi-media health campaign in Tanzania in 1973, noted earlier. The *Mtu ni Afya* (Man Is Health) project used radio programming, small group discussion, and supplementary media to mobilize public efforts in health education, malaria control, and latrine building. The radio programs reached an estimated 1.5 million people, and the discussion groups were conducted by 75,000 specially trained leaders. President Julius Nyerere supported the campaign and instructed the village political organizations to mobilize the public. Special adult education classes were conducted, mosquito breeding areas were cleaned up, and 750,000 latrines were built. The project was successful in substantially reducing the incidence of malaria in Tanzania, and at a cost of under $275,000.

The Korean Mothers' Clubs established under the New Village Movement are the classic example of self-help and cooperative micro-level development efforts. The program was established on the macro level as part of the national development plan. This national commitment ensured the interaction among the clubs, which are organized and administered on a village level.

In 1968, the Planned Parenthood Federation of Korea (PPFK) organized 12,000 Mothers' Clubs in rural villages. The program has subsequently grown, the number of clubs doubling by 1974.[47] The initial objectives of the clubs were (1) to create a grass-roots and voluntary movement encouraging family planning as well as an interpersonal channel for disseminating related information and supplies, and (2) to encourage participation in community development. The clubs undertake self-help social, agricultural, and educational development projects from funds they have raised or saved. They have formed cooperatives, credit unions, and savings banks. Village women take an active role in the planning and implementation of cooperative development projects. The national organization now publishes a women's magazine, which boasts one of the largest readerships in Korea.

A final example of a grass-roots traditional effort is Cuba's literacy campaign in the 1960s. Evolving into a "revolutionary cultural movement involving the whole nation,"[48] the slogan of the campaign was that the people teach the people. The campaign lasted nine months, and the entire Cuban population was mobilized. Poets, artists, and composers provided campaign publicity materials, and volunteers taught or encouraged enrollment in classes conducted by a quarter of a million men, women, and children, who were supplied with 3 million books and with paraffin lamps.[49] At a time when most Latin American nations had literacy rates (reading and writing) of less than 70 percent, Cuba's literacy rate soared to 96 percent.

NOTES

1. Allan M. Kulakow, "Development Communications and the Agency for International Development, 1962–1982," unpublished doctoral dissertation, Washington, DC, The American University, 1983.
2. Emile G. McAnany, *Communications In the Rural Third World: The Role of Information in Development*, New York, Praeger, 1980.
3. See Hamid Mowlana, *International Flow of Information: A Global Report and Analysis*, Reports and Papers on Mass Communication, No. 99, Paris, UNESCO, 1985; his *Global Information and World Communication: New Frontiers in International Relations*, White Plains, NY, Longman, 1985; and his *International Flow of News: An Annotated Bibliography*, Paris, UNESCO, 1983.
4. International Commission for the Study of Communication Problems, *Many Voices, One World*, London, Kogan Page, 1980.
5. Academy for Educational Development, *Integrated Family Life Education Project: Ethiopia*, Washington, DC, Clearinghouse on Development Communication, 1982.
6. For some conclusions and evaluations of the impact of communication and information on development, see McAnany, *Communications in the Rural Third World*. See also Heli E. Perrett, *Using Communication Support in Projects: The World Bank's Experience*, World Bank Staff Working Papers, No. 551, Washington, DC, World Bank, April 22, 1983.
7. Academy for Educational Development, *Tarahumara Radio Schools: Mexico*, Washington, DC, Clearinghouse on Development Communication, 1982.
8. Academy for Educational Development, *Mass Media and Health Practices*, Washington, DC, Clearinghouse on Development Communication, 1983.
9. Academy for Educational Development, *Experimental Nutrition Project: Brazil*, Washington, DC, Clearinghouse on Development Communication, 1982.
10. Wilbur Schramm, *Big Media, Little Media*, Beverly Hills, CA, Sage, 1977, p. 13.
11. See C. P. Epskamp, "Evaluation of RNTC-project 'Training and Research with Regard to the Application of the Mass-media for Education and Information in Latin America and the Caribbean,' Part II, Case-study: La Voz de la Selva (Peru)," The Hague, CESO, November 1981.
12. Colin Cherry, "The Telephone System: Creator of Mobility and Social Change," in Ithiel de Sola Pool, ed., *The Social Impact of the Telephone*, Cambridge, MA, MIT Press, 1977. See also, Heather E. Hudson, "The Role of Telecommunications in Development: A Synthesis of Current Research," paper presented at the Tenth Annual Telecommunications Policy Research Conference, Annapolis, MD, April 25–28, 1982; and her "The Role of Telecommunications in Socio-

Economic Development," for the International Telecommunication Union's Seminar on Rural Telecommunications, New Delhi, September 11–22, 1978.

13. Douglas Goldschmidt, "Financing Telecommunications for Rural Development," *Telecommunication Policy*, September 1984, pp. 190–191.

14. Ibid., pp. 191–192.

15. Ibid., pp. 198–199.

16. Andrew P. Hardy, "The Role of the Telephone in Economic Development," *Telecommunications Policy*, December 1980, pp. 278–286.

17. Figures extracted from *The World's Telephones*, August 1980, and reprinted in Goldschmidt, "Financing Telecommunications for Rural Development," p. 202.

18. Heather E. Hudson, Douglas Goldschmidt, Edwin B. Parker, and Andrew Hardy, *The Role of Telecommunications in Socio-Economic Development: A Review of the Literature with Guideline for Future Investigations*, an ITU Study, 1979. See also her "The Role of Telecommunications in Development," pp. 2–3. See also Anna Casey with Suzanne Douglas, "African Telecommunication Needs," paper prepared for the Workshop on the Relationship Between Communication Technology and Economic Development: A Case Study of Africa, National Science Foundation, Washington, DC, April 9–10, 1984.

19. See Robert J. Saunders, Jeremy J. Warford, and Bjorn Wellenius, *Telecommunications and Economic Development*, Baltimore, MD, Johns Hopkins University Press, for the World Bank, 1983; Bjorn Wellenius "On the Role of Telecommunications in Development," *Telecommunications Policy*, March 1984, pp. 59–66; Heather E. Hudson, "The Role of Telecommunications in Development, and "The Role of Telecommunications in Socio-Economic Development"; and with Andrew P. Hardy and Edwin B. Parker, "Impact of Telephone and Satellite Earth Station Installation on GDP," *Telecommunications Policy*, December 1982, pp. 300–307. See also Hardy, "The Role of the Telephone in Economic Development"; Edwin B. Parker, "Appropriate Telecommunications for Economic Development," *Telecommunications Policy*, September 1984, pp. 173–177; and his "Communications Satellites for Rural Service," *Telecommunications Policy*, March 1981, pp. 12–17.

20. For a description, explanation, and evaluation of this project, see U.S. Department of State, *LAC Regional Project Paper: Rural Communications Services*, Project No. 538-0581, Washington, DC, Agency for International Development, 1979; Angel Velasquez Abarca and Anna Casey-Stahmer, *A Project for Rural Communications in Peru: Considerations for Planning*, Washington, DC, Academy for Educational Development (no date); Angel Velasquez Abarca, "Las Comunicaciones por Satelite Aplicadas a las Areas Rurales del Peru," paper presented at the World Communications Year Conference in San Jose, Costa Rica, August 1983; John K. Mayo, Gary R. Heald, and Steven J. Klees, *The Florida State Evaluation Component of the Peru Rural Communications Services Project Annual Report*, March 1981–1982. See also Abraham F. Lowenthal, *The Peruvian Experiment: Continuity and Change Under Military Rule*, Princeton, NJ, Princeton University Press, 1975.

21. Mayo, Heald, and Klees, *The Florida State Evaluation Component*, pp. 17–18.

22. Hudson, "The Role of Telecommunications in Development," pp. 13–15; and "The Role of Telecommunications in Socio-Economic Development," pp. 2–5.

23. See Mowlana, *Global Information and World Communication.*

24. For descriptions, examples, and case studies of computer application, see *Considerations for Use of Microcomputers in Developing Country Statistical Offices,* Washington, DC, International Statistical Program Center of the Bureau of the Census, U.S. Department of Commerce, 1983, specifically, Chapter 5: "Current Microcomputer Applications," pp. 83–91, and Chapter 15: "Case Studies," pp. 244–263.

25. *Considerations For Use of Microcomputers in Developing Country Statistical Offices,* p. 83.

26. United Nations Development Programme, "Annual Report of the Administrator for 1983," June 1984, English, p. 9.

27. *Considerations For Use of Microcomputers in Developing Country Statistical Offices,* pp. 85–86 and 244–263.

28. Academy for Educational Development, *University of the South Pacific Satellite Extension Services,* Washington, DC, Clearinghouse on Development Communication, April 1983.

29. Academy for Educational Development, *Beyond the Flipchart: Three Decades of Development Communication,* p. 34.

30. Ibid.

31. *Considerations For Use of Microcomputers in Developing Country Statistical Offices,* p. 86.

32. See Hamid Mowlana, "Technology Versus Tradition: Communication In the Iranian Revolution," *Journal of Communication,* 29: 3, Summer 1979, pp. 107–112.

33. For a summary of this project as well as the subsequent projects cited in Honduras, Kenya, and Peru, see Academy for Educational Development, Audio Cassette Listening Forums: Tanzania, Washington, DC, Clearinghouse on Development Communication, 1982; *Integrated Rural Project in Education, Health, and Family Planning: Honduras,* 1983; and *Video-based Training for Rural Development: Peru,* 1983.

34. Academy for Educational Development, *Soybean Promotion Campaign,* Washington, DC, Clearinghouse on Development Communication, December 1983.

35. For more in-depth evaluation, see "Soybean Utilization Project Final Report," Department of Nutrition, School of Public Health, University of North Carolina at Chapel Hill, 1980.

36. Colin Fraser "Video in the Field—A Novel Approach to Farmer Training," *Educational Broadcasting International,* Vol. 13, No. 3, September 1980. See also his "Video for Farmer Training," unpublished paper, November 1981; Manuel Calvelo Rios, "Mass Communication Technology, A Case Study in Training Campesinos," *Development Communication Report,* No. 25, January 1979; and Gerardo Van Alkemade, "Capacitacion Masiva Audiovisual Para el Desarrallo Rural," UNDP/FAO/CENCIRA Report on Media Design, Lima, Peru, 1979.

37. Ibid.

38. See Academy for Educational Development, *The MOBRAL Adult Literacy Experiment: Brazil,* Washington, DC, Clearinghouse on Development Communication, 1978; *Universidad Estatal a Distancia: Costa Rica,* 1983; and *University of the South Pacific Satellite Extension Services.*

39. For a comprehensive report of activities see Christopher A. Nascimento, "The Village Video Network: Progress Report—1983," New York, The Village Network, 1983.

40. See the United Nations Development Programme's Evaluation Study No. 3, "Rural Women's Participation in Development," New York, June 1980.

41. For a complete overview of worldwide national statistics on videorecorder ownership and usage, see "Video Cassette Recorders: National Figures," *InterMedia*, Vol. 11, No. 4/5, September 1983, pp. 38–75.

42. Academy for Educational Development, *My Brother's Children: Nigeria,* Washington, DC, Clearinghouse on Development Communication, 1978; and *Batingaw: Philippines,* 1979. See also their *Barani Project: Pakistan,* 1983; and *Project Poshak: India,* 1979.

43. Academy for Educational Development, *Plan Puebla*, Washington, DC, Clearinghouse on Development Communication, October 1978.

44. Academy for Educational Development, *Plan Puebla.*

45. Academy for Educational Development, *Integrated Family Life Education Project*, Washington, DC, Clearinghouse on Development Communication, January 1978.

46. See Mowlana, "Technology Versus Tradition."

47. See Daniel Lerner and Wilbur Schramm, *Communication and Change in Developing Countries*, Honolulu, University Press of Hawaii, 1967.

48. Goran Hedebro, *Communication and Social Change in Developing Nations: A Critical View*, Ames, Iowa State University Press, 1982, p. 85.

49. Ibid., p. 84.

CHAPTER 7

Telecommunications and Its Impact

Just as mobility and localization are undeniable advantages of the diverse media discussed in Chapter 6, so is the infrastructure of the broadcast media a highly desirable aspect contributing to their success and effectiveness. Although the more mobile media can be very specifically targeted to regions, villages, and demographic groups, the broadcast media have the advantage of far-reaching dissemination. Additionally, as systems and infrastructures become more established and widespread, local participation and programming enter the realm of possibility. In fact, virtually all development efforts, at some point, involve use of the global, national, regional, and/or local infrastructure established for broadcast media. Case studies of development projects are replete with examples focused on the use of traditional telecommunications. Although the technology of space will definitely alter somewhat the nature and application of these media, they will, nevertheless, play a crucial and predominant role in communication and development for some time to come.

RADIO

Initially, efforts to apply communication technology in the development process primarily concentrated on radio. This inexpensive and flexible medium continues to be the most frequently used of all the mass media in development projects. Radio is by far the most diversified and dispersed of the media. Census figures show the number of radios per 100 population in developing countries to be far greater than any of the other media. In 1976, one study reported that a fourth to a third of all inhabitants in the developing world had direct access to radio broadcasts.[1] Communities may also have loudspeaker systems, such as those in the People's Republic of China, which project the reception to the entire village, giving all villagers access to this dynamic and important developmental medium. Additionally, the cost of radio production and broadcast is a fraction of the cost of television, yet it retains many of the advantages of the latter. Further, radio lends itself to a number of formats, from technical programming of moderate length to short public service or persuasive messages. An example of the latter are the Manoff Nutrition Social Marketing Campaigns implemented in the Philippines and Ecuador from 1975 to 1978. The Manoff advertising agency developed and tested short radio messages designed to market inexpensive and "simple nutritional beverages that would counter dehydration" in diarrhea-stricken infants.[2] The messages were mini soap operas that were pre-recorded and frequently repeated. Another example of the use of such short messages to influence nutrition is a project in Tunisia using the fictional "Dr. Hakim" to deliver health and nutrition messages.

A number of writers have stressed the use of radio to stimulate national integration in Third World countries.[3] They note that effective national integration requires a national network of simultaneous relay, more critically objective national news rather than programming that includes only official announcements and the like, and promotion of a national language (which could be a problem in large and diverse nations such as India where there are over 1600 languages and dialects). For example, coverage of national sporting events, such as a nation's participation in the Olympic games, and programming that features traditional and cultural music are powerful integrating forces because they reinforce national identity.

Radio broadcasting is used on national and regional levels in a number of social development projects to educate and disseminate information. Because of the widespread use of radio broadcasting in development projects, it is impossible to address each individual application; the projects discussed here are meant to be representative, not exhaustive.[4]

The evolution of radio broadcasting in Nigeria exemplifies the diversity of this medium as well as its integrative power.[5] Because radio broadcasting was introduced in the early 1940s and has grown and developed as the nation itself has developed, the medium is familiar and widely distributed. Now the Federal Radio Corporation of Nigeria (FRCN) "controls four Zonal stations, an external service, an educational service, two light entertainment services . . . and the State stations (19 in all) which operate alongside the State-owned services in each State."[6] Radio Nigeria 2, or grass-roots broadcasting, is a project of local programming in local languages. Stations gather material locally, including traditional music, news, and current affairs. The mandatory allocation is 45 percent music, 25 percent news and current affairs, 20 percent federal government activities, 5 percent talks, and 5 percent sports. Further, 90 percent of broadcasting time must be in local languages and dialects, and the general manager and 80 percent of the staff of each station are drawn from the local population to ensure knowledge of local culture and tradition.

The FRCN content emphasizes a message of unity and similarity in tradition and culture. It has become a "social mobilizer" in stimulating participation in national development programs such as the Green Revolution, and it has been an effective medium for literacy campaigns, environmental sanitation campaigns, social education, and health care education. It has motivated people to civic activity and is a favorite medium of politicians "because of its reach, depth, immediacy, and effectiveness."[7]

The objective of the Basic Village Education Project in Guatemala, conducted from 1973 to 1978, was to educate and motivate rural farmers in specific experimental areas to adopt agricultural innovations such as improved corn seed and appropriate and timely application of fertilizer and fungicides.[8] The project called for radio broadcasts of technical agricultural information supplemented by general interest programming. The technical messages recorded on audiocassettes were distributed to discussion groups on a weekly basis and were further reinforced in some areas by a visiting agronomist. Prior to implementation, project personnel spent two years surveying and researching to identify participants, priorities, issues and concerns, and schedules. This extensive pre-research may well account for the success of the project. The research design provided control groups; that is, of the four areas, one received only radio broadcasts, a second received the broadcasts as well as discussion leaders, a third had the added element of periodic visits of a specialist, and the fourth received discussion leaders without radio broadcasts.

Evaluation of the project, performed by Florida State University, concludes that the combination of radio and discussion leader (usually the most successful farmer in the village) showed the highest correlation to increased crop yields. The radio broadcast alone did change behavior, but the changes were significantly greater when reinforced by a discussion leader. Access to the agricultural specialist was also shown to be a factor in the adoption of the new ideas and methods presented in the project. Further, it is important to note the length of time involved in inducing significant behavioral change. Evaluation shows that the first year resulted in information acquisition, the second in increased knowledge and acceptance, and the third and fourth in application.

The Tanzanian health campaign, *Mtu ni Afya*, used the group discussion concept in implementing radio listening forums to educate the rural population in disease prevention.[9] Based on the success of other projects in implementing rural radio forums—such as India's campaign, which registered 75 to 80 percent attendance and 65 percent participation in discussions, and Cuba's literacy campaign, which virtually eradicated illiteracy in that country[10]—Tanzania's President Julius K. Nyerere implemented radio "study groups" to ease that nation's transition to socialism, at the same time taking steps toward rural development and mass education. The study groups evolved into the radio forums later implemented in the health campaign in 1973. Study group leaders were trained, and printed materials provided for discussion and education. Health practice surveys showed that an overwhelming majority of participants in the project implemented some kind of health practice advocated, such as digging pit latrines or installing insect netting over windows. More recent efforts in Tanzania have followed this same development methodology in a literacy campaign, which has raised the literacy rate from 25 percent to an incredibly high 75 to 80 percent, and in a "Food is Life" campaign to encourage community feeding programs and planting of gardens.[11]

In an effort to achieve self-sufficiency in agriculture as well as to boost agricultural exports for foreign exchange to fuel development, Radio Bangladesh began a program of farm broadcasting in 1973.[12] Since that time, the broadcasts have grown to include both national (55 minutes daily) and regional (100 minutes daily) programming, and an effort is being made to localize services further, which will mean local field correspondents and production of programs specifically addressing local needs.[13]

On the national level, a daily 30-minute broadcast is aimed at modernizing agricultural practices. These broadcasts explore problems and solutions, encourage cooperation and feedback, advise farmers of assistance programs and marketing opportunities, and caution against exploitation by middlemen. Every two weeks, a program on livestock and domestic animals is included to raise consciousness about breeding and using livestock. A program on nutrition is also broadcast every two weeks to educate the population and decrease the incidence of malnutrition. A daily program on development activities such as literacy programs and village defense forces is incorporated as part of the farm broadcast series. Cooperative farming, marketing, and religious values are also recurring themes in national broadcasts. A daily morning farm bulletin broadcasts weather and reminds farmers of the day's operation. Programs for agricultural colleges and the Bangladesh Agricultural University are also included in the monthly schedule.

On a regional level, a 20-minute daily broadcast more directly addresses the target audience. Ten minutes a day are directed at the women of Bangladesh, who make up 50 percent of the population and are an active part of the agricultural work force. The majority of women are illiterate and the programs help educate them on "more meaningful living."[14] Another program is directed at young people, and the regional schedule also includes a program on self-reliance.

It was only recently that attention on the national level was turned toward evaluation of the farm programs. There are a limited number of farm clubs organized to provide the radio stations with feedback, but systematic analysis is lacking. Radio Bangladesh has commissioned the National Broadcasting Academy in Dacca to study and evaluate the impact of the programs and to provide them with information on listener profiles, barriers, program relevance, and credibility. Such evaluation is critical to shape the farm broadcasts to fit the needs of a growing and diverse population.

Some early evaluation found district officials pleased with the programs, but farmers were critical. They complained that the daily programs were aired too early, offered no solutions, were dull and too technical, and lacked local orientation. Further, most receivers were owned by urban inhabitants: The programs were not reaching the target audience.[15]

In other development sectors, Radio Bangladesh uses a similar combination of national and regional programming.[16] For population planning, a 70-minute national program and a 115-minute regional program are broadcast daily. Literacy programs for school children are broadcast nationally for 40 minutes a day, and mass literacy programs at the primary level are broadcast for 30 minutes four days a week. Other programming further addresses social development issues such as health and participation in nation-building programs. Based on some preliminary research and evaluation of the population planning broadcasts, programming is designed especially to reach and influence opinion leaders who can initiate action and lead community efforts.[17]

In addition to programming for social development, Radio Bangladesh carries normal entertainment programs not associated or related in any way to the development messages. M. N. Mustafa believes that "when a pure entertainment programme is interjected with a social development message, the listener tends to erect a perceptual screen against it."[18]

In Sierra Leone, radio plays an important role in all development sectors.[19] In that nation, the illiteracy rate is 75 to 80 percent among the adult population, and the majority of the people are subsistence farmers. Stimulating the agricultural sector for self-sufficiency as well as export is obviously a high priority. Radio is perceived as the ideal medium for educating farmers and fighting the ills of social underdevelopment. Local programs on disease prevention and self-help tend to integrate the people for collective action. Family planning messages are contained in theatre dramas, and health campaigns are coordinated and publicized through special programs. Rural broadcasters provide some original material that encourages feedback and cooperative programs with extension workers. Every effort is being made "to extend the role of radio to every aspect of . . . daily life so as to enhance the cause of development."[20] These efforts include research on participation and listener priorities to better tailor programming to meet the needs of the people.

The Cotabato Ngayan project in the Philippines was designed to provide local news, weather information, and disaster warning to villages in an area without telephone service.[21] Four people using cassette recorders gather local news and information for a daily hour and a half broadcast. The project is self-supporting and the participants have learned on the job. The format is unstructured but meets the needs of the listeners, who have no other means of communication.

Radio Baha'i in Ecuador has also implemented programming to meet the needs of area inhabitants. Its news programming addresses issues of local concern such as weather conditions, lost livestock, and community work projects. Further, a half-hour segment entitled "Tarpacpac Yuyay" airs interviews and information obtained by surveying area farmers and subsequently interviewing government officials on topics and issues of expressed interest. As a result, the farmers are incorporating modern technology in their farming practices, such as in the treatment of disease. Although 30 other radio stations can be received, more than 94 percent of the target audience listens to Radio Baha'i.[22]

In the realm of formal education, projects in a number of countries apply radio to teaching, particularly in the primary grades.[23] Beginning in 1970, Mexico incorporated the use of radio in the curriculum of primary schools. Lesotho implemented distance teaching radio programs in 1974 for students of all ages who cannot attend conventional classes. In a project supported by UNESCO in 1968, rural radio programming was broadcast to organized listening groups in Senegal to motivate farmers to apply improved agricultural practices.

In Nicaragua, radio has been used in a program to improve the instruction of mathematics in primary schools (1973–1980). Radio Matematica worked with teachers to design radio programs and materials that would be supportive of the teachers' efforts in the classroom.[24] The resulting lessons provided a 30-minute radio broadcast of music, games, and question/response exercises. The programs were designed to hold the interest of the children and were followed by another 30 minutes of student-teacher interaction in activities designed to supplement the radio programming.

One of the keys to the success of Radio Matematica was the institutional commitment at the national level. Evaluation shows that children in the program scored 20 percent higher than those studying the same curriculum in the conventional way. Improvement in program participants in the first grade was as much as 60 percent higher than their counterparts in conventional classrooms. Further, the failure rate of students dropped by nearly 50 percent. The project was popular with the teachers as well. Midway through the project, 92 percent expressed a desire for the program to be continued, reporting that it enabled them to teach material they would ordinarily be unable to teach because of insufficient educational training.

The Radio Language Arts Project (RLAP) in Kenya was patterned after the Nicaraguan Radio Matematica because evaluation showed the success of its design and its applicability to other subjects.[25] In Kenya, primary school children are taught in their native tongue for the first three years; beginning with the fourth year, instruction is in English and students must pass an English proficiency examination for secondary school enrollment. In 1973, primary school enrollment increased dramatically as enrollment fees were eliminated. Materials, facilities, and qualified teachers are at a premium. The RLAP was designed to integrate listening, speaking, reading, and writing and to reinforce and expand other language skills. As in the Radio Matematica project, media instruction requires participation and response, and it is conducted in the presence of the teacher, who reinforces, corrects, and offers encouragement. Subsequent activities are also conducted by the teacher. Use of local facilities and materials, such as chalkboards, is encouraged to lessen the cost and distribution problems of printed material.

As with the Nicaraguan project, emphasis is placed on the crucial role of the classroom teacher. Teachers are given guides on classroom learning activities but are urged to adapt them to meet specific student needs. The teacher's attitude toward the program will greatly affect its acceptance by the children. A related radio project, the Radio Correspondence Education, is designed to provide in-service training for primary school teachers through the use of radio broadcast and correspondence study materials.[26]

The Korean Air and Correspondence High School combined existing local educational facilities with an existing radio network to provide quality education at low cost. The program emphasizes self-study, although local teachers do conduct classes on Saturday to ensure some student-teacher interaction. Since the project uses existing facilities and requires little time of teachers, the service is provided at a very low cost. User fees help to offset the cost of textbooks and educational materials. Although the results have been mixed, a number of students have earned high school diplomas through the program.

In a field where research and evaluation is frequently slighted and more often entirely neglected, it is refreshing to note the research orientation of Radio Gambia.[27] One specific study consisted of personal interviews with 798 women in 20 villages in four divisions of the Gambia. The study sought to determine women's use of radio and other media, including some specific evaluation of several radio programs aimed at improving health and literacy.

Nearly all of the women (98 percent) had access to a radio and 90 percent of the radios were functioning adequately. The cost of batteries was accepted as a regular and worthwhile expense. More than half of the women surveyed listened daily and another 25 percent on a regular basis. Radio

Gambia seems anxious to further analyze the non-listeners possibly to adapt its programming to meet their needs as well. Listeners tune in primarily in the morning (62 percent), early afternoon (59 percent), and evening (96 percent). Further, listeners were pleased with the length and content of programming, finding it useful and practically applicable. Radio Gambia has little competition: Only 6 percent of the women surveyed prefer Radio Senegal, the closest competitor. It is obvious that Radio Gambia is a popular medium with tremendous potential as a development tool.

The versatility of radio is demonstrated by its use for (1) developmental entertainment, as in the radio comedies sponsored by the United Nations Children's Fund (UNICEF) in Kenya that focus on health and nutrition; (2) radio commercials or short spots, such as those used in Jamaica's family planning project; (3) longer topical education programs like the social programming targeted at youth in Iran and families in Thailand; (4) religious programming oriented to social development as is implemented by the National Office of Mass Media and the Catholic church in the Philippines; (5) radio schools and formal education projects such as those in Nicaragua and Kenya discussed previously and the Radio School for Family Education in the Dominican Republic; and (6) news and information programs and forums as have been discussed, such as the programming of All India Radio (AIR).[28] Certainly, these categories do not exhaust the potential of this medium; its capabilities and diversity are great and render radio subject to numerous creative applications.

TELEVISION

More recently, television has been applied in development projects, particularly those in education, health, and community development. Television is used in both macro- and micro-level projects since it lends itself to both centralized and decentralized programming, although the former is by far the most prevalent. In large nations with culturally and linguistically diverse populations, centralized programming presents quite a problem. For example, in India, only 3 percent of the population speaks English and 40 percent speaks Hindi. Yet news programming is national, there being few regional facilities, and is broadcast only in English and/or Hindi. Experiments in decentralized programming, such as the Kadur project to be discussed subsequently, have met with success but are not widespread.

Television is being used widely for educational purposes, both within and without the classroom. Television shares some of the benefits of radio, such as the ability to reach large audiences without regard for literacy.[29] Additionally, it has a practicality not present in radio. Television lends itself to demonstrations and actual scenes of events and places that can transcend language barriers. It can also depict events and processes that extend over lengthy time periods. Television's biggest drawback is the expense of production and the expense and maintenance of infrastructure. Progress in technology, such as direct broadcast satellites and improvements in electronics, as well as consideration of the large numbers of people to be reached and the vast areas to be covered, continually lowers the expense of the medium in relation to its effectiveness and versatility.

The role of television in education is a particularly controversial topic. Criticism of the Western programming that dominates Third World viewing is not directed at entertainment programming alone. The international broadcast of children's educational programs such as "The Electric Company" and "Sesame Street" is being questioned on grounds of cultural applicability.[30] Nevertheless, the cost of producing educational and entertainment programming is far greater than the cost of importing it from the West.

Another concern has been the effect of television programming on behavior, particularly violent behavior. Although several thousand studies have been conducted and the results indicate there is almost surely a relationship between viewing violence on television and violent behavior, the research has a decided English-language bias in addition to a developed-nation bias. There is no evidence that the research findings apply in the developing world.[31] Perhaps more precisely we should say just that there is no evidence. Research of this type is virtually non-existent in developing countries.

Further, the full potential of television is yet to be realized.[32] Production, distribution, and utilization limitations have become evident in projects in developing nations. Technological advances are perhaps the key to overcoming these limitations and unlocking the potential of this medium. For example, satellite technology has done much to alleviate distribution problems. Satellites were predicted to be the dominant video transmission technology by the end of the 1980s.[33] Interactive cable capabilities are also becoming available. One of the latest technologies, teletext or videotext, allows the transmission of text and graphics in the vertical blanking interval of the broadcast signal. The transmission is stored for later use and displayed on command either in conjunction with another broadcast (for example, subtitles or weather warnings) or as a separate viewing frame.

As these previously experimental technological advances become increasingly applied to diverse developmental projects for diverse purposes, their potential may become reality. The possibilities for application lie in the creativity and resourcefulness of planners. For example, television in Pakistan has had an integrating effect for the culturally and linguistically diverse and varied population. In the past, it has been seen as a luxury, but government policy is targeted at making it "an instrument for educating the masses."[34] Although some of Pakistan's ambitious goals for educational television have not materialized, the national station does broadcast 10 hours of educational programming a week. Nevertheless, it has been accepted that, given the limitations of funding and the lack of trained educators, educational programming will not reach a target audience with formal instruction.

In other projects, teleclubs or group viewing seem to have had success in reaching rural farmers and peasants. In India, broadcasts aimed at farmers were found to close the information gap between small and large farmers.[35] In Senegal, 500 women were organized into 10 discussion-viewing groups receiving twice-weekly broadcasts on hygiene, nutrition, and disease treatment. Results indicated that the women learned much valuable information, which they passed on to their families and friends.[36]

A rural television project in the Sudan was also designed around the idea of viewing clubs.[37] The clubs were adapted from already established social clubs at the village level. West German and FAO technical aid provided televisions and generators, and the clubs provided facilities for the equipment. Further, each club selected a TV club monitor, who was responsible for the equipment and able to lead discussions and initiate village action on discussion ideas. Although weather and installation difficulties made the program less effective than had been hoped, ongoing evaluation enabled the modification and intensification of activities to better meet project goals. The project was a learning experience that demonstrated the potential role of television broadcasting in development in the Sudan, as well as the problems that would need to be overcome in subsequent efforts.

In El Salvador, instructional television is used in a project much like the radio mathematics project in Nicaragua.[38] In a project implemented in the late 1960s which encompassed grades one through nine by the early 1980s, programming is broadcast in Spanish, math, social and natural science, and English. The classroom teacher directs learning activities and reinforcement sessions following the programs, and students have workbooks to supplement the lessons. Evaluation shows that students in classrooms using instructional television demonstrate basic skill gains of 15 to 25 percent more than students in traditional classrooms.[39]

SATELLITES

In the 1980s, attention has been drawn to the urban bias, or the concentration of telecommunications services in the cities. For obvious political and economic reasons such as the parallel concentration of people and investment capital in the cities, as well as for practical reasons such as the lack of power and transportation infrastructures, telecommunication services have been all but denied rural inhabitants of developing countries.[40] Recently, however, a number of efforts have focused on extending the infrastructure and the services into rural areas. Although the use of communication satellites and space technology in development is discussed at length in the following chapter, the effects of this new technology on the more traditional telecommunication services is applicable here. Satellite technology has made television broadcasting a much more viable, effective, and economical method of reaching rural populations. It simplifies the infrastructural requirements; consequently, that barrier to extending telecommunication services is less formidable. It also provides the facility for teleconferencing and rural telephony.

A recent comparison of the nature of usage of the International Telecommunications Satellite Organization (INTELSAT) for television shows that developing nations have definitely increased their transmission and reception since the early years of the organization's operation.[41] Because INTELSAT was initially established for telephones and seen as a means for developing nations to compensate for a weak or lacking terrestrial infrastructure, television space was both limited and very expensive. Developing nations were largely passive recipients, the only real mutual exchange being between western Europe and the United States. In 1969, the flow of television transmission resembled a dependency pattern.

In 1982, INTELSAT was in its fifth generation of satellites and moving toward the sixth. Television traffic grew from a total of 40 hours to 21,708 hours a year in 1982. Yet only 5 to 6 percent of total INTELSAT revenues were from television broadcasts. Conventional telecommunications services still dominated. The capital cost per telephone link declined to 1/100th of the cost in 1965 (fixed values). Yet only 68 percent of available circuits were in use in 1982 because of the rapid technological advances.

INTELSAT television links are still too expensive to use for transmission of anything but news and sports (the "perishables"), which accounted for 93 percent of all hours transmitted and received from November 1981 through July 1982. Satellite transmission cannot replace conventional transport of videocassettes.

The comparative study concluded that although the West has retained its dominance in the use of INTELSAT and the North Atlantic traffic is still the heaviest, Asia, the Arab states, Latin America, and Africa increased their usage from 12 percent in 1969 to 20 percent in 1982. Largely because most world news services are based in Europe and because the United States has its own domestic satellite capability, Europe has replaced the United States as the traffic hub. With intra-regional distribution being a new feature of INTELSAT, flows have become more decentralized. In 1969, 25 countries and territories were part of the INTELSAT organization; in 1982, there were 141 member nations. The Arab nations, who were not users in 1969, accounted for 6 percent of the total 1982 use.

Probably the most significant change in the nature of INTELSAT television use is the increase of multi-point transmissions, which have increased from 12 percent to 31 percent of all transmissions (39 percent to 84 percent of total reception time and 19 percent to 49 percent of total transmit time). The greatest volume of multi-point reception is in less developed regions. Point-to-point transmission tends to be almost exclusively between the more affluent regions of the globe.

INTELSAT members must obtain the organization's approval before creating or using other satellite systems. Nevertheless, there has been tremendous growth in national and regional systems. France, Australia, Brazil, Canada, Japan, India, the Soviet Union, and the United States all have domestic satellite systems, including ARABSAT, PALAPA, Soviet STATSIONAR, and EUTELSAT. The creation and use of such systems are expected to increase, as is the use of cable systems. With the advent of fibre optic cables, several new transoceanic cables are planned in addition to those already in use. It is believed that a balance will eventually be achieved between cable and satellite systems to create "optimally efficient hybrid networks."[42]

Satellite use has been a basis for the development of Indian television (Doordarshan). From experimental service of one hour twice a week in 1959, Doordarshan now has[43]

- 183 transmitters reaching an estimated 70 percent of the population
- 11 broadcasting centers, five of which have their own relay transmitters
- Four SITE continuity centers
- Six INSAT stations
- 157 links with New Delhi
- An estimated 6.75 million sets nationwide (1985)

Two significant features of Doordarshan are the urban community viewing centers, called "teleclubs," and a regular programming feature, Krishi Darshan, which routinely addresses such topics as farming techniques, education, personal hygiene, family planning, and social education.

In an effort to develop its television broadcasting efforts more systematically, India initiated the Satellite Instructional Television Experiment (SITE) project in 1975. In 1983, the U.S. Challenger space shuttle launched INSAT, a telecommunications satellite built by Indian planners. Since that time, over 200 earth-receiving stations have been constructed in what is the most ambitious telecommunications project in the Third World. National programming is now relayed simultaneously from different centers. INSAT, coupled with microwave linkage, brings international news and events to viewers. The $130 million satellite is a bargain in comparison to the trillion dollars a comparable ground-based system would have cost. Beyond that, it is a technological upgrade to replace India's outdated and exhausted ground systems.

INSAT is intended to be an infrastructural development project. That is, the system established the infrastructure to support other development projects. INSAT provides 8000 telephone circuits, a continuous weather picture, flood and other disaster predictions, government office links, and computerized hotel and transportation links for the tourist industry. Nevertheless, INSAT's primary purpose is to provide instructional television broadcasts to rural areas, demonstrating India's commitment to using television for social programs. INSAT is used for children's programs and adult education, and plans are being made to establish an air university like that in the People's Republic of China. INSAT broadcasts teacher training programs as well.

Doordarshan recently introduced color, and now very little programming is in black and white. A second channel has been added in some areas to encourage local programming. Recent broadcasts of tremendous proportion have brought even more credibility to the capability of Doordarshan, including the Ninth Asian Games in 1982, the Non-aligned Nations Conference in 1983, the Commonwealth Heads of Government meeting and the general elections in 1984, and the State Assembly Elections in 1985. Indicative of the television system's growth is the fact that from July 1984 until the end of that year, India commissioned a transmitter a day.

The main goal of Doordarshan is still to provide "support to the national developmental plans and policies."[44] In keeping with that goal, Doordarshan supports in-service and institutional training of media professionals. A viewers' panel of 100 socially and demographically stratified viewers evaluates programming daily. A number of bilateral cultural agreements and program exchanges have been instituted with other nations. Perhaps most significantly, "every programme production centre has a team of social scientists, continuously engaged in formative and summative research; they work in close collaboration with the producers, to make teleprogrammes more meaningful and somewhat area specific."[45]

Yash Pal, the secretary of India's Department of Science and Technology and the head of the SITE project, explains that three out of four Indians are illiterate, that same number either not attending school at all or dropping out before the age of 12. Further, because of India's already massive population and the population growth rates, a school would have to be built every five minutes to educate the people and keep children in school. Books are rare. Satellite television is the only feasible way to reach the people in rural India. Pal further observes that communication, specifically telecommunication, in India "is not a luxury; it must be used for *all* development programs."[46]

Opponents of INSAT, however, argue that the money expended on satellite television would be much better spent for teachers, buildings, and facilities. Inadequate maintenance of receiving sets has also been a problem. Opponents remind planners that educational television programming must be followed with material resources such as loans, medical supplies, and agricultural innovations. Communication is not a singular approach to development; development requires interaction, and communication is a facilitator to that interaction. It is, however, deemed requisite for self-sustaining change.

An example of Doordarshan's plans for the future is a micro-level project using INSAT for television broadcasting in the Kadur district.[47] An experimental outgrowth of SITE, the Kadur project's planners advocate decentralized programming as essential in dealing with localized problems. Programs are produced in conjunction with national ministries of health, language, and agriculture, and the local programming is supplemented by some national programming. Nevertheless, local programming to meet local needs with public feedback is the objective of the project. The Kadur district is served by 2500 television sets, 2000 of them privately owned. Although the project has not yet been replicated, it has achieved much success, which its administrators credit to three key factors: a small target population, public access, and audience involvement.

THE IMPORTANCE OF TRAINING, RESEARCH, AND EVALUATION

The variety of projects discussed in chapters 7 and 8 are indicative of the great potential of the conventional media in development efforts. Although much can be learned from reviewing case studies of projects, much more can be gained from their planned and systematic evaluation. Although we have particularly tried to include projects that have made provisions for evaluation, by far the majority have slighted that dimension. For developmental projects to be truly and consistently effective, training, research, and evaluation must be an integral part of planning and implementation.

Recognizing this need, a few projects have been aimed specifically at developing media and media professionals to increase their effectiveness in developmental efforts. An outstanding example is Training and Research with Regard to the Application of the Mass-media for Education and Information in Latin America and the Caribbean, sponsored by the Radio Nederland Training Centre (RNTC).[48] The project, initiated in 1979, focused on training and research and met with such success and uncovered such great developmental potential in selected stations that a second stage was designed and implemented. This stage was designed to extend training at selected stations to link educational programs with relevant social groups, instructing them in development techniques and participatory communication as well as teaching them how to create and execute radio development campaigns.

The RNTC implemented this program with ERPE in Ecuador, Radio Occidente in Venezuela, and La Voz de la Selva (The Voice of the Jungle) in Peru. The changes and impact on the effectiveness of the last is examined here.[49] The objective of this project was to create three models of regional radio stations for development in Latin America that were independent because of self-management and self-financing and schooled in participatory communication. La Voz de la Selva is a licensed cultural station that was created by the 1972 merger of two separate stations begun in the early 1960s by religious organizations for communication support for scattered area missions. The stations also initiated radio schools to promote basic education.

In 1980, the RNTC decided to include La Voz de la Selva in its project. It donated transmitter equipment, increasing the power of the station from 1 KW to 6–10 KW; supplied technical studio equipment, advice on renovation, tion, and cassette recorders for field correspondents; and offered staff training seminars. It has been observed in evaluation that RNTC has not initiated change but rather participated and financially and technically aided the changes already in process. The RNTC continues to conduct training seminars, which in accordance with its policy of participation, now also include local leaders and representatives. The training and advice of an external team of specialists have resulted in local radio information campaigns to encourage sanitation and cleanliness, community participation and interest in news and current events, and education. The project has been successful in helping the existing medium to bring about changes that meet the needs of the people. The training offered to indigenous personnel and the subsequent development campaigns have been shown to be advantageous in a number of ways.[50]

- They ensure cooperation among the station, local authorities, social organizations, and the public.
- They ensure public participation.
- They ensure awareness and social training.
- They ensure relevant content, stimulating collective action.
- They ensure respect for existing culture and tradition.

An example of built-in project evaluation is the Evaluation and Action Research (EAR) unit in Malawi.[51] The Extension Aids Branch of Malawi's Ministry of Agriculture and Natural Resources has been producing media programs for rural development since 1970. This production unit produces media on request from within the ministry in addition to publishing a bimonthly magazine, dispatching a fleet of Land Rovers to show films and puppet shows in rural areas, and broadcasting regularly over the national radio network. As a result of dissatisfaction with traditional methods of post-project evaluation, the media production unit has taken an innovative approach to assessing the quality of media and the effectiveness of individual campaigns: the EAR unit.

The EAR unit works with the media production unit, testing and evaluating the media and the message in the process of its development and performing pre-tests and experiments to ensure its effectiveness. The EAR unit views the following as essential to effective communication:[52]

- Messages relevant to the target audience
- Messages accurate and valid for the specific situation
- Appropriate messages accompanied by necessary and available material support (such as facilities and incentives for performing as requested)
- Messages designed to carry impact and influence

The EAR unit fulfills its role in two stages. First, it collects the necessary information to select a medium and design a message for a particular campaign. The information is gathered from topic documents and proposals, topic specialists, past projects, and individuals who may be affected, such as local farmers. The EAR unit surveys the target audience through interviews, questionnaires, and group discussion. Random sampling is used as much as possible to ensure the most accurate response. All information resulting from this research is analyzed and used to design the message and select the media. In the second stage, the EAR unit actually pre-tests the media and message, making suggestions for alteration and improvement.

Although the process is a little more expensive than traditional evaluation and has to be abridged or eliminated entirely in emergencies, such as a sudden epidemic, preliminary evaluation has shown it to be invaluable in ensuring the effectiveness and pervasiveness of media campaigns as well as ensuring the best use of media production resources.

Ever looking forward to the needs and requirements of developing nations and peoples, those projects that incorporate training, research, and evaluation not only meet immediate developmental needs and goals but also contribute to the unending processes that constitute the positive growth and change in individuals and in their physical, social, and spiritual lives. In our review of case studies and in our efforts at development, we cannot forget that the critical nature of the process is that it is ongoing and that what we learn from today's efforts will help to ensure fewer mistakes and more effective application in tomorrow's endeavors.

NOTES

1. Wilbur Schramm, "An Overview of the Past Decade," in Wilbur Schramm and Daniel Lerner, eds., *Communication and Change: The Last Ten Years and the Next*, Honolulu, University Press of Hawaii, 1976, pp. 1–14.
2. Allan M. Kulakow, "Development Communications and the Agency for International Development, 1962–1982," unpublished doctoral dissertation, Washington, DC, The American University, 1983.
3. See Elihu Katz and George Wedell, *Broadcasting in the Third World*, Cambridge, MA, Harvard University Press, 1977.
4. For an overview of the variety of applications of radio in development, see Hilary Perraton, "How Can Radio Be Usefully Applied to Education and Devel-

opment?" *The Educational Use of Mass Media,* Washington, DC, World Bank Staff Working Paper, No. 491, October 1981; Terry D. Peigh, Martin J. Maloney, and Donald J. Bogue, *The Use of Radio in Social Development,* Chicago, The Communication Laboratory Community and Family Study Center at the University of Chicago, 1979; and Academy for Educational Development, *Beyond the Flipchart: Three Decades of Development Communication,* Washington, DC, 1985.

5. Isola Folorunso, "Grassroots Broadcasting in Nigeria," *COMBROAD,* No. 60, September 1983, pp. 7–9.

6. Ibid., p. 7.

7. Ibid., p. 9.

8. Academy for Educational Development, *The Basic Village Education Project, Guatemala: Final Report,* Washington, DC, 1978.

9. For a complete history, description, and evaluation of this project, see Budd L. Hall, *Mtu ni Afya: Tanzania's Health Campaign,* Washington, DC, Clearinghouse on Development Communication, June 1978.

10. Ibid., pp. 2–7.

11. Ibid., p. 69.

12. S. A. Shahadat, "Farm Broadcasting in Radio Bangladesh," *COMBROAD,* No. 57, December 1982, pp. 15–17.

13. M. N. Mustafa, "Development Programming in Radio Bangladesh," *COMBROAD,* No. 60, September 1983, pp. 33–34.

14. Shahadat, "Farm Broadcasting in Radio Bangladesh," p. 16.

15. Sufia Khanam, "Radio Use in Rural Bangladesh," Dacca, Bangladesh, Radio Bangladesh, 1976–1977.

16. See Mustafa, "Development Programming in Radio Bangladesh."

17. Syed Ashraf Ali, "Population Planning Broadcasts in Bangladesh," *COMBROAD,* No. 55, June 1982, pp. 37–38.

18. Mustafa, "Development Programming in Radio Bangladesh," p. 34.

19. Sama Lengor, "The Role of Radio in Support of Development Activities in Sierra Leone," *COMBROAD*, No. 55, June 1982, pp. 42–44.

20. Ibid., p. 44.

21. Academy for Educational Development, *Cotabato Ngayan: Philippines*, Washington, DC, Clearinghouse on Development Communication, 1983.

22. Academy for Educational Development, *Radio Baha'i: Ecuador*, Washington, DC, Clearinghouse on Development Communication, 1983.

23. Kulakow, "Development Communications and the Agency for International Development, 1962–1982"; see also Hilary Perraton, "How Can Radio Be Usefully Applied to Education and Development?"

24. Ibid.

25. African Council on Communication Education, "Using Radio to Teach Language Arts: Pilot Program in Kenya Addressing Primary Needs," *Africom,* Vol. 6, No. 1, August 1984, p. 7.

26. Marion Kohashi Warren, "PPC/E Education Sector Report: A Summary of Impact Evaluation Findings," Washington, DC, AID Bureau for Program Policy and Coordination, February 1982, Appendix A, p. 8.

27. Statistical results here are extracted from Peter Span-Head and Mark Rasmusson, "Radio Research in the Gambia," *COMBROAD*, No. 58, March 1983, pp. 24–26.

28. For further explanation of these projects and others of related themes, see Piegh, Maloney, Higgins, and Bogue, *The Use of Radio in Social Development*.

29. Janet Jenkins, "Do Audiovisual Media Possess Unique Teaching Capabilities?" in Kathleen Courrier, ed., *The Educational Use of Mass Media*, Washington, DC, World Bank, 1981.

30. Prakash M. Shingi and Bella Mody, "The Communication Effects Gap," in Everett Rogers, ed., *Communication and Development*, Beverly Hills, CA, Sage, 1976, p. 82.

31. See Dennis List, "Effects of Television on Children's Behavior," *COMBROAD*, No. 49, December 1980, pp. 10–12.

32. See Albert Horley, "What Does Educational Television Offer Us Now?" in Courrier, ed., *The Educational Use of Mass Media*, pp. 94–104.

33. Ibid., p. 96.

34. A. F. Kalimullah, "Television in Pakistan," *Pakistan Quarterly*, 15: 268, Summer and Autumn, 1967.

35. K. E. Eapen, "Social Impacts of Television on Indian Villages: Two Case Studies," in Godwin C. Chu, Syed A. Rahim, and D. Lawrence Kincaid, *Institutional Exploration in Communication Technology,* Honolulu, East-West Communications Institute, 1978, pp. 89–108.

36. Frans Lenglet, "The Ivory Coast: Who Benefits from Education/Information in Rural Television," in Emile G. McAnany, *Communications in the Rural Third World: The Role of Information in Development*, New York, Praeger, 1980, pp. 49–70.

37. See Henry T. Ingle, *Communication Media and Technology: A Look at Their Role in Non-formal Education Programs*, Washington, DC, Clearinghouse on Development Communication, 1974; see also their *Rural Television Project: Sudan*, 1983.

38. Academy for Educational Development, *Instructional TV and Educational Reform*, Washington, DC, Clearinghouse on Development Communication, June 1977.

39. Ibid.

40. See Douglas Goldschmidt, "Financing Telecommunications for Rural Development," *Telecommunications Policy*, September 1984, pp. 181–203.

41. Olof Hulten, "The Use of INTELSAT for Television 1982," paper presented at the International Association of Mass Communication Research Conference in New Delhi, August 25–31, 1986.

42. Ibid.

43. Audience Research Unit of the Director General of Doordarshan, "Television India," New Delhi, August 1986.

44. Ibid., p. 11.

45. Ibid., p. 8.

46. NOVA, "Global Village" (television documentary videocassette), Washington, DC, Public Broadcasting System, 1985.

47. Ibid.

48. See C. P. Epskamp, "Evaluation of RNTC-project 'Training and Research with Regard to the Application of the Mass-media for Education and Information in Latin America and the Caribbean,' Part II, Case-study: La Voz de la Selva (Peru)," The Hague, CESO, November 1981.

49. For more information see the bibliographical references and project documents referred to in Epskamp, "Evaluation of RNTC-project."

50. Epskamp, "Evaluation of RNTC-project," p. 28.

51. David Warr, "Evaluating Media in Malawi," *Educational Broadcasting International*, September 1978, pp. 121–123.

52. Ibid., p. 122.

CHAPTER 8

The Use of Modern Space Technology in Social and Economic Development

In our civilization, technological advances represent the management system generally considered responsible for the high standard of living in many nations. To a great extent, technology provides the methods for using energy to communicate information and to shape our environment to meet physical and psychological needs. It has the power to unleash human brain power, of which all nations have an abundance. For example, recent research indicates that telecommunications contributes significantly to socio-economic development.[1] Nevertheless, telecommunications alone does not guarantee economic development. In an environment of development planning, initial intense and productive research has been necessary to demonstrate the benefits, acceptable cost risks, and solutions to potential problems. More research and experimentation may have to be undertaken before some nations will be willing to enter the high-cost phase of technological advancement.

Determining the desired rate of telecommunications and technology development in developing nations has sparked considerable controversy. Three views are generally expounded.[2] First, some believe that technological investment should be restricted because it (1) has little measurable economic effect; (2) engenders social and political instability; and (3) creates an urban-based infrastructure that benefits elite groups and encourages excessive levels of urban migration, thus not promoting indigenous development. Second, others suggest that technological development in response to market demands provides application when it is most cost effective. A third view supports vigorous expansion of telecommunication, information, and space technology and believes that it facilitates knowledge transfers and efficient allocation of resources in the developing world. It is important that nations select the appropriate rate of technological development to support developmental efforts adequately without misusing resources and creating burdensome and unnecessary infrastructures. This step will require research and experimentation.

Communication satellites have been studied in political, economic, commercial, and social contexts. The recent global report on the international flow of information prepared for UNESCO is a detailed examination of all aspects of international information flows, including communication aspects of space technology such as communication satellites, transborder data flows, and remote sensing.[3] The purpose of the UNESCO report was to summarize the results of research done in the 1970s and 1980s and to analyze world information flow patterns and implications.

The purpose of this chapter is to focus on the operational and experimental aspects of space technology and communication in development, specifically as applied to social services, education, culture, agriculture, health, family planning, weather forecasting, and scientific advancement. We will explore the results of experiments and research in such areas as Direct Broadcast Satellites (DBS) and remote sensing, synthesizing the reports of international, regional, and national institutions and organizations on development activities around the world. Particular attention will be given to technological applications with direct and practical relevance for developing nations, and for which further research is desirable. The applications discussed include projects in some of the developing or isolated regions in some nations that would be considered developed, such as Japan, the United States, and the Soviet Union. Such projects present valid and useful information for the application of space technology in developing regions as well, and for this reason are included here.

Although this chapter attempts to cover a broad and diverse range of technological applications in a fairly comprehensive overview and analysis of space technology and development, it is not exhaustive. Given the limited space available and the incredibly rapid rate of technological advance, the purpose here is to address the major areas of activity, outline specific areas of application and interest, and guide the reader to supplementary sources for additional exploration.

After a brief historical outline, we will describe the relevance and potential of space technology to specific areas of socio-economic development. The result of past and current experiments and research is then summarized and synthesized under broad functional categories of community development, resource management, and national integration. The final section will describe, in some detail, case studies of experimental applications in a number of countries and regions as well as the activities of institutions and organizations involved in the use of modern space technology for development.

HISTORICAL DEVELOPMENT

Since 1957, when the Soviet Union launched the first artificial satellite, telecommunications technology has advanced and changed almost daily. Three periods of development can be identified. The first period, from the mid-1950s to the end of the 1960s, was a period of immense growth in the technology itself. During this period, interest in the potential of telecommunications technology in general, and space technology in particular, for developmental purposes was just beginning. In the 1970s, many projects in the application of space technology to development were conducted, primarily on an experimental basis. The third and current period, the decade of the 1980s, is one of operationalization and institutionalization of previously experimental programs on national and regional levels. Efforts were aimed at stimulating regional and international cooperation to incorporate telecommunications innovations and space technology in long-term development planning.

THE RELEVANCE AND APPLICATIONS OF SPACE TECHNOLOGY FOR DEVELOPMENT

Considering developmental needs, particularly in developing nations, it is generally acknowledged that space technology and communication satellites, by virtue of their special characteristics, have potential applications in the following areas:

1. National integration, including mobilization and assimilation processes
2. Administrative, organizational, and managerial effectiveness
3. Delivery of education, both formal and nonformal, including teacher training
4. Agricultural extension services
5. Family planning programs
6. Medical and health care delivery
7. Marketing, banking, and commercial information dissemination
8. Information, news, and cultural programming
9. Political participation and social pluralism
10. Meteorology, navigation, and environmental monitoring
11. Disaster prevention and emergency services
12. Resource management including remote sensing
13. Scientific information exchanges

These are the areas in which some experiments have been undertaken, especially in the 1980s, or are considered to be potential applications for modern space technology. A variety of data and research reports has been accumulated in some of these areas, and it has been argued that many applications, if operationalized nationally or regionally, can be more cost-effective than existing terrestrial systems.

In many developing countries, the infrastructure, technical and managerial skills, and data handling capacity are presently inadequate to accommodate the application of space technology. However, since most developing countries have few established technological methods and are formulating educational, training, and practical development programs, they are in a unique position to design and implement programs appropriate to the application of space technology.[4]

TECHNOLOGY AND INFRASTRUCTURE

Key factors in the application of space innovations to development are (1) appropriate technology and (2) infrastructure. A telecommunications infrastructure is essential, but the economic benefits are likely to be far greater than providing telephone service alone. It will facilitate the flow of information about innovations, new products, and improved techniques and for coordinating large-scale development projects. Rural areas are particularly in need of a telecommunications infrastructure to facilitate their inclusion in development efforts.

For example, satellite, electronics, and computer technology have potential relevance for regional and national integration. High costs and low density have historically hampered communications development in isolated areas. Satellite transmission, however, is a more flexible system with costs unrelated to location or frequency of use. Additionally, the declining costs of earth stations, as low as $20,000 by the mid-1980s, make establishing an extended telecommunications infrastructure a realistic development objective.[5] Further, small nations can share technology. Regional cooperative efforts may allow small nations to develop and/or implement their own satellite system, much like the Indonesian PALAPA and the Australian AUSSAT satellites.

INTERACTIVE VERSUS
ONE-WAY COMMUNICATION

Telecommunication transmission applied to development has been predominantly one way, from urban source to rural receiver without feedback, or more recently, two way, allowing transmission and feedback from rural stations. The latter is sometimes known as interactive communication and is obviously more effective in development programs.

A third methodology, teleconferencing, an interactive method in principle, promises to be beneficial in development efforts. Teleconferencing establishes interactive communication links among several locations simultaneously. This newest innovation is applicable in business, education, training, health care, and a number of other sectors of crucial importance in developing countries.

In the last decade, communication satellite experiments in different geographical regions of the world, and in one case employing "live, interactive satellite transmissions to transfer skills and knowledge across national and cultural boundaries," proved the usefulness of teleconferencing in educational and medical consultation.[6]

In health care, interactive communication links have demonstrated the feasibility of using this technology to combat problems of malnutrition and poor sanitation, as well as to support the efforts of local health care workers in remote regions. The nutrition education programs in the SITE experiment in India demonstrated the need to incorporate local representatives in formulating programs that target specific customs and domestic habits. Other experiments show the advantages of interactive communication in health care as well as in other areas and indicate that the use of this innovation will increase because of its flexibility and incomparable advantages.

The potential application areas of space technology in development cited previously can be viewed as making up three broad functional categories: (1) community development, (2) resource management, and (3) national integration. Of course, as previously indicated, application of space technology in development has spillover effects that overlap and interrelate the functional categories. Nevertheless, it is useful to consider the areas singly as long as it is remembered that they are, in reality, interactive.

COMMUNITY DEVELOPMENT

Community development is the label usually attached to development projects that target specifically health, agricultural extension services, family planning, education, and social welfare. Space technology application to these types of development generally occurs in three phases: identification of potential, experimentation, and implementation of operational services. In the late 1960s and 1970s, many regions and nations experimented with satellite services for rural community development. The U.S. National Aeronautics and Space Administration (NASA) ATS satellite series and the joint U.S.-Canadian CTS system provided the opportunity for abundant and diverse experimental programs.

In conjunction with USAID, NASA made the ATS-6 available to any developing nation in the path of the satellite as it returned to the United States from India in 1976. Small demonstrations of satellite communication between rural areas and capital cities were participated in by 27 countries. A longer experiment linked the campuses of the University of the West Indies for in-service teleconference training of development workers in agriculture, health, and education.[7]

In the 1980s, however, the transition from experimentation was begun, and policy decisions were being made on the role and extent of satellite operational services in community development. The USAID/NASA experimentation with the ATS-6 laid the foundation for the USAID Rural Satellite Program (RSP) currently in operation. The RSP encourages the use of existing satellites in a cooperative effort to support community development programs in health care, agricultural improvement, adult literacy, and education. In Peru, a project using the telephone company's existing lease of INTELSAT service is providing telephone and radio communication with rural areas. Negotiations were conducted with the Philippines to use the PALAPA satellite for agriculture extension, teacher training, and administration in a remote province.

Many of the experiments using the ATS satellite series concerned the application of telecommunications to education, such as India's SITE project. The experiments demonstrated a wide range of applications, including upgrading the skills of educators, improving the quality of primary education, and expanding the scope of college curriculum through sharing among universities. In 1971, the ATS-1 satellite was used by the University of the South Pacific for audioconferencing. By 1979, 10 terminals were operating 23 hours a week for teaching, tutorials, and program administration, as well as applications in health care.[8]

Although it is believed that broadcasting is currently the most important telecommunication medium for education,[9] satellite use in education does face some difficulties, such as the problems encountered in using television in development, discussed in the previous chapter. Most satellite systems have integrated functions, and educational programming, because it is not commercially viable, is frequently at the bottom of the list of priorities. Further, educators themselves often resist distance teaching methods. Suggestions, however, have been made that may help overcome some of the problems.[10] Educational programming will be more readily carried by satellite systems if it is fully paid for at current rates and if it is integrated with another service. It must serve recognized needs and target various economic levels to allow pooling of customers to support broadcast facilities. Broadcasting in off-hours and taping for rebroadcast also helps assure satellite space. Education programs can use satellites that have exhausted their commercial life and are unoccupied or those that are promoting new technologies and services.

A full range of satellite communication for community development has been used successfully in virtually every sector (education, health, agriculture, entertainment, public service) to reach a variety of objectives. In spite of some technical limitations, the primary barriers to implementation are unclear purposes and institutional inadequacies. The unwillingness of the telecommunications sector to supply rural public service because of economic infeasibility is also a problem. Users must be integrated on a common system and cooperate as a unit to create a significant market force.

Another specific area of community development that has proven highly effective through use of space technology is health care. Because of a critical shortage of trained medical personnel, the health care sector in most developing countries is comprised of three or four levels.[11] The first is the primary, or local level, where care is usually dispensed in clinics by paraprofessionals drawn from the local population and given limited training. The primary health care workers focus on preventive, promotive, and simple curative care, including early diagnosis and treatment of common illness, maternal and child care, midwifery, and treatment of injuries. Any more serious cases are referred to higher-level facilities. Local health care workers may also implement programs for immunization, family planning, nutrition, hygiene, and water quality and sanitation. They can monitor epidemics and collect demographic and health data.

The second level of health care usually encompasses small district or regional facilities, including larger health centers and hospitals. Services are provided by nurses, technicians, paramedics, and some physicians.

The third level is more technologically sophisticated and provides a greater range of personnel and services. Such services are normally concentrated in the larger urban areas in hospitals, where physicians provide specialized as well as general care. In some nations a fourth level of health care is provided by further specialization of physicians and hospitals treating specific diseases, such as leprosy, and other physical or mental health problems.

The application of telecommunications to health care, sometimes known as "telemedicine," maintains the health care system by providing emergency assistance as well as routine consultation, facilitating program administration ensuring quality, and providing continued training. Studies on programs in Canada and Alaska, as well as in other locations, have shown that health care can be improved significantly while costs are reduced by establishing a two-way communications link tying local health aides and clinics to hospitals and specialists who assist in diagnosis and treatment of illness and disease. Twenty-four-hour emergency lines provide requisite service for individual cases, as well as in the event of a natural disaster. Not only is health care improved by distance consultations, but also the confidence of villagers in village health care personnel is substantially improved, increasing utilization of local facilities and creating the positive mental attitude frequently crucial in medical treatment.

RESOURCE MANAGEMENT

The second functional category in which space technology and development are having an impact is resource management. This category includes meteorology, navigation, environmental monitoring, disaster prevention, remote sensing, and scientific information exchanges. Telephone and data links have proven valuable in conserving energy and increasing transportation efficiency. Travel is substantially decreased by coordination of efforts through telephone communication. Further, remote sensing satellites, which gather and transmit scientific data on weather patterns and land resources, are proving invaluable in managing and developing those resources as well as in minimizing the devastation of natural disasters.

The 1970s was the decade of technological advance that stimulated the use of satellite observations to monitor earth's resources and environment. Cooperative international programs, such as the World Weather Watch (WWW), have set encouraging precedents for the provision of information and services to developing nations by regional and global networks.

Since the first remote sensing imaging experiments in the 1960s, the growth in the amount of data returned to earth by satellites and space probes has been phenomenal. The United States' LANDSAT network now assures coverage of most of the land surfaces of the globe. Data are made available on a public and non-discriminatory basis from a U.S. distribution facility or from ground stations established and operated in various regions by agreements with NASA. Further, orbiting laboratories such as the United States' SKYLAB, the Soviet Union's SALYUT, and India's BHASKARA provide additional imagery, supplementing high-resolution images obtained from meteorological satellites. A number of socialist countries and developing countries, including Morocco and Angola, have obtained imagery data from the SOYUZ-SALYUT missions through bilateral agreement with the USSR.

For land to be used most advantageously, planners need to know both its current use and potential capability. In Bolivia, for example, 1972 LANDSAT imagery was used to prepare planimetric maps, which assisted in planning a population and housing census and, through comparison with prior topographic maps, facilitated identification of surface changes because of either natural or man-made forces. More detailed studies provided soil maps, terrain maps, and vegetation and land use maps and identified high-potential agricultural or mining zones.

In agriculture, remote sensing imagery supplemented by ground observations and other information can provide data on crop yield estimates, infestations, soil moisture, and soil mineral deficiencies. Satellite monitoring can assist in the selection of planting and harvesting dates and in scheduling irrigation. Agricultural information is also essential in managing the transportation and storage of food as well as in planning imports and exports. A pilot study by the Food and Agriculture Organization (FAO) in 1976 in Algeria, Morocco, Tunisia, and Libya found that interpretation of remote sensing imagery correlated highly with ground observations of locust infestations.

Satellite imagery is used to monitor rangelands and estimate numbers and locations of animals from the distribution and density of vegetation. Burning rangeland to control vegetation is monitored by satellite to determine the appropriate timing and extent of the fires. Such efforts increase the effectiveness of land management techniques, particularly in remote and relatively inaccessible areas.

Forest planning and management is another area in which satellite imagery data are important. In a pilot project on Tropical Forest Cover Monitoring in Benin, Cameroon, and Togo by the FAO and the U.N. Environment Programme, LANDSAT data were interpreted to determine types and density of vegetation. Imagery is used in other areas to distinguish economically valuable stands of trees and to program log harvests and conservation projects.

Management of water resources requires information on both demand for and availability of water. Satellite data are useful in securing rainfall, runoff, storage, and evaporation information and estimating flood damage and the number and location of people affected. Satellite data are also used to monitor siltation patterns and aquatic vegetation.

Satellite imagery has opened new possibilities for investigating geological structure as well. Major faults in the earth's surface can be detected and monitored. LANDSAT data have been used in evaluating earthquake-prone areas in the Philippines. Geological imagery has assisted in mapping tin deposits in Brazil and in locating materials for low-cost road construction in Botswana.

Remote sensing of the oceans has progressed slowly, partially because electromagnetic radiation cannot penetrate much beyond the surface of the water. The first oceanographic satellite was the U.S. SEASAT, launched in 1978. Early on, it was known that remote sensing could primarily detect surface temperature gradients. It is now known that such gradients point to ocean eddies, which transfer heat and affect weather. Further, ocean currents, which can also be detected by temperature variance, influence weather and climate. Experiments using buoys with satellite-trackable sensors showed their ability to track currents, origins and movements of fish stock, and atmospheric circulation. Such experiments have been so successful that a buoy-satellite system is being considered for routine operation.

SEASAT has provided some interesting information on the effects of moving water and gravitational irregularities of the sea surface. Further, shipping and marine operations depend on satellite information for the height of wind-induced waves. Temperature data are used to identify potentially good commercial fishing regions, and monitoring the colors of coastal zones helps in the study of marine productivity. Satellite imagery also aids in tracking oil spills, such as the one in the Gulf of Mexico resulting from a platform blowout. Additionally, monitoring the ocean's ice will contribute to better long-range estimates of climatic changes.

Atmospheric observation is perhaps the best known and most understood use of remote sensing satellites. Satellite data were used in meteorological operations from the first appearance of cloud pictures in the 1960s. Satellite data are used both quantitatively and qualitatively to improve the understanding of atmospheric processes and weather forecasting, particularly in regions where logistical or financial barriers render other methods impractical.

Because remote sensing imagery makes possible the prediction of severe storms and earthquakes, it is an invaluable tool in disaster prediction and relief programs. Major volcanic eruptions, which affect global climate, can also be studied and monitored. Perhaps more critical, though, is the capability to establish communication with disaster areas. A system of transportable earth terminals linked by geostationary communication satellites provide communication with and within affected regions. Navigation satellites such as the U.S. TRANET, NAVSTAR, MARISAT, and the International Maritime Satellite Organization (INMARSAT) provide ships with rapid, reliable, and high-quality voice and data communication links with the shore in times of emergency. Search and rescue satellites such as the international cooperative SARSAT and the Soviet COSPAS, which is compatible with the SARSAT system, assist in detecting and locating land or sea emergencies and communicating to mobilize and assist rescue and disaster relief teams.

NATIONAL INTEGRATION

This final category of development refers primarily to large-scale, or macro, projects, including administrative operations, political participation, information, news, and cultural programming. In this context, telecommunications is used to manage or administer projects and programs, from implementing new techniques and promoting innovations to daily or weekly supervision of the operation of public offices and government. It can be used, as it was, for example, in the People's Republic of China after the fall of the "Gang of Four," to provide political legitimacy and to popularize policies basic to development plans. Telecommunications and space technology aid the process of national integration by converting development programs into cybernetic systems, the feedback from the field being the critical element in adjusting and modifying the efforts to ensure that they continue to progress toward national development objectives.

In this functional category are also the uses of space technology in trade, commerce, and the financial industry. Innovations spread to rural areas to increase agricultural production or resource harvests are of little use if there is no current information on the market and commodity prices. Current and continuous monitoring of demand and pricing enable producers to manage and market their products at the most advantageous times and in the most appropriate places, or the government to plan the appropriate usage and distribution of agricultural products. Further, telecommunications links can provide banking transfers and other financial services that have long been available to the developed world and in the urban centers of the developing world but have been withheld from rural businesspeople and entrepreneurs because of prohibitive geographical and cost considerations.

In short, because of their heterogeneous social composition and vast but diverse geographical areas, often accompanied by such natural barriers as deserts, forests, and mountains, many countries are at a disadvantage in regard to the high cost of road, railway, or telephone line construction neces- sary to establish an integrated communication network and a single polity. The experiments of the 1970s and 1980s have shown domestic distribution satellite systems to be a satisfactory and cost-effective alternative in such situations. The outstanding experiments in this area include the use of com- munication satellites in Indonesia, Canada, Alaska, and Japan.

In Canada, where approximately six million people, or about one-quarter of the population, live in rural areas and remote settlements, satellite com- munications systems have proven to be most effective in ensuring that all Canadians have equal access to communication services. In fact, Canada has pioneered in space technology and national integration by providing services in the northern regions where terrestrial radio communication is hampered by climatic changes.

The PALAPA satellite system of Indonesia, in operation since 1976, is providing telephone, telegraph, radio, and television services to the country's 14,000-island territory encompassing some 3,000 miles. The important aspect of the Indonesian satellite system is that it has increased the government's ability to reach the rural areas, and thus integrate the vastly diverse geo- graphical areas through radio and television with news, government informa- tion, development education, and other social and cultural programs. According to one report "at present [1983] there are about 1.2 million television sets in Indonesia, and the number is increasing rapidly. The current plan for 75 transportable terminals coupled with a terrestrial rural radio system will make possible a satellite based broadcasting system with full national coverage."[12] At present, the PALAPA system is connected to 100 earth stations located throughout the islands. A recent study examining the primary information sectors of a selected Pacific basin economy concluded that Indonesia's significant investment in an information sector based on the most sophisticated technology has not only resulted in "skill formation within the labor force but has been instrumental in the launching of a National Program on Research and Technology."[13] The PALAPA system has also been useful for broadcasting services among ASEAN members. Thailand, Malaysia, and the Philippines are already leasing PALAPA transponders for their own domestic telecommunication services.

As described in the next section of this chapter, satellite communication is being used for national integration in such countries as China, Japan, Thailand, the Philippines, and Brazil to overcome geographical barriers and, in some cases, incomplete traditional telecommunication networks. In fact, based on the existing experiments, it can be said that the application of space technology in this area has been one of the most desired attempts to use modern technology in development.

CASE STUDIES
OF EXPERIMENTAL APPLICATIONS

In the phase of experimentation and pilot study, which is only now coming to a close, innumerable projects were undertaken that can provide significant insights for planning, implementing, and maintaining satellite applications in development. In this section, we systematically review a number of projects, describing purposes, applications, results, and evaluations that may prove useful to other entities involved in development planning. This section is not intended to be an exhaustive overview of every nation's involvement in space technology and satellite communication, but rather, to concentrate on those projects that provide generally applicable information or a data base.

The U.S. and the Canadian Experiments

The United States has employed satellites to reach remote or sparsely populated areas for a variety of purposes.[14] In the Rocky Mountain states, the ATS-6 satellite has been used to provide career education in intermediate schools; teacher training (career upgrading as well as teacher recertification); adult education courses; and distribution of educational materials such as films, videos, and graphics. The WAMI project established satellite links among students in remote areas of Washington, Alaska, Montana, and Idaho and the University of Washington Medical School. The system broadcasts pre-medical school curriculum as well as providing continuing education and medical consultation to medical staffs in those states. In other areas, satellite communication provides a medium for administration teleconferencing for personnel in medical education institutions; dispatch of emergency units and patient evacuation; and inter-hospital consultation, case reviews, and information programs.

The Appalachian Community Service Network has provided, since initial experimentation began in 1971, education and teacher training services to remote areas of mountainous, economically depressed Appalachia in the eastern United States. In 1979, the program switched from the ATS-6 to the RCA SATCOM and expanded its programming efforts to offer a mix of educational, instructional, informational, and public service programming to a variety of audiences, including courses for college credit.[15]

The final example of the extensive internal use of space technology for development in the United States is the well-known Alaska project using experimental satellite programs in health and education, which have now made the transition to permanent operational services. Alaska is characterized by vast distances, mountainous terrain, and harsh climate, making travel and traditional communication difficult. Ionospheric disturbances further interfere with land-based communication systems. The state has recognized the necessity of using satellites to provide telecommunications services, including telephone, television, education, health, and community services. Presently, satellite communication services are established in every community of 25 or more people.[16] After installation of improved public phone service, the major emphasis was on the health care sector. The experiment provided video transmissions from village practitioners in remote communities to physicians and specialists in a small hospital and a larger medical center. The system was designed with the capability of transmitting audio and video as well as electrocardiogram and stethophone information. It also provided a health information system containing comprehensive patient records and requisite information. In addition to consultative and diagnostic assistance, the system provided expeditious patient evacuation, a crisis line for persons with mental and emotional problems, and training courses for medical personnel. The equipment was selected and the system designed for effectiveness, low cost, reliability, and simplicity in operation. The health care experiment demonstrated that broadband satellite communication can be used effectively in the treatment and care of patients in remote areas.[17] It also showed the potential of nurse-practitioners in telemedicine and the capabilities of paraprofessional health workers. It reinforced the advantages of a network connecting health personnel to provide services as well as training.

In education, the Satellite Television Demonstration Project distributed programming to public schools in several independent school districts in

Alaska. The project offered a classroom resource from which teachers in remote areas could select relevant learning material. Evaluations[18] of the project found limitations in one-way broadcasting, the importance of reliable equipment, the need for teacher training on such systems, and the need for greater variety of material at more grade levels. All of the teachers, parents, and students responding to the evaluation wanted the program to continue. The satellite communications system now has educational television channels, a statewide audioconferencing network, and a computer network for self-instruction. Educational programming includes college coursework, and the teleconferencing network focuses on in-service teacher training, continuing education, and program administration. The system also provides programs on fish and game to remote villages dependent on hunting and fishing.

In 1972, Canada launched the ANIK A–1 and became the first nation to use a geostationary satellite system for domestic communications. The rural areas of Canada face many of the same constraints to social and economic development encountered in the developing world. In 1976, Canada began a series of experiments using the HERMES satellite system, a joint venture with the United States. Representative of experiments in education, the University of Quebec explored teledocumentation and teleteaching to provide education and research opportunities to students in remote areas. The Ministry of Education in British Columbia coordinated a cooperative distance teaching effort among more than 20 educational institutions, offering workshops, seminars, phone-ins, films, discussions, and off-air workshops on a variety of vocational and public affairs topics. A two-way video experiment between French-speaking Quebec and a small Francophone community in another province featured cultural exchange programs. HERMES was also used in an engineering coursework exchange between Carleton University in Canada and Stanford University in the United States. Government ministries used HERMES not only for a telehealth care experiment linking rural areas with hospital facilities but also to test the capability to service remote areas in forest fire control, routine conferencing, medical evacuation, and government and scientific research consultations.

The results of the HERMES experiments[19] show that the public service sector can benefit from the reliability and flexibility of a satellite communications system to support effectively efforts in remote areas. The experiments demonstrated that terminals can be operated by minimally trained nontechnical people and that users with different program interests can share facilities. The results also established the necessity of user participation in program planning and flexible plans. Operating experience indicated that users prefer interactive on-air techniques and that resource material should be presented by personnel at all sites, not just at the main resource center. Short messages and discussions were preferred to long films or tapes. It was determined that satellite material should be just a part of a multi-media approach to teaching and that discussions should be stimulated among participating sites and not limited to interaction with the resource people.

The Experiments and Experiences in Asia

The stated objective of Japanese space policy is to strengthen communications (especially broadcasting), weather forecasting, remote sensing, and relay of communication between many parts of the country. It stresses international cooperation, especially with NASA. Japan, however, was late in beginning its program, not having launched a satellite until 1970 and its first domestic communication satellite, SAKURA, in 1977.[20]

In broadcast satellites, Japan is not so determined to push indigenous development as it is to provide services. The first of two BS-2 satellites was tested in May 1984, making Japan the first country in the world with a nationwide Direct Broadcast Satellite (DBS) system.[21] According to a Japanese public broadcasting official, "BS-2 telecasting was scheduled to promote the popularity of satellite broadcasting by allowing some programs to be telecast sooner than in terrestrial services or provide other advantages unique to satellite telecasts, in addition to simultaneous or delayed broadcasts of terrestrial educational programs. The BS-2b scheduled to be launched sometime after August 1985, is expected to eliminate the blind zones . . . and expand the use of satellite broadcasting and its reception throughout the country."[22]

Japan's meteorological satellite plays a vital role in that country's meteorological and navigational observation, especially in the Pacific, where observation points are few. The National Space Development Agency of Japan (NASDA) receives and processes data from NASA LANDSAT-4, providing information to various users. Japan launched its own remote sensing satellite (MDS-1) in 1986.[23]

The People's Republic of China has identified space technology as a fundamental basis for development and achievement of its four "modernizations": industry, agriculture, national defense, and science/technology. That nation has scheduled three new satellite systems to become operational by the end of the 1980s.[24] The first is designed to improve telephone communications and data transmission throughout China and will require lease of satellite space from INTELSAT. The second is a DBS system designed primarily for educational television transmissions, and the third is a remote sensing satellite system for land resource management.

The Ministry of Posts and Telecommunications (MPT) will coordinate the use of leased INTELSAT transponder services among the MPT and other government ministries. The MPT will use the leased services to improve nationwide communication connections, especially linking remote areas with Beijing and other cities. They will also establish dedicated communication links for high-speed data transmission. The Ministry of Petroleum will use the system to facilitate communications and data transmission between oil drilling operations and administrative offices. The system will be used by the Ministry of Coal for communication with isolated mining operations, and the Ministry of Water Resources and Electric Power will use it to improve communications between major hydroelectric power installations.

The second system, the DBS system, was put into operation in the mid-1980s. Its primary purpose is to achieve a comprehensive television and radio network by the year 2000. The immediate application is educational programming, mainly the support of China's Television University. The University, which now enrolls approximately 300,000 students annually, expects to boost enrollment to 1.3 million in 1990, partially through implementation of extensive satellite programming and correspondence coursework.

The final system will be a more comprehensive use of the LANDSAT satellite system, expected to aid agricultural research, hydrological surveying, mineral exploration, and city planning. Although initial plans call for purchase of technology, remote sensing technological research is a top priority under a national five-year plan. The government hopes to develop soon its first generation of domestically designed airborne remote sensors and digital image analysis systems.

Recently, China launched its own orbiting communications satellite. Deployed in April 1984, the satellite will transmit radio and television broadcasts to remote areas as well as facilitate emergency communications with disaster-stricken areas during earthquakes or floods when terrestrial links are temporarily inoperable.

The three systems in conjunction with the new communications satellite will probably have important spillover effects as·well. China plans as much internal production of the equipment as possible and is stipulating that it receive technology transfers as part of satellite purchases. Both ploys are important to the advancement of that nation's aerospace industry and are helping to establish a base in the electronics field.

In 1975, Indonesia announced plans to develop and operate a domestic communications satellite system. It was the first developing country (and fourth nation after the Soviet Union, Canada, and the United States) to acquire its own domestic satellite system.[25] Indonesia has come under some criticism for taking such a giant technological leap when it is a poor and struggling nation. Nevertheless, because of the nature of the country and the benefits of satellites, the decision was made to employ space technology.

Indonesia is a nation of islands: nearly 14,000 islands of which 1,000 are inhabited. It has a population of 170 million people,[26] comprising approximately 300 ethnic groups speaking 250 distinct languages. Terrestrial systems made up of thousands of miles of cables crossing underwater as well as overland through swamps and acres of virgin timber are nearly impossible to maintain. The lack of roads and adequate power supply makes the terrestrial system equally untenable.

Satellites, however, provide a wider area of coverage. They are not sensitive to distance and their ground segments are more easily (and less expensively) maintained. Their service is instantaneous. Furthermore, all of Indonesia was connected with ground stations, which took only 18 months to construct. Today, more than 40 ground stations have been erected throughout the country. Each satellite has 12 transponders and the capacity for telephone, radio, television, telex, and data retrieval. The PALAPA satellite system is tied to a terrestrial microwave system providing extensive coverage. Indonesia is also using the INTELSAT system for access to data networks and overseas telephone circuits.

The objective of the domestic satellite system is to provide growth capacity in telephone, telegraph, and telex services and to back up existing terrestrial networks. Telecommunications is seen by Indonesia as a means to unify, educate, and develop its people. The 1970 oil boom in Indonesia made the PALAPA purchase economically feasible, and now the system uses PALAPA-B, the second generation, which provides coverage to eight nations.[27] The system is more flexible and cost-effective than any alternatives in meeting national development goals.

A primary function of the satellite system is in education and rural development. Currently, less than 20 percent of those applying to Indonesia's 42 universities can be accommodated.[28] The government thus supports an open university program using telecommunications technology. The government's diffusion of the education and technology program in agriculture, health, family planning, transmigration, and education has been effectively disseminated by PALAPA as well. Further, primary school teacher training and open junior secondary schools are operated through the PALAPA system. Disaster relief and medical assistance are program areas in which future projects are planned.

In addition to educational programming, PALAPA television broadcasts local, regional, national, and international news and cultural and religious programming. Entertainment programming, however, takes the largest share of television broadcast time.

PALAPA is predominantly government supported. It is national policy not to allow television advertising; therefore, the system must receive financial backing from other sources. Sales to other nations, to corporations, and to individuals (i.e., phone and telex access) bring some revenue. Further, Indonesia produces most of the necessary ground hardware and receiving sets and exports those products to other ASEAN countries.[29]

Perhaps most beneficial are the lessons learned in Indonesia's experience. The first lesson is that nations can effectively skip some of the predetermined stages or steps in developing technological systems. The second is that hardware is relatively easy to develop, as was seen in the 18-month construction of a ground system; software (programming) takes much more thought and time. Third, the loss of the first PALAPA-B satellite taught that the more sophisticated the technology, the more vulnerable it is. And finally, evaluation is critical to ensure continuing progress and effective application of Indonesia's promising new satellite system.

India's current INSAT system was based on knowledge gained in three experimental satellite programs: SITE, STEP, and APPLE. The Satellite Instructional Television Experiment (SITE), one of the most important satellite applications in development, was conducted during 1975–1976 to demonstrate the use of satellite television for communication and instruction in remote areas and to develop, test, and manage such a system. The U.S. ATS-6 satellite was used, but India was entirely responsible for design, development, deployment, operation, and maintenance of all ground equipment and for the programming transmitted to nearly 2500 villages scattered throughout the country. Earth station reliability was nearly 99.8 percent and receiving sets were 90 percent operational at any one time.

The average audience for each set was 100, limited by available space, not program quality. Many participants had never previously been exposed to mass media and were illiterate and from the poorer sections of rural society. Continuous interview feedback indicated the audience's preference for instructional programming rather than socio-cultural and entertainment programming. Although none of the objectives of SITE was fully realized, later evaluations and surveys showed statistically significant gains in information about and awareness of health and hygiene, politics, modernity, and family planning. New agricultural innovations not requiring expense or infrastructure were individually implemented with success. Children showed gains in language development and in learning to seek information from a variety of sources. Further, 48,000 teachers participated in in-service training. According to one researcher, however, the SITE experiment made no apparent changes in the decision-making structures of the villages.[30]

A number of lessons were learned from SITE, including the necessity for inexpensive, portable, and reliable equipment and for the single-minded cooperation of the agencies, organizations, and people involved. Pre-testing of programming and continuous user evaluation aided in targeting efforts. One of the major findings of SITE was that the planning of software rather than hardware requires more time. A major research recommendation was that both quantitative and qualitative methods of evaluation should be employed. (For a comprehensive overview of Doordarshan—Television India— see Chapter 7.)

In another experiment, the Franco-German Symphonie satellite was used as a basis for emergency communications and disaster relief. Two transportable terminals were also used in the STEP experiment for originating and relaying radio and television programming and news to remote areas.

The APPLE project is conducting digital communication experiments on time division and spread spectrum multiple access and on random access package switching. Computer networking is being investigated, as are data and file transfers and remote job entry. Other experiments include a multiple-language-mode television transmission with four audio and a single video channel, newspaper printing in remote locations by facsimile transmission, and a two-week post-graduate satellite communication course.

These three programs, as well as cooperative efforts with the Soviet Union, have built the foundation for India's INSAT program. This newest program provides telecommunications, meteorology, remote sensing, and broadcasting services and features the cooperative efforts of many government ministries. The services include telephone, data, and facsimile transmission; meteorological monitoring, land mapping, and disaster warning systems; and nationwide radio and television broadcasting. Research efforts are continuing as India is progressing rapidly in the application of space technology in development.[31]

In the 1970s, Pakistan constructed an earth station to use the INTELSAT communications system. A microwave telecommunications system links major cities in Pakistan and enables simultaneous viewing of television programming. Pakistan is only one of many nations using remote sensing technology to conduct research in crop yields estimation, land use, and the environment; to coordinate research with national institutions and organizations; and to promote use of satellite data through awareness seminars and training. LANDSAT imagery is the basis for research in agriculture, hydrology, morphology, geology, and land use.

In Thailand, probably the greatest contribution of LANDSAT data is in agriculture, where it aids in crop differentiation, acreage estimation, yield forecasting, and damage assessment. Economic studies show LANDSAT to be extremely cost-effective and to help determine appropriate crop calendaring and agricultural practices.[32] In forestry, LANDSAT data were applied to identify forest land, shifting cultivation and watershed areas, and areas of cut forest and to map land use for resource planning. Remote sensing data also provide information on potential fishing areas and the location (by habitat) of fish stocks. A number of satellite communication programs have been recommended and approved by the Thai government and are currently operated by several governmental and broadcasting organizations, and "a series of attempts have been made to draw up a national policy to bring these scattering satellite communications programs under the same system."[33]

Europe and the Soviet Union

The Soviet Union's Interkosmos program, which now involves seven eastern Europe countries and three developing countries, has participated in space exploration, remote sensing, biological and medical research, and meteorological research. A number of satellites have been launched, including IN-TERSPUTNIK satellites, the Czech MAGION satellite, and Bulgaria's 1300 satellite. Cuba now has satellite access to the data bases of the International Center of Scientific and Technical Information of the COMECON countries, and it participated in a project to collect oceanographic data. Remote sensing activities are performed by a camera in the SALYUT manned spacecraft and the METEOR meteorological satellites. Bilateral agreements establish data-acquisition and imagery-dissemination projects.[34]

The Soviets began joint scientific space projects with the French in 1966, holding frequent bilateral conferences. There is also substantial cooperation with India, with whom a series of satellites have been launched and more planned. The Soviets participate in joint projects with Sweden as well.

The Soviet Union's stake in INMARSAT, the 40-nation marine navigation satellite program, is 14 percent, second only to the United States' 23 percent stake.[35] Additionally, MARFLOT (the Soviet merchant marine industry) is involved with the Centre Nationale des Etudes Spatiales, the Canadian Department of Communications, NASA, and sometimes Norway in COSPAS-SARSAT, maritime distress and rescue operations systems that had saved 200 lives as of July 1984.

The European Broadcasters Union (EBU), in cooperation with the International Organization of Radio and Television, has developed television and news exchange systems, such as Eurovision and Intervision, using both IN-TELSAT and INTERSPUTNIK satellites. With the support of the European community, successful experiments with regional satellite programming have been conducted. The European ECS system, which was operational in 1984, exemplifies diverse satellite usage.

Of course, almost all western European nations are involved in remote sensing and meteorological applications, most having their own satellite organizations. In-depth discussion of their activities, since they are similar to efforts already described, is beyond the scope of this book.

Applications in Africa

Experimental applications of satellite technology in Africa have been diverse and scattered. There are examples of nearly every kind of experimental application but few large and conclusive projects leading to operational use of space technology on any great scale.

One such project is sponsored by the African Remote Sensing Council (ARSC),[36] including countries in eastern and southern Africa that use satellite data to enhance environmental assessment and management. The ARSC was formed to promote policy for and usage of remote sensing as well as to foster regional cooperation, training, and exchange; it provides comprehensive user training in agriculture and soils, hydrology, cartography, teaching with remote sensing data, geology, transportation engineering, and environmental monitoring. Further, it provides seminars and user reference, interpretation, photographic, and field data collection facilities. The ARSC stresses potential applications in agriculture, disaster forecasting, land use, and resource identification. Meteorological data are virtually unused except in Kenya.

Another project has used remote sensing data in the development of a network of roads in Africa.[37] Satellite imagery allows for appropriate planning of bridges and culverts as well as for identifying the necessary available water and building materials. Ground surveys were found to be much less reliable because of the rapidly changing landscape. Satellite imagery supported low-cost road construction in Libya, Botswana, and Upper Volta.

In the realm of telecommunications, the Pan African Telecommunication Network (PANAFTEL), the Pan African Telecommunications Union (PATU), and the Pan African News Agency (PANA) are among the organizations promoting cooperative telecommunications and satellite development in Africa. Nevertheless, progress is extremely slow even though INTELSAT does operate in some African nations, Algeria being the first to join in 1974. Scattered experiments show the potential for satellite communication application in African development.

In northern Senegal, a study concluded that phone service with audioconferencing and hardcopy transmission capabilities could improve rural production.[38] The study also identified the need for broadcasting for market information, weather forecasting, and training in production techniques. Networking of environmental and health data was recommended to facilitate planning, budgeting, and environmental management.

Educational television programming in Niger and the Ivory Coast is proving successful in primary schools.[39] Radio broadcasting is being used in several countries to support education, and virtually all countries use radio to support public health campaigns. Medical evacuations are coordinated by radio in eastern and southern Africa, and satellite transmission has been used to reach disaster victims. Further, telecommunications has been integrated into a major development project in West Africa for project administration, teleconferences on field problems, and staff meetings and to monitor health care and the environment. In another area, AGRHYMET is used to secure hydrological and meteorological information for farmers, herders, and fishermen.[40]

Examples in Latin America

Remote sensing, meteorology, and communications satellite programs are currently in operation in Brazil. The nation has two programs using remote sensing.[41] The first is the Radar Program, which surveys natural resources with a focus on geology, geomorphology, soil, agriculture, ecology, and land use. The Satellite Remote Sensing Program, established in 1973, receives, processes, and distributes primarily LANDSAT data in a similar vein, with priorities on agriculture and energy. Training of the more than 1400 users is a main concern of the program.

Over 200 applications of remote sensing data have been developed by users, which has led the government to plan upgrades of existing systems and processing stations. By 1990, Brazil plans to have launched two of its own remote sensing satellites. Regional remote sensing centers are being established to encourage both government and private research and technological development.

Meteorological satellite efforts began in 1967 with the construction of a low-resolution receiving station, which has been systematically expanded and upgraded. The program now includes an interactive image-processing system using computer facilities to receive, store, analyze, classify, and transmit images. Satellite weather data combined with conventional data allow Brazil to experiment with atmospheric modeling, weather and climate simulations, and numerical weather forecasting.

Brazil participated in the 1980s in a pilot project with the ATS-6 satellite that transmitted educational programming to schools and a university. The project demonstrated the feasibility of using satellite communications in education, and several such programs are currently offered on both private and government television channels. Further, the Brazilian government developed nationwide programming in education, health care, and agriculture to be transmitted by BRASILSAT, which was launched in 1985.

In addition to the efforts already mentioned in remote sensing and land use planning, Peru has proposed a project for USAID funding, using satellite and terrestrial technologies for rural communication to improve social services and the socio-economic development of rural populations.[42] In education, the system would provide satellite links between zone offices and village educational facilities. Similar links will enable village paramedical personnel to consult with regional hospitals for assistance in diagnosis and treatment and in-service training in preventive health care, family planning, and child care.

A primary purpose of the project will be to provide telephone service to rural towns to connect them with the national network. With these voice channels, the Ministry of Agriculture will attempt to improve and expand its extension programs. Agricultural innovations and market prices will also be transmitted to farmers. The satellite system will further aid in disaster prevention and relief programs and in transmitting defense-related instructions and first aid assistance.

The proposed Peruvian project is the first in a series that will be undertaken cooperatively by USAID and INTELSAT. Similar projects are expected to be implemented in other developing nations.

The Pacific Regions

The Pacific Education and Communication Experiments by Satellite (PEACESAT) illustrates another relatively major approach to satellite uses in development. PEACESAT links some 17 ground stations located in various countries and islands in the Pacific area.

Two separate systems are in operation in the South Pacific. The 2100 islands of Micronesia are linked by use of INTELSAT transponders, and the University of the South Pacific (USP), based in Fiji, uses the ATS-1 satellite, now more than 10 years past its design life. The audio-only system links the university's campuses in 11 nations for distance teaching, discussions, tutorials, student counseling, and program administration. Computer links permit reference search and abstract distribution.

In 1978, USAID funding facilitated an increase in capability, allowing slow-scan transmission of weather maps and pictures, facsimile transmission of X-rays and medical records, and text and electronic mail transmission. The system's application has also been expanded to increase community service, including weekly news exchanges among journalists as well as seminars, discussions, and conferences for a variety of participants and heads of state of the Pacific Island nations—demonstrating an alternative interactive model in contrast with the traditional model of broadcast development. The only serious and detailed evaluation of PEACESAT, however, raises some questions about its long-term benefits in the promotion of indigenous development.[43]

INTERNATIONAL, REGIONAL, AND INSTITUTIONAL APPLICATIONS

A number of satellite systems span national boundaries and provide regional and international services. Some of these systems are sponsored by a developed nation, such as the United States or the Soviet Union, and others are the result of regional cooperative efforts such as ARABSAT and the European ECS system. Although their diverse and numerous endeavors cannot all be discussed in this report, we will attempt to highlight many significant and representative organizations and projects.

International Telecommunications Satellite Organization (INTELSAT)

INTELSAT has initiated a number of programs devoted to encouraging the development of communications systems in developing nations. The organization has reduced rates and technical requirements for earth stations, improved accessibility, and provided technical assistance to users. INTELSAT has also increased transponder power, making small earth stations less expensive. Further, in 1983, they conducted several training conferences on the use of satellite communications in development, attended by 145 participants from 18 countries.

Chapter 7 addresses the increased use of INTELSAT for television. Additionally, two new services, VISTA and INTELNET, are being provided to improve communications in developing areas.[44] VISTA service will support thin-route voice and low-rate data channels using small earth stations in remote areas. It is designed to provide voice, telex, teletype, and low-speed data services in areas with inadequate service and thus at a disadvantage in economic and social development. A primary benefit of VISTA is the simpler, smaller, and less expensive earth station, which consumes less power than previous stations. INTELNET will support spread-spectrum data distribution networks.

INTELSAT's Assistance and Development Program (IADP) will assist users in design and implementation of the two systems, which will facilitate creation and expansion of small domestic networks as well as regional networks supporting development projects. Established in 1978, the IADP provides technical and operational assistance, in many cases without charge. To date, 74 nations have been given such assistance. Further, INTELSAT has created a Communications Development Fund to channel money into various projects using its satellites in development.

INTELSAT's activities for development are exemplified in its newest program, Project SHARE (Satellites for Health and Rural Education), which was instituted in January 1985 and was scheduled to operate for 16 months. During this time, INTELSAT donated "free use of its satellites for tests and demonstrations in the fields of health care and education."[45] The project, facilitating improvement and innovation in the use of telecommunications in social development, emphasized geographic diversity and practical application.

The program was administered by a steering committee, which reviewed and referred organization or country proposals to the International Advisory Council. Proposals were judged for originality; technical, operational, and economic feasibility; results of previous similar undertakings; documentation; and the credibility of the sponsoring organization. The International Institute of Communications, a global non-profit body, assisted in the application of the technology and overall project development. No minimum or maximum time period was inposed on tests or demonstrations.

Project SHARE has received numerous inquiries, including a plan for a telecommunications link in Tanzania to transmit audio-visual educational materials to remote areas, and a proposal to establish an audioconferencing link among hospitals in Canada, Uganda, and Kenya.[46]

INTERSPUTNIK

The INTERSPUTNIK system currently leases three Soviet satellites and operates 14 ground stations in 13 countries.[47] More earth stations are planned in a variety of other nations. The only major inhabited area of the globe not covered is central and western North America, but plans are being made to cover those areas as well.

The system is used by organization members, which in 1984 included the six eastern European COMECON nations, Afghanistan, Cuba, Laos, Mongolia, North Korea, Vietnam, South Yemen, and the Soviet Union. Additionally, channels are also used by other nations, and relations with PANAFTEL are being expanded and consolidated.[48] Further, about 40 percent of European Intervision's television transmissions are sent via INTERSPUT-NIK.[49] In 1984, the Harriman Institute at New York's Columbia University demonstrated that signals can be received by any appropriately constructed satellite receiving dish. The Soviet communication satellites also have a cost advantage over comparable systems because they have very large transponders, which make ground stations less expensive to construct.

INTERSPUTNIK coordinates its activities with the ITU and other international organizations and has established agreements with organizations and nations on areas and methods of cooperation.

United States Agency for International Development (USAID)

USAID's efforts are diverse and include technical assistance, training, fieldwork, conference participation, and financial assistance. In November 1984, a report of the Senior Interagency Group for International Communications and Information Policy (SIG) was delivered to the United States' National Security Council (NSC).[50] The report is the first serious attempt of the U.S. government to define the problem of world communications development in terms of U.S. national interests. Previously, such assistance has been provided only as secondary support within other programs, but a decade of worldwide experiments and experience show communications development to be a priority crucial to the success of other projects, whether social or economic.

The SIG report made several recommendations on increasing U.S. efforts in development communications assistance. USAID is the primary U.S. government agency providing such assistance and has pioneered in satellite communications applications to education, health care, agriculture, and rural development. Yet less than 2 percent of USAID's budget is dedicated to development communications assistance, and the programs are not structurally formalized within the agency. SIG recommends administrative action to formalize such efforts within USAID. Since INTELSAT has aggressively promoted telecommunications services in remote areas of the world, the report advocated continued U.S. support for the effort to increase the access of developing countries to INTELSAT. The system has played a significant role in USAID projects and may play an even greater role in the future.

Nevertheless, USAID's efforts in development communications represent 18 years of research and project application, including, among others, the Rural Satellite Program, the Radio Mathematics Project, the Radio Language Arts Project, and the Basic Village Education Project. The agency currently supports projects in 70 developing countries; 50 of these projects include communications applications.[51]

The National Oceanic and Atmospheric Administration (NOAA) in the U.S. Department of Commerce has been involved in USAID projects to exchange satellite weather information and provide in-service training. NASA also coordinates with USAID for projects using its ATS series of satellites.

Finally, the five-year experimental Rural Satellite Program (RSP) encourages the use of existing communications satellites for domestic communications in rural areas.[52] The program, previously discussed in light of its emphasis on community development, uses the INTELSAT system as well as existing independently owned satellites such as Indonesia's PALAPA. The use of television is not anticipated in the pilot projects, which will concentrate instead on thin-route, two-way telecommunications for public use and rural project administration.

Additionally, USAID is conducting studies and research in connection with the RSP pilot projects to assess the financial, technical, regulatory, and international considerations facing developing countries in rural telecommunications projects and to guide future efforts. Research is in progress on solar energy power for earth stations, as well as the overall development of less expensive earth station technology appropriate to the rural environment. Evaluation of the program is also in progress and includes service surveys, cost-benefit analyses, institution-building effects, impact assessments, and comparison with conventional communications alternatives.[53]

Regional Organizations

The ARABSAT organization, established in 1976 to link the countries in the Arab League, consists of three satellites covering 22 countries and provides telephone and data transmission, telex and telegraphy, radio and television broadcasting, and community television reception. Launched in 1987, the organization produces cooperative programming on development, adult education, teaching, training, and general culture. Program and news exchanges are encouraged as well.

ARABSAT can be used for national, regional, or international transmission. The organization's planning commission advocates studies on national educational needs and educational broadcasting potential. It recommends expanding data banks and information networks as well as investigating the possibility of disseminating a regional newspaper by satellite.

UNESCO and UNDP

United Nations agencies, specifically the UN Development Programme (UNDP) and UNESCO, have been involved in space communications technology for the purpose of development for years. Satellites are seen as potential aids in literacy campaigns, free flow of information, education, and cultural exchange. UNESCO, acting as a clearing house for information, works to create normative instruments and plan and implement new communications tools.[54]

UNESCO itself is not permitted to operate systems, assist in their operation, or finance them, but it does collect, analyze, and disseminate information for planners. It has thus performed in an advisory capacity on a number of national and regional satellite projects. It has conducted feasibility studies and designed schemes for pilot projects. On request, it provides "neutral and comparative evaluations" of alternative satellite systems.[55] Further, UNESCO organizes regional conferences such as LACOM (1976) and AFRICOM (1980) to draw the attention of planners to the potential of satellite communications in development. Through the International Programme for the Development of Communication (IPDC), UNESCO has been able to sponsor a trial Global Satellite Project for the exchange of news in developing countries. Other similar projects will undoubtedly follow.

PADIS and DEVENET

In the area of regional cooperation, mention must be made of the Pan African Documentation and Information System (PADIS) and Development Information Network (DEVENET) proposed by UNDP. PADIS, which was created in 1980 within the working system of the UN Economic Commission for Africa (ECA), was designed to provide information to policy makers and development planners in African states. The PADIS telecommunication system will include the use of satellite facilities to disseminate information and data to regional and sub-regional levels in Africa, depending on the adequacy of satellite communication links connecting the African regions with the data base centers, as well as with other countries. DEVENET, which "will provide information flow between developing countries to promote and support cooperation for development," is also planned to take advantage of satellite facilities for distribution.[56]

International Telecommunications Union (ITU)

The ITU is the international body that coordinates the assignment of frequencies for terrestrial and satellite broadcasting. In the past, the spectrum appeared to be infinite, but now that satellite technology has proven its value in development efforts, the resource needs to be conserved and cooperatively used.

In the area of remote sensing satellites, the ITU's International Radio Consultative Committee has undertaken studies on the performance and interrelationships of space and terrestrial systems and their use of the electromagnetic spectrum. Further research will be conducted in rural communications satellite applications for the benefit of development planners. The research is seen as a way to strengthen the role of the ITU and to give its members the flexibility to participate in the technology revolution.

The ITU is currently evolving and changing in an attempt to better assist developing countries in meeting the problems of development communications. One planned project involves a global satellite system designed to provide telephone services in rural areas.[57]

The World Bank

The World Bank approach to communications development is to improve project implementation. As such, it becomes a component of projects rather than a project in and of itself. The communications component usually includes radio broadcasts, audio-visual media, and printed materials. Distance teaching has been emphasized as a valuable communication application, as in education projects in the Philippines and in Malawi.

A key objective of the communications support is also to provide evaluation and ensure that the project meets the needs of the target community. As would be expected, communications technology is changing both the nature of World Bank projects and their implementation.

NOTES

1. International Telecommunications Union case studies show remarkable benefits in remote and developing areas. Cost-benefit ratios were as high as 85:1 in rural Egypt and more than 200:1 in Kenya. See Heather E. Hudson, Andrew P. Hardy,

and Edwin B. Parker, "Impact of Telephone and Satellite Earth Station Installations on GDP," *Telecommunications Policy*, December 1982, pp. 300–307.

2. Robert J. Saunders, Jeremy J. Warford, and Bjorn Wellenius, *Telecommunications and Economic Development*, Baltimore, MD, Johns Hopkins University Press, 1982, pp. 16–18; and Hamid Mowlana, "The Myths and Realities of the Information Age: A Conceptual Framework for Theory and Policy," *Telematics and Informatics*, Vol. 1, No. 4, 1984, pp. 427–438.

3. Hamid Mowlana, *International Flow of Information: A Global Report* and *Analysis*, Reports and Papers on Mass Communication, No. 99, Paris, UNESCO, 1985; and *Global Information and World Communication: New Frontiers in International Relations*, White Plains, NY, Longman, 1985. See also his "Political and Social Implications of Communications Satellite Applications in Developed and Developing Countries," in Joseph Pelton and Marcellus Snow, eds., *Economic and Policy Problems in Satellite Communication*, New York, Praeger, 1977, pp. 124–142.

4. Neville D. Jayaweera, "Communication Satellites—A Third World Perspective," *Communication Manual: New Communication Technologies and Their Impact on Western Industrialized Countries* (Summary Report of a Colloquium held in Bonn, December 17–19, 1982), Singapore, Parkland Press for Friedrich-Ebert-Stiftung, and Bonn, 1984, pp. 108–130.

5. Second United Nations Conference on the Exploration and Peaceful Uses of Outer Space, "Application of Space Telecommunications for Development—Service Prospects for the Rural Areas," Vienna, ITU, 1982.

6. See Andrea Kavanaugh, "International Education Through Satellite: The NCIES Satellite Project," *The International Teleconference Symposium Proceedings, April 3–5, 1984*, Washington, DC, INTELSAT, 1984, pp. 432–433; also, Timothy Prynne, "Health Communications and International Teleconferencing: An Overview," *The International Teleconference Symposium Proceedings, April 3–5, 1984*, pp. 446–451.

7. Anna Casey-Stahmer, "Overview and Assessment of Satellite Communications Systems for Education and Development: The United States Experience, with Implications for Developing Countries," Washington, DC, Academy for Educational Development, 1981, p. 8.

8. Ibid., p. 7.

9. UNESCO, "Satellites for Education and Development," prepared for the United Nations Committee on the Peaceful Uses of Outer Space, June 1983, p. 37.

10. Ibid., pp. 5–6, 28, and 43–45.

11. Saunders, Warford, and Wellenius, *Telecommunications and Economic Development*, pp. 297–300.

12. Syed A. Rahim, "Telecommunications Technology and Policy: The Case of Satellite Communication," *Keio Communication Review*, No. 4, March 1983, pp. 52–53.

13. Mehroo Jussawalla and Neil Karunaratne, "An Overview of the Primary Information Sectors of Selected Pacific Basin Economies," Honolulu, unpublished manuscript, East-West Center, Institute of Culture and Communication, 1985, p. 38.

14. See Second United Nations Conference on the Exploration and Peaceful Uses of Outer Space, "Relevance of Space Activities to Monitoring of Earth Resources

and the Environment," Rural Satellite Library, Academy for Educational Development, Washington, DC, 1981.

15. Casey-Stahmer, "Overview and Assessment of Satellite Communications Systems for Education and Development," pp. 5–6.

16. Ibid., p. 6.

17. Martha Richardson Wilson and Charles Brady, "Health Care in Alaska Via Satellite," prepared for the Indian Health Service of the U.S. Public Health Service, Washington, DC, no date, p. 7.

18. Jennifer L. Wilke, "Satellite ITV in Alaska," *Development Communication Report*, No. 26, April 1979, p. 6.

19. Anna Casey-Stahmer, "Satellite Applications for Public Services: Canadian Experiences with Worldwide Implications," *Development Communication Report*, No. 26, April 1979, pp. 1, 4–5.

20. *Space in Japan 1983–1984*, Tokyo, Science and Technology Agency, Research Coordination Bureau, 1984, pp. 10–14.

21. Testsuro Tomita, Deputy Director-General, Telecommunication Policy Bureau, Ministry of Post and Telecommunication, "Prospectus: New Media Policy in Japan," Tokyo, no date. See also, "Japan's Satellite Development Program," Washington, DC, Japan Economic Institute, Report No. 11A, 1984, p. 6.

22. Yoshinaga Ishii, "The New Media and Public Broadcasting," Tokyo, New Media Department, NHK Headquarters, 1985, pp. 6–7.

23. National Space Development Agency of Japan, "NASDA '83, '84," Tokyo, 1984.

24. See Madelyn C. Ross, "China's Great Leap Skyward," *The China Business Review*, January-February 1984, pp. 8–11; also, Jeffrey M. Lenorovitz, "China Plans Upgraded Satellite Network," *Aviation Week and Space Technology*, November 11, 1983, pp. 71–74. There were three major telecommunications and satellite exhibitions in the People's Republic of China during 1984: POSTEL '84, October 30 through November 5 in Beijing; China COMM '84, November 5–13 in Beijing; and ADVANTECH '84, December 4–10 in Shanghai.

25. Marwah Daud, "The Use of Satellite Communication PALAPA in Indonesia: A Historical Overview," paper presented at the IAMCR Conference in New Delhi, August 25–31, 1986.

26. *World Development Report 1985*, Oxford, England, World Bank, 1985, p. 174.

27. Daud, "The Use of Satellite Communication PALAPA in Indonesia," p. 15.

28. "An Overview of the Indonesian Rural Satellite Project Summative Evaluation," Cambridge, MA, Abt Associates, March 1984, p. 1.

29. Daud, "The Use of Satellite Communication PALAPA in Indonesia," p. 18.

30. K. E. Eapen, "The Cultural Component of the SITE," *Journal of Communication*, Vol. 29, No. 4, Autumn 1979, pp. 89–144. For the latest data on the SITE evaluation, see Binod C. Agrawal, *SITE Social Evaluation: Results, Experiences and Applications*, Ahmedabad, India, Space Applications Center, 1981. See also Arbind Sinha, *Role of Mass Media in Rural Development: Study of Village Communication in Bihar*, New Delhi, Coveepr Publishing Company, 1984.

31. Second United Nations Conference on the Exploration and Peaceful Uses of Outer Space, "Relevance of Space Activities to Economic and Social Develop-

ment," Rural Satellite Library, Academy for Educational Development, Washington, DC, 1981, p. 13.

32. "Remote Sensing Activities in Thailand," paper presented at the Regional Meeting on Remote Sensing in Southeast Asia, Bangkok, March 23–24, 1981.

33. Boomlert Supadhiloko, "Satellite Communications Programs in Thailand," *Keio Communication Review*, No. 4, 1983, p. 65.

34. United Nations Committee on the Peaceful Uses of Outer Space, "Report on the United Nations Regional Seminar on Remote Sensing Applications and Satellite Communications for Education and Development," Buenos Aires, April 7–14, 1981.

35. John D. H. Downing, "Competition and Cooperation in Satellite Communication: The Soviet Union," paper prepared for the conference "Tracing New Orbits," Columbia University, November 30, 1984, p. 6. (Cited with the permission of the author.)

36. David K. Andere, "Regional Requirements in the Applications of Remote Sensing Technology: A Case Study," prepared for the United Nations International Seminar on Remote Sensing Applications and Satellite Communications for Education and Development," Toulouse, France, April 21–25, 1981.

37. Second United Nations Conference on the Exploration and Peaceful Uses of Outer Space, "Relevance of Space Activities to Economic and Social Development."

38. Anna Casey-Stahmer, "African Telecommunication Needs," prepared for the Workshop on the Relationship Between Communication Technology and Economic Development: A Case Study of Africa, Washington, DC, National Science Foundation, April 9–10, 1984, p. 2.

39. Ibid.

40. Ibid., p. 18.

41. Nelson de Jesus Parada, "A Brief Description of the Current Status and Future Plans of the Brazilian Application Satellite Program," paper presented at the First Intergovernmental Meeting of Space Technology Experts, Columbia University, February 4–6, 1983.

42. Angel Velasquez, "Rural Communications for Social Services in Peru," *Development Communication Report*, No. 26, April 1979, p. 8.

43. Christopher Plant, "PEACESAT: A Classic Wolf in Sheep's Clothing: Evaluating Interactive Technology in Education and Culture," in Liora Salter, ed., *Communication Studies in Canada*, Toronto, Butterworths, 1981, pp. 147–160; See also D. M. Lamberton, "From PEACESAT to GLODOM: Models of Telecommunication Development," *Media Information Australia*, No. 25, August 1982, pp. 64–67.

44. *New Directions for INTELSAT: Satellite Communications for Development*, Washington, DC, INTELSAT, 1985.

45. Ibid., p. 51.

46. Ibid., p. 53.

47. *Mass Media Manual: Television News in a North-South Perspective*, Third International Broadcast News Workshop, Jakarta, February 1981, Bonn, Friedrich-Ebert-Stiftung, 1982, p. 137.

48. Downing, "Competition and Cooperation in Satellite Communication," p. 9.

49. Ibid., p. 13.
50. Academy for Educational Development, *Communications Development: A Preliminary Review of U.S. Government Communications Activities for Developing Countries*, prepared for the Office of the Coordinator for International Communication and Information Policy of the U.S. Department of State, October 1, 1984.
51. Ibid., p. 25.
52. USAID, "Rural Satellite Program Evaluation Management," Washington, DC, no date.
53. Ibid., p. 2.
54. UNESCO, "Satellites for Education and Development," p. 47.
55. Ibid., p. 49.
56. Edward Ploman, *Space, Earth and Communication*, London, Frances Printer, 1984, pp. 105–109.
57. Ibid., p. 92.

CHAPTER 9

Individuals and Communities: Communication and the Transformation of Society

As Thomas Kuhn points to scientific revolutions brought about by paradigmatic shifts in dominant scientific and social theories, so have we identified the ground swell of a great human revolution that is challenging the dominant theories and models of political, social, and economic development.[1] The overwhelming Western perspective, both theoretically and historically, has resulted in what is largely a secular theory of salvation.

Regardless of the diversity within the dominant paradigm, or the Western perspective of development (including both modernization and dependency approaches), impersonality, rationalization, large-scale organization, and increase in production have been the prevailing emphases. In the technological area, the application of science and technology to increases in production has been the emphasis. Although there has been little clarification between means and ends, more attention has been given to the means of development.

Although emerging Third World views and approaches have generated considerable controversy over the meaning of development, it has, nevertheless, been largely explained in terms of plans and strategies rather than in the context of culture and prevailing world views. Thus, static and asymmetrical notions of people and society have been the core of developmental policies and planning.

TRANSFORMATION OF TOTAL SOCIETIES

This book looks at development from the perspective of communication and the transformation of society, focusing on the centrality of the world view in the process. The ordinary dictionary meaning of *communication* is "to make known," and *development* means "to unfold." Therefore, communication and development, as a phrase in and of itself, can be defined as the "unfolding of knowledge," a transformation from being to becoming. It is through transformation that societies create new semiotics, a regime of signs and expressions that translates itself into action. This process of order through chaos is as much revolutionary as evolutionary. The relationship between "reality in itself" (ontology) and our "knowledge of reality" is placed within the individual's and the society's world view.

One of the schools of thought examined earlier has been termed the Western liberal framework. This framework moves through the instrumental rationality of Thomas Hobbes and the political thought of Jeremy Bentham to the Protestant Reformation and its emphasis on the ethics of achievement and individuality to the scientific-industrial era and its emphasis on value-free knowledge and the domination of nature by technology.[2] With the succeeding forms of capitalist economic structure and bureaucratic organization, we find a clear path through which the unfolding of knowledge occurs. Here, individuals are seen to exist as self and other, and knowledge is accumulated in the communication process between a sender and receiver through a communication channel. With instrumental rationality and the capitalist economic system, the power or ability of one to control and be active within the communication process is determined by the ownership of capital and the technological medium through which communication occurs. This relationship is expressed in the bureaucratic ethic of organizational man. The unfolding of knowledge is equated with what means the individual or organization has available to determine the allocation of values and the transmission of communication symbols.

An extension of this world view in a somewhat different school of Western thought began with Kant's positing of the transcendental subject and its inheritance in Hegel's dialectic between the subject and object in the unfolding of knowledge. From here, one can move to the phenomenologists, beginning with Husserl and continuing through Merleau-Ponty.[3] The phenomenologists, as with Kant and Hegel, were concerned with the idea of the essence of the transcendental subject; their divergence was in response to Hegel's inability to unite individual freedom and social order. To the phenomenologists, it was a mistake in logical typing to believe that the transcendental subject was constituted within the individual. To Merleau-Ponty, the transcendental subject was constituted by the living experience of our bodies. As rooted in the natural world and the social world, the transcendental subject gives the intersubjective process of communication its ability to create and re-create meaningful systems of symbolic reality. Communication and development, or the unfolding of knowledge, is constituted at the cultural level of analysis, in which the intersubjective meaning of shared symbol systems constitutes reality.

A radical departure within the Western world view begins with the politico-economic thought of Karl Marx. Marx was discontent with both the capitalist division of labor and Hegel's idealism. In response, he posited a structural and material system of relationship, which occurs between the forces of production and the relations of production. To Marx, every system, as an interconnected web of relations, generates its own contradictions, which are resolved as the forces of production overcome the outmoded relations of production in ever more whole relationships between man and nature and man and man.

The Frankfurt school of critical theory was unhappy with both Marx's materialism and Hegel's idealism. Max Horkheimer, the director of that group of scholars in the 1920s, criticized the notion of value-neutrality in science and constitutive subjectivity. Horkheimer emphasized the emancipatory interest of knowledge and the natural relationship between subject and object.[4] In the 1960s and 1970s, Jurgen Habermas continued by recognizing the two moments of consciousness as critical reflection and radical praxis. To Habermas, knowledge has an inherent emancipatory interest from both internal and external constraints.[5] The means of emancipative knowledge is communicative interaction in culture and the praxis of labor in work. The final test of knowledge is overcoming the blending force of power relations.

These are some of the main ontological and epistemological frameworks that under the broader terminology of world views have shaped the current discourses of communication development originating in the West—the Western attempt to understand the process of social change. Moving to the East and examining the world views inherent in the societies and cultures of the non-European and non-Western peoples, we find fundamental differences in the way such internal and external transformations might take place. For example, one can look at Islamic thought as interpreted by many writers within these societies and throughout the past centuries.[6] The Islamic world view rejects both idealism and materialism. There seem to be three dialectic moments in Islamic thought. First, and most important, is the relationship between the world view of *tawhid* and that of *shirk*. With *tawhid*, there is an essential unity among God, humankind, and nature. Humanity has inherited the divine essence of God, as a trustee in nature. As willful beings, human beings are to come in touch with their divine essence through self-knowledge. In correspondence with this divine essence, humankind comes to value a harmonious relationship with nature.

With the world view of *shirk*, we can express the second and third moments of the dialectic. Humans are constituted of both the spirit of God and putrid clay. These elements represent the dual movements in which humans embark in an ascent from earth to heaven and a descent from heaven to earth. In *shirk's* view, which is based on fragmentation, humanity succumbs to the putrid clay and the descent from heaven to earth. Although scientific knowledge, or the principle of the "names," is valued in Islamic thought, it is as a means to an end, not an end in itself. Through the use of symbols and knowledge, humans come to a recognition of the unity among themselves, God, and nature. The world view of *shirk*, unlike that of *tawhid*, is based on the drive for power. As power becomes usurped from its living presence in the spirit of God to early heroic figures, the world view of *tawhid* becomes fragmented.

Because in Islam life is considered as an organic whole, the society does not arise from institutions, such as tribes, family, or nations, but originates in the immutable Divine Law. Thus every individual is considered as a social unit as well as the center of social communication. History is viewed not from the perspective of nation or country but from a certain grouping of humanity called society, regardless of time and place. Therefore, Islam does not see any transformation in human society merely by economic or physical powers; rather it views transformation as a change in the inner being of a human as a social unit which crystallizes itself in a change in the external condition of society.

The emphasis on unity also finds its place in Indian thought.[7] *Brahman*, or the ultimate reality of being, constitutes the one reality toward which thought and experience can offer only the illusionary understanding of the phenomenal world. Knowledge is the relationship between *atman*, the innermost essence of each individual, and *Brahman*, which is offered a direct link through *dharma*. Knowledge is contained within a radical experience of an eternal now, never changing, just being in the ultimate unity of absolute spirit. Nagarjuna, a spiritual descendent of Buddha and founder of Madhyamika Buddhism, exposes the illusion of becoming in any system of thought that posits an absolute level of reality. He goes on to show that cause and effect, as well as being an agent of action, are negated at the level of unity, or *dharma*. Gandhi transplants Indian thought into the present day by positing his dialectic of *satyagraha*. In *satyagraha*, the truth is abandoned as an end in itself because it is relegated to an end in its becoming. To Gandhi, truth in its becoming is offered through non-action, which is not equated with passivity but is a very subtle and radical form of action in which a rational actor confronts his or her enemy with his or her own contradiction.

With Confucius, Chinese thought reacted to Indian thought in a fashion similar to Marx's reaction to Hegel. Confucius believed that the truth was handed down through civilization by the noble elite. Confucius was a conservative, believing that the morals that should prevail in everyday life were in accord with traditional role models. The Taoists criticized Confucian thought for not penetrating the archetypal and universal depth of reality. To the Taoists, reality of the Tao is constituted by the polar *yin* and *yang* aspects of reality. The *yin* and *yang* are in a ceaseless motion from which everything flows, returns, and then is reconstructed. The whole reality is encompassed in the totality of every moment, although in different patterns or configurations. The *I Ching*, or book of changes, identifies 64 different constellations of wholeness. The important point here is that wholeness is flowing and dynamic, constantly changing while remaining whole in itself. Mao relied on Chinese metaphysics—although not as much as he did on the thoughts of Marx and Lenin—in constituting his dialectic materialism, which was based on the all-pervasive quality of the unity of opposites.

Viewing these varied world views inspires an important question. What are the productive forces and how do they come into existence? Are they mainly economic, technological, and political, or do they find their roots in some different and higher level of abstraction and reality? In short, what is the principle that governs all human relations? The field of development has not addressed this question in any depth.

THE THEORETICAL AND PRACTICAL CRISIS

The overall field of development continues to be plagued with a number of epistemological and practical difficulties, which are barriers to applying communication comprehensively and fully realizing its potential. Development has been treated in either a very general or a very narrow sense. Consequently, the question of how its definition can relate to specific technological, economic, political, and cultural factors has been a puzzle since its inception as a discrete and independent idea. Although the problems are extremely complex and their solutions somewhat elusive, they need to be addressed if we are to understand completely the development process and effectively apply communication and related technology.

The analysis and the writing on development itself, even by those who have criticized the notion of development as ethnocentric or ahistorical, have been incomplete. Nearly the entire body of literature on development, no matter what the epistemological basis, considers the history of the phenomenon from its classical period in the 17th century. Therefore, a prerequisite for understanding the social history of development is a more comprehensive historical analysis that can trace the process to earlier times, both in time and in space. By so tracing the notion of development, we hope that we have exposed the reader to the process in a much broader and more comprehensive context.

Further, the notion of development as societal had its earlier roots in both human and political and socio-economic analysis. Indeed, one can say that the writings on societal development prior to classic and neoclassic times were very much multi-dimensional yet human-centered, and thus, more comprehensive if less rigorous. The industrial revolution and the neo-classical economic and social thinkers shaped the notion of development to suit the exogenous development of the time, basically in economic and industrial dimensions. For the next two generations, and one can safely conclude even up to the present day, the tendency has been to return to a broader notion of societal, national, and human development—but from economic, technological, political, and sociological aspects, without the cohesion and grand overarching theories of the human-oriented writings. The comprehensive, ideal, and universal terminologies of development for which we are now searching are rooted in the work of the early writers on societal development: those who addressed the concept at a time when the term itself was not yet acceptable and fashionable. Nevertheless, the analysis is less comprehensive and less cohesive at the present time, when the term is widely used.

A related problem is exposed by a review of the development literature, which reveals that the incorporation of other cultural and philosophical notions of development are missing. It is clear that there is an intellectual imbalance in the literature. For example, if a writer does not use the term *development*, the work is not included in the body of development literature even though it may directly address the concepts and realities of the field. Additionally, after almost three decades of experiments with donors and agencies in development, no comprehensive picture of the relationship between communication and development has appeared. Of the numerous experimental projects to date, particularly with technological applications, few have been fully or coherently evaluated. We have no systematic research or justifiable theory on which to base efforts in this direction. We operate under assumptions, the ultimate assumption being that those assumptions are correct.

Critiques and controversies of the proliferate models abound, but few coherent alternatives have been proposed. Yet the lack of coherent alternative models has not diminished the shortcomings of existing models; nor has the lack of alternative models impeded the process of searching for new ideas. One outcome is the division of developmental literature, theories, and policies into the micro-macro dichotomy: community versus national, bottom-up versus top-down, cultural/social versus political economy. As a result, since the 1950s, there have been several programs that are directed toward indigenous revivals and community movements. Although some have succeeded, many have failed.

In specific reference to communication technology and development, excessive emphasis has been placed on media-driven or technology-oriented models of utility. Programs are built around the use of new technology or a favorite medium rather than seeing technology as a tool to be incorporated into development efforts as appropriate and necessary. Further, the popularization of the mass society notion in sociology and the mass media and mass culture concepts in communication and in political science have had a tremendous influence on the theories and practice of development.

Expanding further on the theoretical and practical crisis that is facing development scholars and practitioners alike, we have herein developed a number of theses that are descriptive of the state of development theory and practice, and which recommend new directions and foci for academic and practical efforts in this field. Our observations in this area are summarized in the paragraphs that follow.

1. Early on, we examined the notion of development that is rooted in prevailing ideologies. Although it is impossible to extract entirely the processes of change from ideological biases, we must identify a way to recognize the bias and to dilute it. The notion of development in current application lacks the rigor necessary to stimulate any major breakthrough in the area of human and societal change. The lesson learned is that we must go beyond developmentalism and either replace the concept and terminology with a clear theoretical as well as practical formulation or henceforth only use the term *development* in conjunction with a descriptive modifier, which clearly identifies meaning, context, and limitations of the term's usage. Otherwise, the generality and ambiguity of the term renders it meaningless. To this end, we have proposed that the re-examination of the process and its intellectual history go beyond the classical economics of Adam Smith. The emergence of more fundamental questions of a cultural, social, political, and psychological nature necessitates that we study the phenomenon from the perspective of communication and the transformation of society, focusing on the centrality of different world views.

2. Just as the term *development* has lent itself generally to a plethora of ideological discourses, so has the term *Third World*. There is perhaps more diversity than commonality within the so-called Third World, and the term has made more than its due contribution to the confusion. We propose that the general and stereotypical notions of the Third World be broken down into more specific and concrete functional and geopolitical areas. For example, the term *Islamic world* more accurately describes a sociological/cultural system than does the term *Third World*. Unless we make progress in this area, we will remain imprisoned by our terminology; nevertheless, progress is difficult, and we ourselves have occasionally used the term *Third World* because the development of alternative designations was not the purpose of this book. The use of economic and technological concepts since the 1950s as major underlying elements of the definition, division, and superficial integration of the world into the broad categories "First," "Second," and

"Third" has distorted perspectives. It has, further, resulted in a better/worse, best/least, right/wrong judgment of values, beliefs, and cultures—judgments that have little to do with the economic and technological criteria initially used to "rank order" the nations of the world. We propose a more modest, but more definitive, criterion, with socio-cultural elements as a common ground for description and designation rather than a narrow economic criterion.

3. The existing developmental theories and models are so tightly interwoven with the world system that they impede any alternative development on a macro level, and they have become highly irrelevant on a micro or community level. The world system and its accompanying ideological mindset is so pervasive that, unless we divorce ourselves from it, we are tied by existing models. This separation is possible only on the micro level; nevertheless existing models and mind-sets continue to interfere in the transition to the macro level. In no work is this difficulty better documented than in studies of economic development and in the use of modern communication technologies, both on local and on national levels.

4. The most important recent occurrence in the field of development has been a slow but sustained and systematic drive toward the processes of human and societal evolution, which we have encompassed under a broader concept termed a monistic/emancipatory perspective. Still in a critical period of formation but manifesting itself more rigorously of late, this trend is evidenced by religio-political movements in a number of geographical areas and by nations that have isolated themselves to pursue development within their traditional cultural and philosophical perspectives. Nevertheless, it is not limited to less industrialized societies and to "Third World" nations but has become evident in the industrialized world as well in campaigns such as the ecological and environmental movements.

5. To better understand these processes of evolution and social change, and to appreciate and overcome the complexities and shortcomings of the term *development*, we propose a framework of analysis with its focus on the central world view that underpins culture as an integrating element in the process of change. We specifically emphasize values and belief systems that permeate the process and help us proceed to the parameters of both individual and societal change in a more systematic and coherent way. We do not separate communication from development; nor do we think that they ought to be viewed as different but interrelated terms. We propose that development, in all its complexity, is communication and that communication is development. Therefore, communication development, if fused as an area of inquiry and research, should be referred to as a single term. It should encourage the construction of development programs to fit the society, rather than orienting society to fit development programs.

6. Similarly, the level of analysis and discourse in the field of develop-

ment has consistently been the individual versus the nation-state, or small communities versus the national system. Less attention has been paid to the fact that levels of analysis are on a continuum, which begins with the individual and surpasses the nation-state. Consequently, there has been little analysis on levels other than those noted, although of that analysis that has been done, the supra-national level has received some attention. It would be interesting to see what would become of development projects if human beings were viewed in terms of larger socio-cultural systems transcending the nation-states. What happens to ethnic or minority groupings if considered as a part of supra-national systems as well as of communities and nation-states? The notion of development since the 1950s, implicitly and explicitly, has been connected, exploited, used, and abused in regard to the concept of nationalism. The decline of nationalism and secular national ideologies patterned on European and Western schools of thought, and the concurrent discourse and revival of notions of community along socio-cultural lines, opens an entirely new area of inquiry and research that needs to be studied by those interested in societal change and evolution.

7. The development of modern media and transportation has led us in two separate directions of study: technological media and human media. These processes should be viewed in a broader and integrated framework of social communication; otherwise we have the tendency to move from the real to the superficial, from the personal to the impersonal, from social interaction to mass society. This misperception is especially dangerous in regard to the "Third World" because it has given and will continue to give the impression that there is something unique and terribly promising about new technology. Technology is then viewed as an end in itself rather than as part of a larger process of social communication. Development and developmental projects must, therefore, be discussed in more comparative ways and on horizontal levels so that the study of any given phenomenon related to social change can examine the problem, not only in the "Third World" or the less developed world's laboratory, but also in the industrialized world as well. In short, our research and the findings of others in both industrialized and less industrialized societies show that the functions and dysfunctions of developmental projects are not unique to the "Third World" but are experienced in some form in the rest of the world as well. It is the discourse of development that has determined that the East needs development and not the West; these propositions must be tested in both "worlds."

8. Finally, as our review of the literature and the evaluation of projects shows, implicit and explicit in the discourse of development, especially as it relates to communication technology, is the notion that there is indeed a communications revolution and that the phenomena under consideration are in the realm of the "information" society. We believe that this notion has not been critically analyzed or sufficiently examined. What is termed an "infor-

mation" society can really, at best, be described only as a "data" society. Information is knowledge, but the abundance and increase in the quantity of data and their utility and relevance to different societies do not necessarily indicate information and knowledge as a unique phenomenon of this age.

The information society in the literature of the post-industrial age has been associated with the division of labor and the increase of services. We propose, however, that the society depicted is neither an information society nor a services society, for if the prevalence of services is the predominant aspect of the economics of this newest society, "Third World" nations would be the leading candidates for such designation. In the West, where government and society have become increasingly secular (despite some recent evidence of a contrary movement), it is assumed that knowledge comes only from empirical "facts."

In the West, discursive knowledge shows the limitation of reason; and the sense perception, which is a key to the physical sciences, has also not led to a complete explanation or exposition of truth. The function of discursive reason which characterized the age of modernity is only partial. Unless we learn to recognize its limitation, it is likely that it will lead us to a unidimensional perspective which neglects the very essence of those on which it is focused.

Dynamism in development rejects setting goals for the final completion of the processes of change in societies. Whereas projects and plans may have specific goals and objectives, change in a society is continual movement in time and space—it never ends. Transformation is not an external object. It lies deep within the individual.

NOTES

1. See Thomas A. Kuhn, *The Structure of Scientific Revolutions*, Chicago, University of Chicago Press, 1962.
2. See Thomas Hobbes, *Leviathan*, Hamondsworth, England, Penguin Books, 1961; and Hans Reichenbach, *The Rise of Scientific Philosophy*, Berkeley, University of California Press, 1963.
3. For a useful survey, see Richard J. Bernstein, *The Restructuring of Social and Political Theory*, New York, Harcourt Brace Jovanovich, 1976; Carl J. Friedrich, *The Philosophy of Hegel*, New York, Random House, 1953; and Edmund Husserl, *Ideas: General Introduction to Pure Phenomenology*, London, Collier-MacMillan, 1931.
4. See Martin Jay, *The Dialectical Imagination: A History of the Frankfurt School and the Institute of Social Research*, Boston, Little, Brown, 1973; and David Held, *Introduction to Critical Theory*, Berkeley, University of California Press, 1980.

5. See Jurgen Habermas, *Knowledge and Human Interests*, Boston, Beacon Press, 1968.

6. For example, see Ayatullah Murteza Mutahhari, *Fundamentals of Islamic Thought*, Berkeley, CA, Mizan Press, 1985; Ali Shari'ati, *On the Sociology of Islam*, Berkeley, CA, Mizan Press, 1979; and Ayatullah Ruhollah Khomeini, *Islam and Revolution: Writings and Declarations of Imam Khomeini*, Berkeley, CA, Mizan Press, 1981.

7. See, for example, Hajime Nakamura, *Ways of Thinking of Eastern Peoples: India—China—Tibet—Japan*, Honolulu, East-West Center Press, 1964; and Robert T. Oliver, *Communication and Culture in Ancient India and China*, Syracuse, NY, Syracuse University Press, 1971.

Selected Bibliography

This is a selected bibliography representing the different dimensions of communication and development. For further references please see the text.

Academy for Educational Development. *The Basic Village Education Project, Guatemala: Final Report.* Washington, DC: Clearinghouse on Development Communication, 1978.

———. *Correspondence Course Unit: Kenya.* Washington, DC: Clearinghouse on Development Communication, 1978.

———. *ETV Maranhao: Brazil.* Washington, DC: Clearinghouse on Development Communication, 1979.

———. *Instructional TV for Educational Reform.* Washington, DC: Clearinghouse on Development Communication, 1977.

———. *Radio Matematica: Nicaragua.* Washington, DC: Clearinghouse on Development Communication, 1977.

———. *Radioprimaria: Mexico.* Washington, DC: Clearinghouse on Development Communication, 1978.

———. *Social Values Through TV Soap Operas: Mexico.* Washington, DC: Clearinghouse on Development Communication, 1983.

———. *University of the South Pacific Satellite Extension Services.* Washington, DC: Clearinghouse on Development Communication, 1983.

Adelman, Irma, and Cynthia Taft Morris: *Economic Growth and Social Equity in Developing Countries.* Stanford, CA: Stanford University Press, 1973.

An African Experiment in Radio Forums for Rural Development: Ghana, 1964/1965. Reports and Papers on Mass Communication, No. 51; Paris: UNESCO, 1968.

Agrawal, Binod C. "Satellite Instructional Television Experiment: SITE Social Evaluation." Ahmadabad, India: Indian Space Center Organization, November 7, 1977.

———. "Satellite Instructional Television: SITE in India." In George Gerbner and Marsha Siefert, eds. *World Communications: A Handbook.* White Plains, NY: Longman, 1984. pp. 354–359.

Ali, Ovid. "Renovation of Adult Education by the New Media." *Educational Media International*, 4, 1979, pp. 14–21.

Ali, Syed Ashraf. "Population Planning Broadcasting in Bangladesh." *COMBROAD*, No. 55, June 1982.

Allbeck, S. "Renovation of Educational Systems by the New Media." *Educational Media International*, 4, 1972, pp. 5–14.

Alliband, Terry. *Catalysts of Development—Voluntary Agencies in India*. West Hartford, CT: Kumarian Press, 1983.

Almond, Gabriel A. "A Developmental Approach to Political Systems." *World Politics*, XVII, January 1965, pp. 183–214.

Amin, Samir. *Accumulation on a World Scale: A Critique of the Theory of Underdevelopment*. New York: Monthly Review Press, 1974.

————. *Unequal Development: An Essay on the Social Transformations of Peripheral Capitalism*. New York: Monthly Review Press, 1976.

Apter, David E. *The Politics of Modernization*. Chicago: University of Chicago Press, 1965.

Arena, E., D. Jamison, J. Olivera, and F. Orivel. "Economic Analysis of Educational Television in Maranhao, Brazil." Paris: UNESCO, 1977.

Aurora, D. "Communication for Development." *Communicator*, April 1975, pp. 23–26.

Australian Post Office. *Report on the Proposed National Telecommunications Plan*, Sydney, Australia, July 1973.

Baeyer, H. von. "The Quest for Public Policies in Computer/Communications: Canadian Approaches." *Telecommunications, International Edition*, September 1975, pp. 34–44.

Bahro, Rudolph. *Building the Green Movement*. Philadelphia: New Society Publishers, 1986.

Balassa, Bela. *Development Strategies in Semi-Industrial Economies*. Baltimore: Johns Hopkins University Press, 1982.

Balcomb, John. "Communication for Development: From Propaganda To Dialogue." *Educational Broadcasting International*, March 1975, pp. 10–14.

Barghouti, S. "The Role of Communication in Jordan's Rural Development." *Journalism Quarterly*, 51: 418–424, 1974.

Barnet, Richard J., and Ronald E. Muller. *Global Reach: The Power of the Multinational Corporations*. New York: Simon & Schuster, 1974.

Barrett, Hugh. "Health Education: A Campaign for Radio Study Groups in Tanzania." *Educational Broadcasting International*, June 1974, pp. 90–92.

Barrett, Mike. "Rural TV in the Sudan." *Educational Broadcasting International*, 10: 2, June 1977.

Bath, C. Richard, and Dilmus D. James. "Dependency Analysis of Latin America." *Latin American Research Review*, XI: 3, 1976, pp. 3–54.

Bava, Noorjahan. *People's Participation in Development Administration in India*. New Delhi: Uppal Publishing House, 1984.

Bell, Geoffrey. "Talking and Listening: Problems of Communication in Rural Communities in Developing Countries." *Educational Broadcasting International*, March 1971, pp. 12–15.

Beltran, Luis Ramiro. "National Communication Policies in Latin America: A Glance at the First Step." In Syed A. Rahim and John Middleton, eds. *Perspectives in*

Communication Policy and Planning. Honolulu: East-West Center, 1977. pp. 185–228.
————. "Rural Development and Social Communication: Relationships and Strategies." In *Communication Strategies for Rural Development: Proceedings of the Cornell—CIAT International Symposium.* Ithaca, NY: Cornell University Press, 1974.
————. "Social Structure and Rural Development Communication In Latin America: The 'Radiophonic Schools' of Columbia." *Communication for Group Transformation in Development.* Honolulu: East-West Communication Institute, 1976. pp. 217–252.
Berger, Peter. *Pyramids of Sacrifice: Political Ethics and Social Change.* Garden City, NY: Anchor Books, 1976.
Bertrand, Jane T., Marie Antonieta Pineda, and Fidel Enrique Soto. *Communicating Family Planning to Rural Guatemala.* Guatemala: Association Pro-Bienestar de la Familia; and Chicago: Community and Family Study Center, University of Chicago, 1978.
Bertrand, Jane T., Marie Antonieta Pineda, and Robert Santiso. "Ethnic Differences in Family Planning Acceptance in Rural Guatemala." *Studies in Family Planning,* 10: 8/9, August/September 1979.
Binder, Leonard. *Crises and Sequences in Political Development.* Princeton, NJ: Princeton University Press, 1971.
Block, Clifford, Dennis R. Foote, and John K. Mayo. "SITE Unseen: Implications for Programming and Policy." *Journal of Communication,* 29: 4, Autumn 1979, pp. 114–124.
Bodenheimer, Susanne J. "The Ideology of Developmentalism: American Political Science's Paradigm Surrogate for Latin American Studies." *Berkeley Journal of Sociology,* XV, 1970, pp. 95–137.
Bordenave, Juan E. Diaz. *Communication and Rural Development.* Paris: UNESCO, 1977.
————. "Communication of Agricultural Innovations in Latin America." *Communication and Development.* Beverly Hills, CA: Sage, 1976. pp. 43–62.
Boyd, Paul D. "Causes and Cures of Communication Neglect in Development Planning." *Educational Broadcasting International,* March 1975, pp. 5–9.
Brandt, W., ed. *North-South: A Programme for Survival.* London: Pan Books, 1980.
Bratton, Michael. *The Local Politics of Rural Development—Peasant and Party-State in Zambia.* London: University Press of New England, 1980.
Bronzon, Simeion. "Cotabato Now." *Rural Radio: Program Formats.* UNESCO Monographs of Communication Technology and Utilization. Paris: UNESCO, 1979.
Bunnay, Jane. *Communication and Community Development.* New York: United Nations Development Programme, 1982.
Burell, G., and G. Morgan. *Sociological Paradigms and Organizational Analysis.* London: Heinemann, 1979.
Cardoso, Fernando Henrique. "Dependency and Development in Latin America." *New Left Review,* 74, July-August 1972, pp. 83–95.
Carpenter, M. B., L. G. Chestler, H. S. Dordick, and S. A. Haggart. *Analyzing the Use of Technology to Upgrade Education in a Developing Country.* Santa Monica, CA: Rand Corporation, 1970.
Cassirer, Henry. "Rural Development and the Flow of Communication." International Commission for the Study of Communication Problems, document #49. Paris: UNESCO, no date.

Cassirer, Henry, and Carlos V. Penna. *Communication in Rural Areas.* Paris: UN-ESCO, 1973.

Chandler, Romesh, and Kiran Karnik. "Planning for Satellite Broadcasting: The Indian Instructional Television Experiment." Paris: UNESCO, 1976.

Chavan, J. P. *The Mass Media: Their Use in Agricultural Training, Education, Extension and Information Services.* Paris: UNESCO, 1973.

Chikulo, B. C. "Popular Participation and Development: The Zambian Model." *African Quarterly,* XIX, July-September 1979, pp. 170–180.

Chilcote, Ronald H. "Dependency: A Critical Synthesis of the Literature." *Latin American Perspectives,* I, Fall 1974, pp. 4–29.

Chodak, Szymon. *Societal Development: Five Approaches with Conclusions from Comparative Analysis.* New York: Oxford University Press, 1973.

Chu, Godwin. "Communication and Group Transformation in the People's Republic of China: The Mutual Aid Teams." *Communication for Group Transformation in Development.* Honolulu: East-West Communication Institute, 1976. pp. 151–174.

―――. "Group Communication and Development in Mainland China—The Functions of Social Pressure." *Communication and Change: The Last Ten Years—and the Next.* Honolulu: University Press of Hawaii, 1978. pp. 119–133.

Chu, Godwin, Syed A. Rahim, and D. Lawrence Kincaid, eds. *Communication for Group Transformation in Development.* Honolulu: East-West Communication Institute, 1976.

Clippinger, John H. *Who Gains by Communication Development: Studies of Information Technologies in Developing Countries.* Program on Information Technologies and Public Policy. Working Paper 76-1. Cambridge, MA: Harvard University Press, 1976.

Colchester, Marcus. "The World Bank Ignores Human Suffering and Is in Breach of International Law." *The Ecologist,* 15: 5/6, 1985, pp. 286–292.

Communication in the Service of Women: A Report on Action and Research Programmes, 1980–1985. Document prepared for the World Conference to Review and Appraise the Achievements of the United Nations Decade for Women, Nairobi, July 15–26, 1985. Paris: UNESCO, 1985.

Davies, John, and Terrence D. J. Louis. "Measuring the Effectiveness of Contraceptive Marketing Programs: Preethi in Sri Lanka." *Studies in Family Planning,* Population Council, 8: 4, April 1977.

Deleuze, Gilles, and Felix Guattari. *A Thousand Plateaus: Capitalism and Schizophrenia.* Minneapolis: University of Minnesota Press, 1987.

Dervin, B. "Communication with the Urban Poor: An Alternative Perspective." Paper presented at the meeting of the International Communication Association, Chicago, 1978.

Deutsch, Karl W. *Nationalism and Social Communication: An Inquiry into the Foundations of Nationality.* New York: Technology Press of MIT and Wiley, 1953.

"Development Communications: A.I.S. Policy Determination." PD-10. Washington, DC, U.S. Agency for International Development, February 17, 1984.

Dhungel, Dipak P. "The People's Movement and Experiment in Nepal." *Community Development Journal,* 21: 3, 1986, pp. 217–227.

Dissanayake, Wimal. "Development and Communication: Four Approaches." *Media Asia,* 8: 4, 1981.

Dogra, Bharat. "The World Bank vs. the People of Bastar." *The Ecologist*, 15: 1/2, 1985, pp. 44–48.

Dos Santos, Theotonio. "The Structure of Dependency." *American Economic Review*, LX, May 1970, pp. 231–236.

Eapen, K. E. "The Cultural Component of SITE." *Journal of Communication*, 29: 4, 1979, pp. 106–113.

Edgar, Patricia, and Syed A. Rahim, eds. *Communication Policy in Developed Countries*. London: Routledge & Kegan Paul, 1983.

Eicher, Jean-Claude, David Hawkridge, Émile McAnany, François Mariet, and François Orvel. *The Economics of New Educational Media*. Paris: UNESCO, 1982.

Ekong, Ekong E., and Kamorudeen L. Sokoya. "Success and Failure in Rural Community Development Efforts: A Study of Two Cases in Southwestern Nigeria." *Community Development Journal*, 17: 3, 1982, pp. 217–223.

Ellul, Jacques. *The Technological Society*. Translated by John Wilkinson. New York: Knopf, 1964.

———. *The Technological System*. Translated by Joachim Nuegroschel. New York: Continuum Books, 1980.

Erikson, Erik H. *Childhood and Society*. New York: Norton, 1950.

Esman, M. "Popular Participation and Feedback Systems in Rural Development." *Proceedings of the Cornell-CIAT Symposium*. Ithaca, NY: Cornell University Press, 1974.

Falk, Richard. "Satisfying Human Needs in a World of Sovereign States: Rhetoric, Reality, and Vision." In Charles K. Wilber, ed. *The Political Economy of Development and Underdevelopment*. 3rd Edition. New York: Random House, 1983.

Falls-Borda, Orlando. "Participatory Action Research." *Development: Seeds of Change*, No. 2, 1984. pp. 18–20.

Fanon, Franz. *The Wretched of the Earth*. Hormondswort, England: Penguin, 1967.

Feliciano, Gloria, "Networking and Local Broadcasting." *The Educational Use of Mass Media*. Washington, DC: World Bank, 1981. pp. 31–34.

Fisher, D., and L. S. Harms, eds. *The Right to Communicate: A New Human Right*. Dublin: Beele Press, 1983.

Fisher, Heinz-Dietrich, and John Calhoun Merrill, eds. *Intercultural Communication*. New York: Hastings House, 1976.

Folorunso, Isola. "Grassroots Broadcasting in Nigeria." *COMBROAD*, No. 60, September 1983.

Foster-Carter, Aiden. "Neo-Marxist Approaches to Development and Underdevelopment." In Emanuel de Kant and Gavin Williams, eds. *Sociology and Development*. London: Tavistock Publication, 1974. pp. 60–105.

Frank, André Gunder. *Capitalism and Underdevelopment in Latin America: Historical Studies of Chile and Brazil*. New York: Monthly Review Press, 1976.

———. *Reflections on the World Economic Crisis*. New York: Monthly Review Press, 1981.

Fraser, Colin. "Video in the Field—A Novel Approach to Farmer Training." *Educational Broadcasting International*, 13: 3, September 1980.

Freire, Paulo. *Education for Critical Consciousness*. New York: Seabury Press, 1973.

———. *Pedagogy of the Oppressed*. New York: Herder and Herder, 1970.

Furtado, Celso. *Development and Underdevelopment.* Berkeley: University of California Press, 1964.

Futagami, Shigenari. "Marshalling, Managing, and Evaluating the Mass Media." *The Educational Use of Mass Media.* Washington, DC: World Bank, 1981. pp. 1–10.

Galtung, J. "A Structural Theory of Imperialism." *Journal of Peace Research,* 8: 2, 1971, pp. 81–117.

———. *The True Worlds.* New York: Free Press, 1980.

Galtung, J., P. O'Brien, and R. Preiswerk, eds. *Self-reliance: A Strategy for Development.* New York: Praeger, 1980.

Gerbner, George, ed. *Mass Media Policies in Changing Cultures.* New York: Wiley, 1977.

Gerbner, George, and Marsha Siefert, eds. *World Communications: A Handbook.* White Plains, NY: Longman, 1983.

Gilbert, Alan, and Peter Ward. "Community Action by the Urban Poor: Democratic Involvement, Community Self-Help or a Means of Social Control?" *World Development,* 12: 8, 1984, pp. 769–782.

Gillis, Malcolm, Dwight A. Perkins, Michael Roemer, and Donald Snodgrass. *Economics of Development.* New York: Norton, 1983.

Golding, Peter. "Media Role in National Development: Critique of a Theoretical Orthodoxy." *Journal of Communication,* 24: 3, Summer 1974, pp. 39–53.

Goldschmidt, Douglas. "Financing Telecommunications for Rural Development." *Telecommunication Policy,* September 1984, pp. 181–203.

Gondolf, Ed. "Community Development Amidst Political Violence—Lessons from Guatemala." *Community Development Journal,* 16: 3, 1981.

Gopalakrishna, P. V., and Paul Gonsalves. *Programme Evaluation of Indian Cultural Development Centre.* Madras: ICDC, 1985.

Goulet, Denis A. *The Cruel Choice: A New Concept in the Theory of Development.* New York: Atheneum, 1971.

———. "Development for What?" *Comparative Political Studies,* 1, July 1968, pp. 295–312.

Gran, Guy. *Development by People: Citizen Construction of a Just World.* New York: Praeger, 1983.

Gutierrez, G. *A Theology of Liberation.* New York: Orbis Press, 1973.

Gwyn, Robert J. "Rural Radio in Bolivia: A Case Study." *Journal of Communication,* 33: 2, Spring 1983.

Habermas, Jurgen. *Communication and the Evolution of Society.* Boston: Beacon Press, 1976.

Hall, B., and A. Dodds. "Voices for Development: The Tanzanian Radio Study Campaign." In P. Spain, D. Jamison, and E. McAnany, eds. *Radio for Education and Development: Case Studies.* Working paper no. 266, 2 vols. Washington, DC: World Bank, 1977.

Hamelink, Cees J. *Communication Research In Third World Realities.* The Hague: Institute of Social Studies, 1980.

———. *Cultural Autonomy in Global Communication: Planning National Information Policy.* White Plains, NY: Longman, 1973.

———. *The Technology Gamble: Informatics and Public Policy: A Study of Technology Choice.* Norwood, NJ: Ablex Publishing, 1988.

Hancock, A. *Communication Planning for Development: An Operational Framework.* Paris: UNESCO, 1981.

———. "Local Broadcasting and Community Media." *The Educational Use of Mass Media.* Washington, DC: World Bank, 1981. pp. 35–44.

———. "Mass Media and National Development." *Educational Broadcasting International,* June 1974, pp. 58–68.

———. *Planning for Educational Mass Media.* London: Longman, 1977.

Haque, Wahidul. "Our Brave New World—Grass Roots Initiatives and Strategies in Response." *Development: Seeds of Change,* No. 1, 1983.

Hawkridge, David. *New Information Technology in Education.* Baltimore: Johns Hopkins University Press, 1983.

Heath, Carla W. "Telecommunications Policy and Projects in Zambia, Kenya and Nigeria: A Dilemma of Development." In Vickie A. Sigman, ed. *Development Communications in the Third World.* Urbana-Champaign: College of Agriculture, University of Illinois, May 1984.

Hedebro, Goran. *Communication and Social Change in Developing Nations: A Critical View.* Ames: Iowa State University Press, 1982.

Hein, Kurt. "Community Radio in Ecuador Meeting People's Needs." *Development Communication Report,* No. 42, June 1983.

———. "Community Radio Thriving in Ecuador: Otavalo Indians Running Their Own Show." *Development Communication Report,* No. 40, December 1982.

Hendrata, Lukas, and David L. Piet. "KARET KB and Jamu: An Integrated Approach to Condom Marketing." *International Development Review,* Vol. 4, 1974.

Hirschman, Albert. "The Rise and Decline of Development Economics." *Essays in Tresspassing.* Cambridge, MA: Cambridge University Press, 1981. pp. 1–24.

Hobson, J. A. *Imperialism: A Study.* Ann Arbor: University of Michigan Press, 1965.

Holdcroft, Lane. *The Rise and Fall of Community Development in Developing Countries, 1950–65: A Critical Analysis and an Annotated Bibliography.* East Lansing: Michigan State University (Office of Rural Development and Development Administration) and USAID, 1978.

Horley, Albert L. "An Approach to Planning Investment in Telecommunications for Development." *Stanford Journal of International Studies,* 5, June 1970, pp. 114–137.

———. "What Does Educational Television Offer Us Now?" *The Educational Use of the Mass Media.* Washington, DC: World Bank, 1981. pp. 94–99.

Horley, A., and A. Sanfridsson. *Communication Policies and Planning: Indonesia.* Paris: UNESCO, 1973.

Hornik, Robert. "Communication as Complement in Development." *Journal of Communication,* 30: 2, Spring 1980, pp. 10–24.

———. *Development Communication: Information, Agriculture, and Nutrition in the Third World.* White Plains, NY: Longman, 1988.

Hudson, Heather. "Three Case Studies on the Role of Telecommunications in Socio-Economic Development." Geneva: International Telecommunications Union, 1981.

Huntington, Samuel P. *Political Order in Changing Societies.* New Haven, CT: Yale University Press, 1968.

Huntington, Samuel P., and Joan M. Nelson. *No Easy Choice: Political Participation in Developing Countries.* Cambridge, MA: Harvard University Press, 1976.

Illich, Ivan. *Shadow Work*. Boston: Marion Boyars, 1981.

Indian Cultural Development Centre. *Development, Law and Indigenous Resources*. Madras: ICDC, 1986.

Inkeles, Alex, and David Smith. *Becoming Modern*. Cambridge, MA: Harvard University Press, 1974.

Innis, Harold A. *The Bias of Communication*. Toronto, Ontario: Toronto University Press, 1951.

International Commission for the Study of Communication Problems. *Many Voices One World*. London: Kogan Page, 1980.

Jacobson, Thomas. "An Epistemological Shift in Development Communications Theory." In Brenda Dervin and Melvin Voight, eds. *Progress in Communication Sciences*. Vol. VI. Norwood, NJ: Ablex Publishing, 1985.

Jamison, P., and E. McAnany. *Radio for Education and Development*. Beverly Hills, CA: Sage, 1978.

Jantsch, Erich. *Design for Evolution*. New York: Braziller, 1975.

Jenkins, Janet. "Do Audiovisual Media Possess Unique Teaching Capabilities?" *The Educational Use of Mass Media*. Washington, DC: World Bank, 1981. pp. 11–25.

Jussawalla, Meheroo, and Debra Lynn Hughes. "The Information Economy and Indigenous Development." In Georgette Wang and Wimal Dissanayake. *Continuity and Change in Communication Systems: An Asian Perspective*. Norwood, NJ: Ablex Publishing, 1984.

Karunaratne, Garvin. "The Failure of the Community Development Programme in India." *The Journal of Community Development*, No. 11, April 1976, pp. 95–119.

Kato, Hidetoshi. *Japanese Research on Mass Communication: Selected Abstracts*. Honolulu: University Press of Hawaii, 1974.

Kautsky, Karl. *The Dictatorship of Proletariat*. Ann Arbor: University of Michigan Press, 1964.

Kaldun, Ibn. *The Muqaddimah* (An Introduction to History). Translated from the Arabic by Franz Rosenthal. London: Routledge & Kegan Paul, 1967.

Khomeini, Ruhollah. *Islam and Revolution: Extracts from the Writings and Declarations of Iman Khomeini*. Translated with an Introduction by Hamid Algar. Berkeley, CA: Mizan Press, 1980.

Kitching, Gavin. *Development and Underdevelopment in Historical Perspective*. London: Methuen, 1982.

Kuhn, T. *The Structure of Scientific Revolutions*. Chicago: University of Chicago Press, 1962.

Larn, Karani Zareen. *Interpersonal Factors Facilitating Community Participation: Methods and Media in Community Participation*. Uppsala, Sweden: University of Lund, 1984.

Lasch, Christopher. *The Culture of Narcissism: American Life in an Age of Diminishing Expectations*. New York: Norton, 1979.

Lengor, Sama. "The Role of Radio in Support of Development Activities in Sierra Leone." *COMBROAD*, No. 55, June 1982.

Lenin, V. I. *Imperialism: The Highest Stage of Capitalism*. New York: International Publishers, 1939.

Lerner, Daniel. *The Passing of Traditional Society*. Glencoe, IL: Free Press, 1958.

Lerner, Daniel, and Wilbur Schramm. *Communication and Change in Developing Countries.* Honolulu: University Press of Hawaii, 1967.

Liu, Alan P. L. *Communication and National Integration in Communist China.* Berkeley: University of California Press, 1971.

Luyken, Georg-Michael. "25 Jahre 'Communication and Development' Forschung in den USA: Wissenschaft Oder Ideologie?" *Rundfunk und Fernsehen,* 28, Jahrgangs 1980/1 (Federal Republic of Germany, Hamburg), pp. 110–122.

McAnany, Émile G., ed. *Communications in the Rural Third World: The Role of Information in Development.* New York: Praeger, 1980.

————. "Does Information Really Work?" *Journal of Communication,* 28: 1, Winter 1978, pp. 84–90.

McClelland, D. *The Achieving Society.* New York: Van Nostrand, 1961.

McLuhan, Marshal. *Understanding Media: The Extension of Man.* New York: McGraw-Hill, 1964.

McNelly, John. "Mass Communication and the Climate for Modernization in Latin America." *Journal of Inter-American Studies,* 8, 1966, pp. 345–357.

Marx, Karl. *Capital.* Moscow: Foreign Language Publishing House, 1959. 3 volumes.

Masuda, Yoneji. *The Information Society as a Post-Industrial Society.* Tokyo: Institute for the Information Society, 1980.

Matta, F. R. "A Model for Democratic Communication." *Development Dialogue,* 2, 1981.

Mattelart, Armand. *Mass Media, Ideologies and the Revolutionary Movement.* Atlantic Heights, NJ: Humanities Press, 1980.

————. *Multi-National Corporations and the Control of Culture.* Atlantic Heights, NJ: Humanities Press, 1979.

Mayo, John K., Robert C. Hornik, and Émile G. McAnany. *Educational Reform with Television: The El Salvador Experience.* Stanford, CA: Stanford University Press, 1976.

Meadows, Donella H., Dennis L. Meadows, Jorgen Randers, and William W. Behrens III. *Limits to Growth.* New York: Universe Books, 1972.

Meier, Gerald M. *Leading Issues in Economic Development.* New York: Oxford University Press, 1984.

Melody, William H. "The Role of Communication in Development Planning." In Syed Rahim and John Middleton, eds. *Perspectives in Communication and Development.* Honolulu: East-West Center, 1977. pp. 25–40.

Merrill, J. C. "The Role of the Mass Media in National Development: An Open Question for Speculation." *Gazette,* 17: 4, 1971, pp. 236–242.

Middleton, John, ed. *Approaches to Communication Planning.* Paris: UNESCO, 1980.

Middleton, John, with Yvonne Hsu Lin. *Planning Communication for Family Planning.* (A Professional Development Module.) Honolulu: East-West Communication Institute, East-West Center, 1975. 3 volumes.

Miller, Jay K. "Media for Distance Education in the South Pacific." *Media in Education and Development,* 14: 4, December 1981.

Mishra, S. N. *Rural Development and Panchayati Raj.* New Delhi: Concept Publishing Company, 1981.

Mkapa, Benjamin. "Media Are Priority in National Development Needs." *Democratic Journalist*, XXIX: 5, May 1982, pp. 9–11.

Mody, Bella. "Planning Development-Communication Software: Lessons From SITE." *Development Communication Report*, No. 23, July 1983.

Mosco, Vincent, and Janet Wasko, eds. *Political Economy of Information*. Madison, WI: University of Wisconsin Press, 1988.

Mowlana, Hamid. "Capital Formation in the Middle East: A Study of Human Factors in Economic Development." *Tennessee Survey of Business*. Knoxville: University of Tennessee, September 1967. III: 1, pp. 1–8.

————. "The Communication Dimension of International Studies in the United States: A Quantitative Assessment." *International Journal of Communication Research* (University of Koln, FRG), 1: 1, 1974, pp. 3–22.

————. "Communication for Political Change: The Iranian Revolution." In George Gerbner and Marsha Siefert, eds. *World Communications: A Handbook*. White Plains, NY: Longman, 1983.

————. "Communications Media in Africa: A Critique in Retrospect and Prospect." In Gwendolen M. Carter and Ann Paden, eds. *Expanding Horizons in African Studies*. Evanston, IL: Northwestern University Press, 1969.

————. "Cross-National Comparison of Economic Journalism: A Study of Mass Media and Economic Development." *Gazette*, XIII: 4, 1967, pp. 363–378.

————. *Global Information and World Communication: New Frontiers in International Relations*. White Plains, NY: Longman, 1985.

————. "Mass Communication and National Development Objectives." In Albert L. Hester and Richard R. Cole, eds. *Mass Communications in Mexico: Proceedings of the March 11–15, 1974 Seminar in Mexico, D.E.* International Communication Division of the Association for Education in Journalism. Brookings: Department of Journalism and Mass Communication, South Dakota State University, December 1975. pp. 115–120.

————. "Mass Media and Culture: Toward an Integrated Theory." In William B. Gudykunst, ed. *Intercultural Communication: Current Perspectives*. Beverly Hills, CA: Sage, 1983.

————. "Mass Media Systems and Communication Behavior." In Michael Adams, ed. *The Middle East: A Handbook*. London: Anthony Blond, 1971.

————. "Multinational Corporations and the Diffusion of Technology." In A. A. Said and L. R. Simmons, eds. *The New Sovereigns: Multinational Corporations as World Powers*. Englewood Cliffs, NJ: Prentice-Hall, 1975.

————. "A Paradigm for Comparative Mass Media Analysis." In H. D. Fischer and J. C. Merrill, eds. *International and Intercultural Communications*. New York: Hastings House, 1976.

————. "Political and Social Implications of Communication Satellite Applications in Developed and Developing Countries." In Joseph N. Pelton and Marcellus S. Snow, eds. *Economic and Policy Problems in Satellite Communications*. New York: Praeger, 1977.

————. "Technology Versus Tradition: Communication in the Iranian Revolution." *Journal of Communication*, 29: 3, Summer 1979, pp. 107–112.

————. "Toward a Theory of Communication Systems: A Developmental Approach."

Gazette, XVII: 1/2, 1971, pp. 17–28.

———. "Trends in Middle Eastern Societies." In George Gerbner, ed. *Mass Media Policies in Changing Cultures.* New York: Wiley, 1977.

———. "Trends in Research on International Communication in the United States." *Gazette,* XIX: 2, 1973, pp. 79–90.

Mowlana, Hamid, and Ann Elizabeth Robinson. "Ethnic Mobilization and Communication Theory." In A. A. Said and L. R. Simmons, eds. *Ethnicity in an International Context.* New Brunswick, NJ: Transaction Books, 1976.

Mowlana, Hamid, and Laurie J. Wilson. *Communication and Development: A Global Assessment.* Paris: UNESCO, 1987.

Mumford, Lewis. *Technics and Civilization.* New York: Harcourt Brace Jovanovich, 1963.

Mustafa, M. N. "Development Programming in Radio Bangladesh." *COMBROAD,* No. 60, September 1983.

Mutahhari, Murtaza. *Fundamentals of Islamic Thought: God, Man and Universe.* Berkeley, CA: Mizan Press, 1984.

Myrdal, Gunnar. *Asian Drama: An Inquiry into the Poverty of Nations.* New York: The Twentieth Century Fund, 1968. 3 volumes.

Nakamura, Hajime. *Ways of Thinking of Eastern Peoples.* Honolulu: East-West Center, 1968.

Nayar, Baldev Raj. *National Communication and Language Policy in India.* New York: Praeger, 1969.

Nordenstreng, K., and H. I. Schiller, eds. *National Sovereignty and International Communication.* Norwood, NJ: Ablex Publishing, 1979.

Nyerere, Julius K. *Ujamaa: Essays on Socialism.* Dar es Salaam, Tanzania: Oxford University Press, 1968.

Oakely, Peter, and David Marsden. *Approaches to Participation in Rural Development.* Geneva: International Labour Office (ACC Task Force on Rural Development), 1984.

Parker, Edward. "Planning Communication Technologies and Institutions for Development." In Syed Rahim and John Middleton, eds. *Perspectives in Communication and Development.* Honolulu: East-West Center, 1977. pp. 43–76.

Parker, Edwin B. "An Information-Based Hypothesis." *Journal of Communication,* 28: 1, Winter 1978, pp. 70–79.

Parsons, Talcott. *The Structure of Social Action.* New York: MacGraw-Hill, 1937.

Pelton, Joseph N., and Marcellus S. Snow, eds. *Economic and Policy Problems in Satellite Communications.* New York: Praeger, 1977.

Perrett, Heli. "Planning of Communication Support (Information, Motivation and Education) in Sanitation Projects and Programs." TAG Technical Note, No. 2. Washington, DC: World Bank, 1983.

Perraton, Hilary. "How Can Radio Be Usefully Applied to Education and Development?" *The Educational Use of Mass Media.* Washington, DC: World Bank, 1981.

Perroux, F. *A New Concept of Development.* Paris: UNESCO, 1983.

Ploman, Edward. *Space, Earth and Communication.* London: Frances Pinter, 1984.

Polanyi, Karl. *The Great Transformation: The Political and Economic Origins of Our Times.* Boston: Beacon Press, 1944.

Pool, Ithiel de Sola. "The Influence of International Communication on Development." In Syed Rahim and John Middleton, eds. *Perspectives in Communication and Development.* Honolulu: East-West Center, 1977. pp. 101–110.

———. "The Rise of Communications Policy Research." *Journal of Communication,* Spring 1974, pp. 31–42.

Pool, Ithiel de Sola, Philip Stone, and Alexander Szalai. *Communications, Computers and Automation for Development.* UNITAR Research Report No. 6. New York: U.N. Institute for Training and Research, 1971.

Pye, L. *Aspects of Political Development.* Boston: Little, Brown, 1966.

———. *Communication and Political Development.* Princeton, NJ: Princeton University Press, 1963.

Pye, L., and S. Verba. *Political Culture and Political Development.* Princeton, NJ: Princeton University Press, 1965.

Radio and Television in the Service of Education and Development in Asia. Reports and Papers on Mass Communication, No. 49. Paris: UNESCO, 1967.

Rahim, Syed A. *Communication Policy and Planning for Development: A Selected Annotated Bibliography.* Honolulu: East-West Center, 1976.

Rahim, Syed, and John Middleton, eds. *Perspectives in Communication and Development.* Honolulu: East-West Center, 1977.

Recent Developments in Communication for Agricultural Education and Training in Latin America. Paris: UNESCO, 1973.

Report of the Meeting of Experts on Communication Policies and Planning. Paris: UNESCO, 1972.

Report of the Meeting of Experts on Communication Policies in Latin America, Bogota, 4-13 July 1974. Paris: UNESCO, 1974.

Roden, Hanne. *The World Bank—Introduction to Its Involvement in the Urbanization in the 3rd World: The Case of Botswana.* Washington, DC: World Bank, 1984.

Rogers, Everett M., ed. *Communication and Development: Critical Perspectives.* Beverly Hills, CA: Sage, 1976.

———. "The Rise and Fall of the Dominant Paradigm." *Journal of Communication,* 28: 1, Winter 1978, pp. 64–69.

Rogers, E., and L. Shoemaker. *Communication of Innovations: A Cross-cultural Approach.* New York: Free Press, 1971.

Rogers E., and L. Svenning. *Modernization Among Peasants: The Impact of Communication.* New York: Holt, Rinehart and Winston, 1969.

Rostow, Walt W. *The Stages of Economic Growth: A Non-Communist Manifesto.* New York: Cambridge University Press, 1960.

Sardar, Ziauddin. *Information and the Muslim World: A Strategy for the Twenty-first Century.* London: Mansell Publishing Limited, 1988.

Saunders, Robert J., Jeremy J. Warford, and Bjorn Wellenius. *Telecommunications and Economic Development.* Baltimore, MD: Johns Hopkins University Press, 1982.

Sathe, Vasant. "How Satellites Will Extend India's Development Communications." *Intermedia,* 9: 5, September 1981.

Schiller, Herbert I. *Communication and Cultural Domination.* New York: International Arts and Sciences Press, 1978.

————. *Who Knows: Information in the Age of the Fortune 500*. Norwood, NJ: Ablex Publishing, 1981.

————. *Information and the Crisis Economy*. Norwood, NJ: Ablex Publishing, 1984.

————. *Mass Communications and American Empire*. New York: Kelly, 1969.

Schramm, Wilbur. *Mass Media and National Development*. Stanford, CA: UNESCO and Stanford University Press, 1964.

Schramm, W., and D. Lerner, eds. *Communication and Change: The Last Ten Years— and the Next*. Honolulu: University Press of Hawaii, 1976.

Schumacher, E. F. *Small Is Beautiful: Economics as if People Mattered*. New York: Harper & Row, 1973.

Serves, Jan. "The Context for Communication Planning." *Media Asia*, 11: 3, 1984, pp. 129–133.

Seumahu, E. Steve. "Kangaroo Network: Annual Report, 1984." Peacerat Australia Project (Kangaroo Network). Mimeograph.

Shari'ati, Ali. *Marxism and Other Western Fallacies*. Berkeley, CA: Mizan Press, 1980.

————. *On the Sociology of Islam*. Berkeley, CA: Mizan Press, 1979.

Sigman, Vickie, ed. *Development Communications in the Third World*. Proceedings of a Midwest Regional Symposium at the University of Illinois at Urbana-Champaign, April 15, 1983. International Agricultural Publications No. 2. Urbana-Champaign: College of Agriculture, University of Illinois, May 1984.

Shukla, Snehlata. "The Impact of SITE on Primary School Children." *Journal of Communication*, 29: 4, Autumn 1979, pp. 104–105.

Smith, Adam. *The Wealth of Nations*. New York: Modern Library, Random House, 1937.

Somavia, J. "The Democratization of Communication: From Minority Social Monopoly to Majority Social Representation." *Development Dialogue*, No. 2, 1981.

Sommerland, E. Lloyd. *National Communication Systems: Some Policy Issues and Options*. Paris: UNESCO, 1975.

Sorokin, Pitirim A. *Social and Cultural Dynamics*. New York: The Bedminster Press, 1937. 4 volumes.

Stevenson, Robert L. *Communication, Development, and the Third World: The Global Politics of Information*. White Plains, NY: Longman, 1988.

Stover, William James. *Information Technology in the Third World*. Boulder, CO: Westview Press, 1984.

"Symposium on the Cultural, Social and Economic Impact of the New Communication Technologies." Rome, Italy, December 12–16, 1983 (Final Report). Paris: UNESCO, 1984.

Tehranian, Majid, "Development Theory and Communication Policy: The Changing Paradigms." In Melvin J. Voigt and Gerhard J. Hanneman, eds. *Progress in Communication Science*. Vol 1. Norwood, NJ: Ablex Publishing, 1979. pp. 119–166.

Tehranian, Majid, Farhad Hakimzadeh, and Marcello L Vidale, eds. *Communication Policy for National Development: A Comparative Perspective*. London: Rutledge & Kegan Paul, 1977.

Thomas, Clive Y. *Dependence and Transformation: The Economic Transition to Socialism*. New York: Monthly Review Press, 1974.

Tilakaratna, S. *The Animator in Participatory Rural Development: Some Experiences from Sri Lanka.* Geneva: International Labour Office, 1986.

Tipps, Dean C. "Modernization Theory and the Comparative Study of Societies: A Critical Perspective." *Comparative Studies in Society and History,* No. 15, March 1973, pp. 199–226.

Toynbee, Arnold J. *A Study of History.* Oxford, England: Oxford University Press, 1946. 4 volumes.

United Nations Development Programme. Developing Training and Communication Planning Reports, Numbers 376, 377, 378, and 379.

————.*Resource Base.* Bangkok, Thailand. May–August 1980.

————. *Rural Women's Participation in Development.* Evaluation Study No. 3. New York: UNDP, 1980.

Van Soest, Jaap. *The Start of International Development Cooperation in the United Nations 1945–1952.* Assen, The Netherlands: Van Gorcum, 1978.

Wallerstein, Immanuel. *The Capitalist World-Economy.* Cambridge, England: Cambridge University Press, 1979.

Weber, Max. *The Protestant Ethic and the Spirit of Capitalism.* London: G. Allen & Unwin, 1930.

Wedemeyer, Dan, ed. "Telecommunication for Pacific Development." PTC '85, Toward a Digital World, Pacific Telecommunication Council, January 13–16, 1985, Conference, Honolulu, Hawaii.

Wellenius, Bjorn. "On the Role of Telecommunications in Development." *Telecommunication Policy,* March 1984, pp. 59–66.

Wilber, Ken. *Up From Eden: A Transpersonal View of Human Evolution.* Boulder, CO: Shambhala, 1981.

Yamanak, Hayato, and Elisabeth Buck, H. Kato, and Jack Lyle, eds. *Japanese Abstracts on Communication Research.* Honolulu: East-West Center, 1985.

Index

N